T0312116

Dynamic Economics

Dynamic Economics

Quantitative Methods and
Applications

Jérôme Adda and
Russell Cooper

The MIT Press
Cambridge, Massachusetts
London, England

This book was set in Palatino on 3B2 by Asco Typesetters, Hong Kong.

Library of Congress Cataloging-in-Publication Data

Adda, Jérôme.
 Dynamic economics : quantitative methods and applications / Jérôme Adda and Russell Cooper.
  p. cm.
 Includes bibliographical references and index.
 ISBN 978-0-262-54788-8 (paperback)
 ISBN 978-0-262-01201-0 (hc. : alk. paper)
  1. Economics, Mathematical. 2. Macroeconomics—Mathematical modes.
 3. Econometric models. I. Cooper, Russell W., 1955– II. Title.
 HB135.D935 2003
 330′.01′5195—dc21   2003042126

à Lance Armstrong, notre maitre à tous

Contents

Dynamic Economics

1   Overview

In this book we study a rich set of applied problems in economics that emphasize the dynamic aspects of economic decisions. Although our ultimate goals are the applications, we provide some basic techniques before tackling the details of specific dynamic optimization problems. This way we are able to present and integrate key tools such as dynamic programming, numerical techniques, and simulation based econometric methods. We utilize these tools in a variety of applications in both macroeconomics and microeconomics. Overall, this approach allows us to estimate structural parameters and to analyze the effects of economic policy.

The approach we pursue to studying economic dynamics is structural. As researchers we have frequently found ourselves inferring underlying parameters that represent tastes, technology, and other primitives from observations of individual households and firms as well as from economic aggregates. When such inferences are successful, we can then test competing hypotheses about economic behavior and evaluate the effects of policy experiments.

To appreciate the benefits of this approach, consider the following policy experiment. In recent years a number of European governments have instituted policies of subsidizing the scrapping of old cars and the purchase of new cars. What are the expected effects of these policies on the car industry and on government revenues?

At some level this question seems easy if a researcher "knows" the demand function for cars. But of course that demand function is, at best, elusive. Further the demand function estimated in one policy regime is unlikely to be very informative for a novel policy experiment, such as this example of car scrapping subsidies.

An alternative approach is to build and estimate a model of household dynamic choice of car ownership. Once the parameters of this model are estimated, then various policy experiments can be evaluated.[1] This approach seems considerably more difficult than just estimating a demand function, and of course this is the case. It requires the specification and solution of a dynamic optimization problem and then the estimation of the parameters. But, as we argue in this book, this methodology is feasible and yields exciting results.

The integration of dynamic optimization with parameter estimation is at the heart of our approach. We develop this idea by organizing the book in two parts.

Part I provides a review of the formal theory of dynamic optimization. This is a tool used in many areas of economics, including macroeconomics, industrial organization, labor economics, and international economics. As in previous contributions to the study of dynamic optimization, such as by Sargent (1987) and by Stokey and Lucas (1989), our presentation starts with the formal theory of dynamic programming. Because of the large number of other contributions in this area, our presentation in chapter 2 relies on existing theorems on the existence of solutions to a variety of dynamic programming problems.

In chapter 3 we present the numerical tools necessary to conduct a structural estimation of the theoretical dynamic models. These numerical tools serve both to complement the theory in teaching students about dynamic programming and to enable a researcher to evaluate the quantitative implications of the theory. In our experience the process of writing computer code to solve dynamic programming problems has proved to be a useful device for teaching basic concepts of this approach.

The econometric techniques of chapter 4 provide the link between the dynamic programming problem and data. The emphasis is on the mapping from parameters of the dynamic programming problem to observations. For example, a vector of parameters is used to numerically solve a dynamic programming problem that is used to simulate moments. An optimization routine then selects a vector of parameters to bring these simulated moments close to the moments observed in the data.

Part II is devoted to the application of dynamic programming to specific areas of economics such as the study of business cycles, consumption, and investment behavior. The presentation of each

---

1. This exercise is described in some detail in the chapter on consumer durables in this book.

application in chapters 5 through 10 contains four elements: presentation of the optimization problem as a dynamic programming problem, characterization of the optimal policy functions, estimation of the parameters, and policy evaluation using this model.

While the applications might be characterized as macroeconomics, the methodology is valuable in other areas of economic research, in terms of both the topics and the techniques. These applications utilize material from many other parts of economics. For example, the analysis of the stochastic growth model includes taxation and our discussion of factor adjustment at the plant level is certainly relevant to researchers in labor and industrial organization. Moreover we envision these techniques to be useful in any problem where the researcher is applying dynamic optimization to the data. The chapters contain references to other applications of these techniques.

What is new about our presentation is the use of an integrated approach to the empirical implementation of dynamic optimization models. Previous texts have provided a mathematical basis for dynamic programming, but those presentations generally do not contain any quantitative applications. Other texts present the underlying econometric theory but generally without specific applications. Our approach does both, and thus aims to link theory and application as illustrated in the chapters of part II.

Our motivation for writing this book should be clear. From the perspective of understanding dynamic programming, explicit empirical applications complement the underlying theory of optimization. From the perspective of applied macroeconomics, explicit dynamic optimization problems, posed as dynamic programming problems, provide needed structure for estimation and policy evaluation.

Since the book is intended to teach empirical applications of dynamic programming problems, we have created a Web site for the presentation of computer codes (MATLAB and GAUSS) as well as data sets useful for the applications. This material should appeal to readers wishing to supplement the presentation in part II, and we hope that the Web site will become a forum for further development of codes.

Our writing this book has benefited from joint work with Joao Ejarque, John Haltiwanger, Alok Johri, and Jonathan Willis. We thank these co-authors for their generous sharing of ideas and computer code as well as their comments on the final draft. Thanks also go to Victor Aguirregabiria, Yan Bai, Joyce Cooper, Dean Corbae, Zvi Eckstein, Simon Gilchrist, Hang Kang, Peter Klenow, Sam Kortum, Valérie Lechene, Nicola Pavoni, Aldo Rustichini, and Marcos Vera for comments on various parts of the book. We also appreciate the comments of outside reviewers and the editorial staff at The MIT Press. Finally, we are grateful to our many masters and doctoral students at Tel Aviv University, University of Texas at Austin, the IDEI at the Université de Toulouse, the NAKE PhD program in Holland, the University of Haifa, the University of Minnesota, and University College London for their numerous comments and suggestions during the preparation of this book.

The book's Web site can be found at http://mitpress.mit.edu/dynamic-economics.

I

Theory

2

Theory of Dynamic Programming

2.1 Overview

The mathematical theory of dynamic programming as a means of solving dynamic optimization problems dates to the early contributions of Bellman (1957) and Bertsekas (1976). For economists, the contributions of Sargent (1987) and Stokey and Lucas (1989) provide a valuable bridge to this literature.

2.2 Indirect Utility

Intuitively, the approach of dynamic programming can be understood by recalling the theme of indirect utility from basic static consumer theory or a reduced form profit function generated by the optimization of a firm. These reduced form representations of payoffs summarize information about the optimized value of the choice problems faced by households and firms. As we will see, the theory of dynamic programming takes this insight to a dynamic context.

2.2.1 Consumers

Consumer choice theory focuses on households that solve

$$V(I, p) = \max_c \ u(c)$$

$$\text{subject to} \quad pc = I,$$

where c is a vector of consumption goods, p is a vector of prices and I is income.[1] The first-order condition is given by

---

1. Assume that there are J commodities in this economy. This presentation assumes that you understand the conditions under which this optimization problem has a solution and when that solution can be characterized by first-order conditions.

$$\frac{u_j(c)}{p_j} = \lambda \qquad \text{for } j = 1, 2, \ldots, J,$$

where λ is the multiplier on the budget constraint and $u_j(c)$ is the marginal utility from good j.

Here $V(I, p)$ is an indirect utility function. It is the maximized level of utility from the current state (I, p). Someone in this state can be predicted to attain this level of utility. One does not need to know what that person will do with his income; it is enough to know that he will act optimally. This is very powerful logic and underlies the idea behind the dynamic programming models studied below.

To illustrate, what happens if we give the consumer a bit more income? Welfare goes up by $V_I(I, p) > 0$. Can the researcher predict what will happen with a little more income? Not really since the optimizing consumer is indifferent with respect to how this is spent:

$$\frac{u_j(c)}{p_j} = V_I(I, p) \qquad \text{for all } j.$$

It is in this sense that the indirect utility function summarizes the value of the households optimization problem and allows us to determine the marginal value of income without knowing more about consumption functions.

Is this all we need to know about household behavior? No, this theory is static. It ignores savings, spending on durable goods, and uncertainty over the future. These are all important components in the household optimization problem. We will return to these in later chapters on the dynamic behavior of households. The point here was simply to recall a key object from optimization theory: the indirect utility function.

2.2.2 Firms

Suppose that a firm must choose how many workers to hire at a wage of w given its stock of capital k and product price p. Thus the firm must solve

$$\Pi(w, p, k) = \max_l pf(l, k) - wl.$$

A labor demand function results that depends on (w, p, k). As with $V(I, p)$, $\Pi(w, p, k)$ summarizes the value of the firm given factor prices, the product price p, and the stock of capital k. Both the flexible and fixed factors can be vectors.

Think of $\Pi(w,p,k)$ as an indirect profit function. It completely summarizes the value of the optimization problem of the firm given (w,p,k).

As with the households problem, given $\Pi(w,p,k)$, we can directly compute the marginal value of allowing the firm some additional capital as $\Pi_k(w,p,k) = pf_k(l,k)$ without knowing how the firm will adjust its labor input in response to the additional capital.

But, is this all there is to know about the firm's behavior? Surely not, for we have not specified where k comes from. So the firm's problem is essentially dynamic, though the demand for some of its inputs can be taken as a static optimization problem. These are important themes in the theory of factor demand, and we will return to them in our firm applications.

2.3 Dynamic Optimization: A Cake-Eating Example

Here we will look at a very simple dynamic optimization problem. We begin with a finite horizon and then discuss extensions to the infinite horizon.[2]

Suppose that you are presented with a cake of size W_1. At each point of time, $t = 1, 2, 3, \ldots, T$, you can eat some of the cake but must save the rest. Let c_t be your consumption in period t, and let $u(c_t)$ represent the flow of utility from this consumption. The utility function is not indexed by time: preferences are stationary. We can assume that $u(\cdot)$ is real valued, differentiable, strictly increasing, and strictly concave. Further we can assume $\lim_{c \to 0} u'(c) \to \infty$. We could represent your lifetime utility by

$$\sum_{t=1}^{T} \beta^{(t-1)} u(c_t),$$

where $0 \leq \beta \leq 1$ and β is called the **discount factor**.

For now, we assume that the cake does not depreciate (spoil) or grow. Hence the evolution of the cake over time is governed by

$$W_{t+1} = W_t - c_t \tag{2.1}$$

---

2. For a very complete treatment of the finite horizon problem with uncertainty, see Bertsekas (1976).

for $t = 1, 2, \ldots, T$. How would you find the optimal path of consumption, $\{c_t\}_1^T$?[3]

2.3.1 Direct Attack

One approach is to solve the constrained optimization problem directly. This is called the **sequence problem** by Stokey and Lucas (1989). Consider the problem of

$$\max_{\{c_t\}_1^T, \{W_t\}_2^{T+1}} \sum_{t=1}^{T} \beta^{(t-1)} u(c_t) \tag{2.2}$$

subject to the transition equation (2.1), which holds for $t = 1, 2, 3, \ldots,$ T. Also there are nonnegativity constraints on consuming the cake given by $c_t \geq 0$ and $W_t \geq 0$. For this problem, W_1 is given.

Alternatively, the flow constraints imposed by (2.1) for each t could be combined, yielding

$$\sum_{t=1}^{T} c_t + W_{T+1} = W_1. \tag{2.3}$$

The nonnegativity constraints are simpler: $c_t \geq 0$ for $t = 1, 2, \ldots, T$ and $W_{T+1} \geq 0$. For now, we will work with the single resource constraint. This is a well-behaved problem as the objective is concave and continuous and the constraint set is compact. So there is a solution to this problem.[4]

Letting λ be the multiplier on (2.3), the first-order conditions are given by

$$\beta^{t-1} u'(c_t) = \lambda \qquad \text{for } t = 1, 2, \ldots, T$$

and

$$\lambda = \phi,$$

where ϕ is the multiplier on the nonnegativity constraint on W_{T+1}. The nonnegativity constraints on $c_t \geq 0$ are ignored, as we can assume that the marginal utility of consumption becomes infinite as consumption approaches zero within any period.

---

3. Throughout, the notation $\{x_t\}_1^T$ is used to define the sequence $(x_1, x_2, \ldots, x_T)$ for some variable x.

4. This comes from the Weierstrass theorem. See Bertsekas (1976, app. B) or Stokey and Lucas (1989, ch. 3) for a discussion.

Combining the equations, we obtain an expression that links consumption across any two periods:

$$u'(c_t) = \beta u'(c_{t+1}). \tag{2.4}$$

This is a necessary condition of optimality for **any** t: if it is violated, the agent can do better by adjusting c_t and c_{t+1}. Frequently (2.4) is referred to as a **Euler equation**.

To understand this condition, suppose that you have a proposed (candidate) solution for this problem given by $\{c_t^*\}_1^T$, $\{W_t^*\}_2^{T+1}$. Essentially the Euler equation says that the marginal utility cost of reducing consumption by ε in period t equals the marginal utility gain from consuming the extra ε of cake in the next period, which is discounted by β. If the Euler equation holds, then it is impossible to increase utility by moving consumption across adjacent periods given a candidate solution.

It should be clear though that this condition may not be sufficient: it does not cover deviations that last more than one period. For example, could utility be increased by reducing consumption by ε in period t saving the "cake" for two periods and then increasing consumption in period $t+2$? Clearly, this is not covered by a single Euler equation. However, by combining the Euler equation that hold across period t and $t+1$ with that which holds for periods $t+1$ and $t+2$, we can see that such a deviation will not increase utility. This is simply because the combination of Euler equations implies that

$$u'(c_t) = \beta^2 u'(c_{t+2})$$

so that the two-period deviation from the candidate solution will not increase utility.

As long as the problem is finite, the fact that the Euler equation holds across all adjacent periods implies that any finite deviations from a candidate solution that satisfies the Euler equations will not increase utility.

Is this enough? Not quite. Imagine a candidate solution that satisfies all of the Euler equations but has the property that $W_T > c_T$ so that there is cake left over. This is clearly an inefficient plan: satisfying the Euler equations is necessary but not sufficient. The optimal solution will satisfy the Euler equation for each period until the agent consumes the entire cake.

Formally, this involves showing that the nonnegativity constraint on W_{T+1} must bind. In fact, this constraint is binding in the solution above: $\lambda = \phi > 0$. This nonnegativity constraint serves two important purposes. First, in the absence of a constraint that $W_{T+1} \geq 0$, the agent would clearly want to set $W_{T+1} = -\infty$. This is clearly not feasible. Second, the fact that the constraint is binding in the optimal solution guarantees that cake does not remain after period T.

In effect the problem is pinned down by an initial condition (W_1 is given) and by a terminal condition ($W_{T+1} = 0$). The set of $(T - 1)$ Euler equations and (2.3) then determine the time path of consumption.

Let the solution to this problem be denoted by $V_T(W_1)$, where T is the horizon of the problem and W_1 is the initial size of the cake. $V_T(W_1)$ represents the maximal utility flow from a T-period problem given a size W_1 cake. From now on, we call this a **value function**. This is completely analogous to the indirect utility functions expressed for the household and the firm.

As in those problems, a slight increase in the size of the cake leads to an increase in lifetime utility equal to the marginal utility in any period. That is,

$$V_T'(W_1) = \lambda = \beta^{t-1} u'(c_t), \qquad t = 1, 2, \ldots, T.$$

It doesn't matter when the extra cake is eaten given that the consumer is acting optimally. This is analogous to the point raised above about the effect on utility of an increase in income in the consumer choice problem with multiple goods.

2.3.2 Dynamic Programming Approach

Suppose that we change the problem slightly: we add a period 0 and give an initial cake of size W_0. One approach to determining the optimal solution of this augmented problem is to go back to the sequence problem and resolve it using this longer horizon and new constraint. But, having done all of the hard work with the T period problem, it would be nice not to have to do it again.

Finite Horizon Problem
The dynamic programming approach provides a means of doing so. It essentially converts an (arbitrary) T-period problem into a two-period problem with the appropriate rewriting of the objective function. This way it uses the value function obtained from solving a shorter horizon problem.

By adding a period 0 to our original problem, we can take advantage of the information provided in $V_T(W_1)$, the solution of the T-period problem given W_1 from (2.2). Given W_0, consider the problem of

$$\max_{c_0} u(c_0) + \beta V_T(W_1), \tag{2.5}$$

where

$$W_1 = W_0 - c_0, \qquad W_0 \text{ given}.$$

In this formulation the choice of consumption in period 0 determines the size of the cake that will be available starting in period 1, W_1. Now, instead of choosing a sequence of consumption levels, we just find c_0. Once c_0 and thus W_1 are determined, the value of the problem from then on is given by $V_T(W_1)$. This function completely summarizes optimal behavior from period 1 onward. For the purposes of the dynamic programming problem, it does not matter how the cake will be consumed after the initial period. All that is important is that the agent will be acting optimally and thus generating utility given by $V_T(W_1)$. This is the **principle of optimality**, due to Richard Bellman, at work. With this knowledge, an optimal decision can be made regarding consumption in period 0.

Note that the first-order condition (assuming that $V_T(W_1)$ is differentiable) is given by

$$u'(c_0) = \beta V_T'(W_1)$$

so that the marginal gain from reducing consumption a little in period 0 is summarized by the derivative of the value function. As noted in the earlier discussion of the T-period sequence problem,

$$V_T'(W_1) = u'(c_1) = \beta^t u'(c_{t+1})$$

for $t = 1, 2, \ldots, T-1$. Using these two conditions together yields

$$u'(c_t) = \beta u'(c_{t+1})$$

for $t = 0, 1, 2, \ldots, T-1$, a familiar necessary condition for an optimal solution.

Since the Euler conditions for the other periods underlie the creation of the value function, one might suspect that the solution to the $T+1$ problem using this dynamic programming approach is identical to that of the sequence approach.[5] This is clearly true for this problem: the set of first-order conditions for the two problems are identical, and thus, given the strict concavity of the $u(c)$ functions, the solutions will be identical as well.

The apparent ease of this approach, however, may be misleading. We were able to make the problem look simple by pretending that we actually know $V_T(W_1)$. Of course, the way we could solve for this is by either tackling the sequence problem directly or building it recursively, starting from an initial single-period problem.

On this recursive approach, we could start with the single-period problem implying $V_1(W_1)$. We would then solve (2.5) to build $V_2(W_1)$. Given this function, we could move to a solution of the $T = 3$ problem and proceed iteratively, using (2.5) to build $V_T(W_1)$ for any T.

Example
We illustrate the construction of the value function in a specific example. Assume $u(c) = \ln(c)$. Suppose that $T = 1$. Then $V_1(W_1) = \ln(W_1)$.

For $T = 2$, the first-order condition from (2.2) is

$$\frac{1}{c_1} = \frac{\beta}{c_2},$$

and the resource constraint is

$$W_1 = c_1 + c_2.$$

Working with these two conditions, we have

$$c_1 = \frac{W_1}{1 + \beta} \quad \text{and} \quad c_2 = \frac{\beta W_1}{1 + \beta}.$$

From this, we can solve for the value of the two-period problem:

$$V_2(W_1) = \ln(c_1) + \beta \ln(c_2) = A_2 + B_2 \ln(W_1), \tag{2.6}$$

where A_2 and B_2 are constants associated with the two-period problem. These constants are given by

$$A_2 = \ln\left(\frac{1}{1+\beta}\right) + \beta \ln\left(\frac{\beta}{1+\beta}\right), \qquad B_2 = 1 + \beta.$$

---

5. By the sequence approach, we mean solving the problem using the direct approach outlined in the previous section.

Importantly, (2.6) does not include the *max* operator as we are substituting the optimal decisions in the construction of the value function, $V_2(W_1)$.

Using this function, the $T = 3$ problem can then be written as

$$V_3(W_1) = \max_{W_2} \ln(W_1 - W_2) + \beta V_2(W_2),$$

where the choice variable is the state in the subsequent period. The first-order condition is

$$\frac{1}{c_1} = \beta V_2'(W_2).$$

Using (2.6) evaluated at a cake of size W_2, we can solve for $V_2'(W_2)$ implying:

$$\frac{1}{c_1} = \beta \frac{B_2}{W_2} = \frac{\beta}{c_2}.$$

Here c_2 the consumption level in the second period of the three-period problem and thus is the same as the level of consumption in the first period of the two-period problem. Further we know from the two-period problem that

$$\frac{1}{c_2} = \frac{\beta}{c_3}.$$

This plus the resource constraint allows us to construct the solution of the three-period problem:

$$c_1 = \frac{W_1}{1 + \beta + \beta^2}, \quad c_2 = \frac{\beta W_1}{1 + \beta + \beta^2}, \quad c_3 = \frac{\beta^2 W_1}{1 + \beta + \beta^2}.$$

Substituting into $V_3(W_1)$ yields

$$V_3(W_1) = A_3 + B_3 \ln(W_1),$$

where

$$A_3 = \ln\left(\frac{1}{1 + \beta + \beta^2}\right) + \beta \ln\left(\frac{\beta}{1 + \beta + \beta^2}\right) + \beta^2 \ln\left(\frac{\beta^2}{1 + \beta + \beta^2}\right),$$

$$B_3 = 1 + \beta + \beta^2.$$

This solution can be verified from a direct attack on the three-period problem using (2.2) and (2.3).

2.4   Some Extensions of the Cake-Eating Problem

Here we go beyond the T-period problem to illustrate some ways to use the dynamic programming framework. This is intended as an overview, and the details of the assertions, and so forth, will be provided below.

2.4.1   Infinite Horizon

Basic Structure

Suppose that for the cake-eating problem, we allow the horizon to go to infinity. As before, one can consider solving the infinite horizon sequence problem given by

$$\max_{\{c_t\}_1^\infty, \{W_t\}_2^\infty} \sum_{t=1}^{\infty} \beta^t u(c_t)$$

along with the transition equation of

$$W_{t+1} = W_t - c_t \qquad \text{for } t = 1, 2, \ldots.$$

In specifying this as a dynamic programming problem, we write

$$V(W) = \max_{c \in [0, W]} u(c) + \beta V(W - c) \qquad \text{for all } W.$$

Here $u(c)$ is again the utility from consuming c units in the current period. $V(W)$ is the value of the infinite horizon problem starting with a cake of size W. So in the given period, the agent chooses current consumption and thus reduces the size of the cake to $W' = W - c$, as in the transition equation. We use variables with primes to denote future values. The value of starting the next period with a cake of that size is then given by $V(W - c)$, which is discounted at rate $\beta < 1$.

For this problem, the **state variable** is the size of the cake (W) given at the start of any period. The state completely summarizes all information from the past that is needed for the forward-looking optimization problem. The **control variable** is the variable that is being chosen. In this case it is the level of consumption in the current period c. Note that c lies in a compact set. The dependence of the state tomorrow on the state today and the control today, given by

$$W' = W - c,$$

is called the **transition equation**.

Alternatively, we can specify the problem so that instead of choosing today's consumption we choose tomorrow's state:

$$V(W) = \max_{W' \in [0, W]} u(W - W') + \beta V(W') \qquad \text{for all } W. \tag{2.7}$$

Either specification yields the same result. But choosing tomorrow's state often makes the algebra a bit easier, so we will work with (2.7).

This expression is known as a **functional equation**, and it is often called a Bellman equation after Richard Bellman, one of the originators of dynamic programming. Note that the unknown in the Bellman equation is the value function itself: the idea is to find a function $V(W)$ that satisfies this condition for all W. Unlike the finite horizon problem, there is no terminal period to use to derive the value function. In effect, the fixed point restriction of having $V(W)$ on both sides of (2.7) will provide us with a means of solving the functional equation.

Note too that time itself does not enter into Bellman's equation: we can express all relations without an indication of time. This is the essence of **stationarity**.[6] In fact we will ultimately use the stationarity of the problem to make arguments about the existence of a value function satisfying the functional equation.

A final very important property of this problem is that all information about the past that bears on current and future decisions is summarized by W, the size of the cake at the start of the period. Whether the cake is of this size because we initially have a large cake and can eat a lot of it or a small cake and are frugal eaters is not relevant. All that matters is that we have a cake of a given size. This property partly reflects the fact that the preferences of the agent do not depend on past consumption. If this were the case, we could amend the problem to allow this possibility.

The next part of this chapter addresses the question of whether there exists a value function that satisfies (2.7). For now we assume that a solution exists so that we can explore its properties.

The first-order condition for the optimization problem in (2.7) can be written as

$$u'(c) = \beta V'(W').$$

---

6. As you may already know, stationarity is vital in econometrics as well. Thus making assumptions of stationarity in economic theory have a natural counterpart in empirical studies. In some cases we will have to modify optimization problems to ensure stationarity.

This may look simple, but what is the derivative of the value function? It is particularly hard to answer this, since we do not know $V(W)$. However, we can use the fact that $V(W)$ satisfies (2.7) for all W to calculate V'. Assuming that this value function is differentiable, we have

$$V'(W) = u'(c),$$

a result we have seen before. Since this holds for all W, it will hold in the following period, yielding

$$V'(W') = u'(c').$$

Substitution leads to the familar Euler equation:

$$u'(c) = \beta u'(c').$$

The solution to the cake-eating problem will satisfy this necessary condition for all W.

The link from the level of consumption and next period's cake (the controls from the different formulations) to the size of the cake (the state) is given by the **policy function**:

$$c = \phi(W), \quad W' = \varphi(W) \equiv W - \phi(W).$$

Substituting these values into the Euler equation reduces the problem to these policy functions alone:

$$u'(\phi(W)) = \beta u'(\phi(W - \phi(W))) \qquad \text{for all } W.$$

The policy functions above are important in applied research, for they provide the mapping from the state to actions. When elements of the state as well as the action are observable, these policy functions will provide the means for estimating the underlying parameters.

An Example

In general, it is not actually possible to find closed form solutions for the value function and the resulting policy functions. So we try to characterize certain properties of the solution, and for some cases, we solve these problems numerically.

Nevertheless, as indicated by our analysis of finite horizon problems, there are some specifications of the utility function that allow us to find a closed form solution to the value function. Suppose, as above, that $u(c) = \ln(c)$. From the results of the T-period problem, we might conjecture that the solution to the functional equation takes the form of

$$V(W) = A + B \ln(W) \qquad \text{for all } W.$$

By this expression we have reduced the dimensionality of the unknown function $V(W)$ to two parameters, A and B. But can we find values for A and B such that $V(W)$ will satisfy the functional equation?

Let us suppose that we can. For these two values the functional equation becomes

$$A + B \ln(W) = \max_{W'} \ln(W - W') + \beta(A + B \ln(W')) \qquad \text{for all } W.$$

$$(2.8)$$

After some algebra, the first-order condition becomes

$$W' = \varphi(W) = \frac{\beta B}{1 + \beta B} W.$$

Using this in (2.8) results in

$$A + B \ln(W) = \ln \frac{W}{1 + \beta B} + \beta\left(A + B \ln\left(\frac{\beta B W}{1 + \beta B}\right)\right) \qquad \text{for all } W.$$

Collecting the terms that multiply $\ln(W)$ and using the requirement that the functional equation holds for all W, we find that

$$B = \frac{1}{1 - \beta}$$

is required for a solution. After this, the expression can also be used to solve for A. Thus we have verified that our guess is a solution to the functional equation. We know that because we can solve for (A, B) such that the functional equation holds for all W using the optimal consumption and savings decision rules.

With this solution, we know that

$$c = W(1 - \beta), \quad W' = \beta W.$$

This tells us that the optimal policy is to save a constant fraction of the cake and eat the remaining fraction.

The solution to B can be estimated from the solution to the T-period horizon problems where

$$B_T = \sum_{t=1}^{T} \beta^{t-1}.$$

Clearly, $B = \lim_{T \to \infty} B_T$. We will be exploiting the idea of using the value function to solve the infinite horizon problem as it is related to the limit of the finite solutions in much of our numerical analysis.

Below are some exercises that provide some further elements to this basic structure. Both begin with finite horizon formulations and then progress to the infinite horizon problems.

EXERCISE 2.1 Utility in period t is given by $u(c_t, c_{t-1})$. Solve a T-period problem using these preferences. Interpret the first-order conditions. How would you formulate the Bellman equation for the infinite horizon version of this problem?

EXERCISE 2.2 The transition equation is modified so that

$$W_{t+1} = \rho W_t - c_t,$$

where $\rho > 0$ represents a return from holding cake inventories. Solve the T-period problem with this storage technology. Interpret the first-order conditions. How would you formulate the Bellman equation for the infinite horizon version of this problem? Does the size of ρ matter in this discussion? Explain.

2.4.2 Taste Shocks

A convenient feature of the dynamic programming problem is the ease with which uncertainty can be introduced.[7] For the cake-eating problem, the natural source of uncertainty has to do with the agent's appetite. In other settings we will focus on other sources of uncertainty having to do with the productivity of labor or the endowments of households.

To allow for variations of appetite, suppose that utility over consumption is given by

$$\varepsilon u(c),$$

where ε is a random variable whose properties we will describe below. The function $u(c)$ is again assumed to be strictly increasing

---

7. To be careful, here we are adding shocks that take values in a finite and thus countable set. See the discussion in Bertsekas (1976, sec. 2.1) for an introduction to the complexities of the problem with more general statements of uncertainty.

and strictly concave. Otherwise, the problem is the original cake-eating problem with an initial cake of size W.

In problems with stochastic elements, it is critical to be precise about the timing of events. Does the optimizing agent know the current shocks when making a decision? For this analysis, assume that the agent knows the value of the taste shock when making current decisions but does not know the future values of this shock. Thus the agent must use expectations of future values of ε when deciding how much cake to eat today: it may be optimal to consume less today (save more) in anticipation of a high realization of ε in the future.

For simplicity, assume that the taste shock takes on only two values: $\varepsilon \in \{\varepsilon_h, \varepsilon_l\}$ with $\varepsilon_h > \varepsilon_l > 0$. Further we can assume that the taste shock follows a first-order Markov process,[8] which means that the probability that a particular realization of ε occurs in the current period depends **only** the value of ε attained in the previous period.[9] For notation, let π_{ij} denote the probability that the value of ε goes from state i in the current period to state j in the next period. For example, π_{lh} is defined from

$$\pi_{lh} \equiv \text{Prob}(\varepsilon' = \varepsilon_h \,|\, \varepsilon = \varepsilon_l),$$

where ε' refers to the future value of ε. Clearly, $\pi_{ih} + \pi_{il} = 1$ for $i = h, l$. Let Π be a 2×2 matrix with a typical element π_{ij} that summarizes the information about the probability of moving across states. This matrix is logically called a **transition matrix**.

With this notation and structure, we can turn again to the cake-eating problem. We need to carefully define the state of the system for the optimizing agent. In the nonstochastic problem, the state was simply the size of the cake. This provided all the information the agent needed to make a choice. When taste shocks are introduced, the agent needs to take this factor into account as well. We know that the taste shocks provide information about current payoffs and, through the Π matrix, are informative about the future value of the taste shock as well.[10]

---

8. For more details on Markov chains, we refer the reader to Ljungqvist and Sargent (2000).

9. The evolution can also depend on the control of the previous period. Note too that by appropriate rewriting of the state space, richer specifications of uncertainty can be encompassed.

10. This is a point that we return to below in our discussion of the capital accumulation problem.

Formally the Bellman equation is written

$$V(W, \varepsilon) = \max_{W'} \; \varepsilon u(W - W') + \beta E_{\varepsilon'|\varepsilon} V(W', \varepsilon') \qquad \text{for all } (W, \varepsilon),$$

where $W' = W - c$ as before. Note that the conditional expectation is denoted here by $E_{\varepsilon'|\varepsilon} V(W', \varepsilon')$ which, given Π, is something we can compute.[11]

The first-order condition for this problem is given by

$$\varepsilon u'(W - W') = \beta E_{\varepsilon'|\varepsilon} V_1(W', \varepsilon') \qquad \text{for all } (W, \varepsilon).$$

Using the functional equation to solve for the marginal value of cake, we find that

$$\varepsilon u'(W - W') = \beta E_{\varepsilon'|\varepsilon}[\varepsilon' u'(W' - W'')]. \tag{2.9}$$

This, of course, is the stochastic Euler equation for this problem.

The optimal policy function is given by

$$W' = \varphi(W, \varepsilon).$$

The Euler equation can be rewritten in these terms as

$$\varepsilon u'(W - \varphi(W, \varepsilon)) = \beta E_{\varepsilon'|\varepsilon}[\varepsilon' u'(\varphi(W, \varepsilon) - \varphi(\varphi(W, \varepsilon), \varepsilon')))].$$

The properties of the policy function can then be deduced from this condition. Clearly, both c' and c' depend on the realized value of ε so that the expectation on the right side of (2.9) cannot be split into two separate pieces.

2.4.3 Discrete Choice

To illustrate the flexibility of the dynamic programming approach, we build on this stochastic problem. Suppose that the cake must be eaten in one period. Perhaps we should think of this as the wine-drinking problem, recognizing that once a good bottle of wine is opened, it must be consumed. Further we can modify the transition equation to allow the cake to grow (depreciate) at rate ρ.

The cake consumption example becomes then a dynamic, stochastic discrete choice problem. This is part of a family of problems called **optimal stopping problems**.[12] The common element in all of

---

11. Throughout we denote the conditional expectation of ε' given ε as $E_{\varepsilon'|\varepsilon}$.
12. Eckstein and Wolpin (1989) provide an extensive discussions of the formulation and estimation of these problems in the context of labor applications.

these problems is the emphasis on the timing of a single event: when to eat the cake, when to take a job, when to stop school, when to stop revising a chapter, and so on. In fact, for many of these problems, these choices are not once in a lifetime events, so we will be looking at problems even richer than those of the optimal stopping variety.

Let $V^E(W, \varepsilon)$ and $V^N(W, \varepsilon)$ be the values of eating size W cake now (E) and waiting (N), respectively, given the current taste shock $\varepsilon \in \{\varepsilon_h, \varepsilon_l\}$. Then

$$V^E(W, \varepsilon) = \varepsilon u(W)$$

and

$$V^N(W) = \beta E_{\varepsilon' | \varepsilon} V(\rho W, \varepsilon'),$$

where

$$V(W, \varepsilon) = \max(V^E(W, \varepsilon), V^N(W, \varepsilon)) \qquad \text{for all } (W, \varepsilon).$$

To understand this better, the term $\varepsilon u(W)$ is the direct utility flow from eating the cake. Once the cake is eaten, the problem has ended. So $V^E(W, \varepsilon)$ is just a one-period return. If the agent waits, then there is no cake consumption in the current period, and in the next period the cake is of size (ρW). As tastes are stochastic, the agent choosing to wait must take expectations of the future taste shock, ε'. The agent has an option in the next period of eating the cake or waiting some more. Hence the value of having the cake in any state is given by $V(W, \varepsilon)$, which is the value attained by maximizing over the two options of eating or waiting. The cost of delaying the choice is determined by the discount factor β while the gains to delay are associated with the growth of the cake, parameterized by ρ. Further the realized value of ε will surely influence the relative value of consuming the cake immediately.

If $\rho \leq 1$, then the cake doesn't grow. In this case there is no gain from delay when $\varepsilon = \varepsilon_h$. If the agent delays, then utility in the next period will have to be lower due to discounting, and with probability π_{hl}, the taste shock will switch from high to low. So waiting to eat the cake in the future will not be desirable. Hence

$$V(W, \varepsilon_h) = V^E(W, \varepsilon_h) = \varepsilon_h u(W) \qquad \text{for all } W.$$

In the low ε state, matters are more complex. If β and ρ are sufficiently close to 1, then there is not a large cost to delay. Further, if π_{lh} is sufficiently close to 1, then it is likely that tastes will switch from low to high. Thus it will be optimal not to eat the cake in state (W, ε_l).[13]

Here are some additional exercises.

EXERCISE 2.3   Suppose that $\rho = 1$. For a given β, show that there exists a critical level of π_{lh}, denoted by $\bar{\pi}_{lh}$ such that if $\pi_{lh} > \bar{\pi}_{lh}$, then the optimal solution is for the agent to wait when $\varepsilon = \varepsilon_l$ and to eat the cake when ε_h is realized.

EXERCISE 2.4   When $\rho > 1$, the problem is more difficult. Suppose that there are no variations in tastes: $\varepsilon_h = \varepsilon_l = 1$. In this case there is a trade-off between the value of waiting (as the cake grows) and the cost of delay from discounting.

Suppose that $\rho > 1$ and $u(c) = c^{1-\gamma}/(1 - \gamma)$. What is the solution to the optimal stopping problem when $\beta\rho^{1-\gamma} < 1$? What happens if $\beta\rho^{1-\gamma} > 1$? What happens when uncertainty is added?

2.5   General Formulation

Building on the intuition gained from the cake-eating problem, we now consider a more formal abstract treatment of the dynamic programming approach.[14] We begin with a presentation of the non-stochastic problem and then add uncertainty to the formulation.

2.5.1   Nonstochastic Case

Consider the infinite horizon optimization problem of an agent with a payoff function for period t given by $\tilde{\sigma}(s_t, c_t)$. The first argument of the payoff function is termed the **state vector** (s_t). As noted above, this represents a set of variables that influences the agent's return within the period, but by assumption, these variables are outside of the agent's control within period t. The state variables evolve over time in a manner that may be influenced by the **control vector** (c_t), the second argument of the payoff function. The connection between the state variables over time is given by the transition equation:

---

13. In the following chapter on the numerical approach to dynamic programming, we study this case in considerable detail.

14. This section is intended to be self-contained and thus repeats some of the material from the earlier examples. Our presentation is by design not as formal as say that provided in Bertsekas (1976) or Stokey and Lucas (1989). The reader interested in more mathematical rigor is urged to review those texts and their many references.

$s_{t+1} = \tau(s_t, c_t)$.

So, given the current state and the current control, the state vector for the subsequent period is determined.

Note that the state vector has a very important property: it completely summarizes all of the information from the past that is needed to make a forward-looking decision. While preferences and the transition equation are certainly dependent on the past, this dependence is represented by s_t: other variables from the past do not affect current payoffs or constraints and thus cannot influence current decisions. This may seem restrictive but it is not: the vector s_t may include many variables so that the dependence of current choices on the past can be quite rich.

While the state vector is effectively determined by preferences and the transition equation, the researcher has some latitude in choosing the control vector. That is, there may be multiple ways of representing the same problem with alternative specifications of the control variables.

We assume that $c \in C$ and $s \in S$. In some cases the control is restricted to be in a subset of C that depends on the state vector: $c \in C(s)$. Further we assume that $\tilde{\sigma}(s, c)$ is bounded for $(s, c) \in S \times C$.[15]

For the cake-eating problem described above, the state of the system was the size of the current cake (W_t) and the control variable was the level of consumption in period t, (c_t). The transition equation describing the evolution of the cake was given by

$W_{t+1} = W_t - c_t$.

Clearly, the evolution of the cake is governed by the amount of current consumption. An equivalent representation, as expressed in (2.7), is to consider the future size of the cake as the control variable and then to simply write current consumption as $W_{t+1} - W_t$.

There are two final properties of the agent's dynamic optimization problem worth specifying: **stationarity** and **discounting**. Note that neither the payoff nor the transition equations depend explicitly on time. True the problem is dynamic, but time per se is not of the essence. In a given state the optimal choice of the agent will be the same regardless of "when" he optimizes. Stationarity is important

---

15. Ensuring that the problem is bounded is an issue in some economic applications, such as the growth model. Often these problems are dealt with by bounding the sets C and S.

both for the analysis of the optimization problem and for empirical implementation of infinite horizon problems. In fact, because of stationarity, we can dispense with time subscripts as the problem is completely summarized by the current values of the state variables.

The agent's preferences are also dependent on the rate at which the future is discounted. Let β denote the discount factor and assume that $0 < \beta < 1$. Then we can represent the agent's payoffs over the infinite horizon as

$$\sum_{t=0}^{t=\infty} \beta^t \tilde{\sigma}(s_t, c_t). \tag{2.10}$$

One approach to optimization is to maximize (2.10) through the choice of $\{c_t\}$ for $t = 0, 1, 2, \ldots$ given s_0 and subject to the transition equation. Let $V(s_0)$ be the optimized value of this problem given the initial state.

Alternatively, one can adopt the dynamic program approach and consider the following equation, called Bellman's equation:

$$V(s) = \max_{c \in C(s)} \tilde{\sigma}(s, c) + \beta V(s') \qquad \text{for all } s \in S, \tag{2.11}$$

where $s' = \tau(s, c)$. Here time subscripts are eliminated, reflecting the stationarity of the problem. Instead, current variables are unprimed while future ones are denoted by a prime.

As in Stokey and Lucas (1989), the problem can be formulated as

$$V(s) = \max_{s' \in \Gamma(s)} \sigma(s, s') + \beta V(s') \qquad \text{for all } s \in S. \tag{2.12}$$

This is a more compact formulation, and we will use it for our presentation.[16] Nonetheless, the presentations in Bertsekas (1976) and Sargent (1987) follow (2.11). Assume that S is a convex subset of $\Re^k$.

Let the policy function that determines the optimal value of the control (the future state) given the state be given by $s' = \phi(s)$. Our interest is ultimately in the policy function, since we generally observe the actions of agents rather than their levels of utility. Still, to determine $\phi(s)$, we need to "solve" (2.12). That is, we need to find the value function that satisfies (2.12). It is important to realize that while the payoff and transition equations are primitive objects that

---

16. Essentially this formulation inverts the transition equation and substitutes for c in the objective function. This substitution is reflected in the alternative notation for the return function.

models specify a priori, the value function is derived as the solution of the functional equation, (2.12).

There are many results in the lengthy literature on dynamic programming problems on the existence of a solution to the functional equation. Here we present one set of sufficient conditions. The reader is referred to Bertsekas (1976), Sargent (1987), and Stokey and Lucas (1989) for additional theorems under alternative assumptions about the payoff and transition functions.[17]

THEOREM 1   Assume that $\sigma(s,s')$ is real-valued, continuous, and bounded, $0 < \beta < 1$, and that the constraint set, $\Gamma(s)$, is nonempty, compact-valued, and continuous. Then there exists a unique value function $V(s)$ that solves (2.12).

Proof   See Stokey and Lucas (1989, thm. 4.6).

Instead of a formal proof, we give an intuitive sketch. The key component in the analysis is the definition of an operator, commonly denoted as T, defined by[18]

$$T(W)(s) = \max_{s' \in \Gamma(s)} \sigma(s,s') + \beta W(s') \qquad \text{for all } s \in S.$$

So by this mapping we take a guess on the value function, and working through the maximization for all s, we produce another value function, $T(W)(s)$. Clearly, any $V(s)$ such that $V(s) = T(V)(s)$ for all $s \in S$ is a solution to (2.12). So we can reduce the analysis to determining the fixed points of $T(W)$.

The fixed point argument proceeds by showing the $T(W)$ is a contraction using a pair of sufficient conditions from Blackwell (1965). These conditions are (1) monotonicity and (2) discounting of the mapping $T(V)$. **Monotonicity** means that if $W(s) \geq Q(s)$ for all $s \in S$, then $T(W)(s) \geq T(Q)(s)$ for all $s \in S$. This property can be directly verified from the fact that $T(V)$ is generated by a maximization problem. That is, let $\phi_Q(s)$ be the policy function obtained from

$$\max_{s' \in \Gamma(s)} \sigma(s,s') + \beta Q(s') \qquad \text{for all } s \in S.$$

When the proposed value function is $W(s)$, then

---

17. Some of the applications explored in this book will not exactly fit these conditions either. In those cases we will alert the reader and discuss the conditions under which there exists a solution to the functional equation.
18. The notation dates back at least to Bertsekas (1976).

$$T(W)(s) = \max_{s' \in \Gamma(s)} \sigma(s,s') + \beta W(s') \geq \sigma(s, \phi_Q(s)) + \beta W(\phi_Q(s))$$

$$\geq \sigma(s, \phi_Q(s)) + \beta Q(\phi_Q(s)) \equiv T(Q)(s) \qquad \text{for all } s \in S.$$

Discounting means that adding a constant to W leads $T(W)$ to increase by less than this constant. That is, for any constant k, $T(W + k)(s) \leq T(W)(s) + \beta k$ for all $s \in S$ where $\beta \in [0, 1)$. The term "discounting" reflects the fact that β must be less than 1. This property is easy to verify in the dynamic programming problem:

$$T(W + k) = \max_{s' \in \Gamma(s)} \sigma(s,s') + \beta[W(s') + k] = T(W) + \beta k \qquad \text{for all } s \in S,$$

since we assume that the discount factor is less than 1.

The fact that $T(W)$ is a contraction allows us to take advantage of the contraction mapping theorem.[19] This theorem implies that (1) there is a unique fixed point and (2) this fixed point can be reached by an iteration process using an arbitrary initial condition. The first property is reflected in the theorem given above.

The second property is used extensively as a means of finding the solution to (2.12). To better understand this, let $V_0(s)$ for all $s \in S$ be an initial guess of the solution to (2.12). Consider $V_1 = T(V_0)$. If $V_1 = V_0$ for all $s \in S$, then we have the solution. Or else, consider $V_2 = T(V_1)$, and continue iterating until $T(V) = V$ so that the functional equation is satisfied. Of course, in general, there is no reason to think that this iterative process will converge. However, if $T(V)$ is a contraction, as it is for our dynamic programming framework, then the $V(s)$ that satisfies (2.12) can be found from the iteration of $T(V_0(s))$ for any initial guess, $V_0(s)$. This procedure is called **value function iteration**, and it will be a valuable tool for applied analysis of dynamic programming problems.

The value function that satisfies (2.12) may inherit some properties from the more primitive functions that are the inputs to the dynamic programming problem: the payoff and transition equations. As we will see, the property of strict concavity is useful for various applications.[20] The result is given formally by

THEOREM 2   Assume that $\sigma(s, s')$ is real-valued, continuous, concave, and bounded, $0 < \beta < 1$, that S is a convex subset of $\Re^k$, and that the constraint set is nonempty, compact-valued, convex, and contin-

---

19. See Stokey and Lucas (1989) for a statement and proof of this theorem.
20. Define $\sigma(s, s')$ as concave if $\sigma(\lambda(s_1, s_1') + (1 - \lambda)(s_2, s_2')) \geq \lambda\sigma(s_1, s_1') + (1 - \lambda)\sigma(s_2, s_2')$ for all $0 < \lambda < 1$ where the inequality is strict if $s_1 \neq s_2$.

uous. Then the unique solution to (2.12) is strictly concave. Further $\phi(s)$ is a continuous, single-valued function.

Proof See theorem 4.8 in Stokey and Lucas (1989).

The proof of the theorem relies on showing that strict concavity is preserved by $T(V)$: namely, if $V(s)$ is strictly concave, then so is $T(V(s))$. Given that $\sigma(s,c)$ is concave, then we can let our initial guess of the value function be the solution to the one-period problem:

$$V_0(s) \equiv \max_{s' \in \Gamma(s)} \sigma(s,s').$$

$V_0(s)$ is strictly concave. Since $T(V)$ preserves this property, the solution to (2.12) will be strictly concave.

As noted earlier, our interest is in the policy function. Note that by this theorem, there is a stationary policy **function** that depends only on the state vector. This result is important for econometric application as stationarity is often assumed in characterizing the properties of various estimators.

The cake-eating example relied on the Euler equation to determine some properties of the optimal solution. However, the first-order condition from (2.12) combined with the strict concavity of the value function is useful in determining properties of the policy function. Beneveniste and Scheinkman (1979) provide conditions such that $V(s)$ is differentiable (Stokey and Lucas 1989, thm. 4.11). In our discussion of applications, we will see arguments that use the concavity of the value function to characterize the policy function.

2.5.2 Stochastic Dynamic Programming

While the nonstochastic problem may be a natural starting point, in actual applications it is necessary to consider stochastic elements. The stochastic growth model, consumption/savings decisions by households, factor demand by firms, pricing decisions by sellers, search decisions, all involve the specification of dynamic stochastic environments.

Also empirical applications rest upon shocks that are not observed by the econometrician. In many applications the researcher appends a shock to an equation prior to estimation without being explicit about the source of the error term. This is not consistent with the approach of stochastic dynamic programming: shocks are part of the state vector of the agent. Of course, the researcher may not observe all of the variables that influence the agent, and/or there may be measurement error. Nonetheless, being explicit about the source of error in empirical applications is part of the strength of this approach.

While stochastic elements can be added in many ways to dynamic programming problems, we consider the following formulation in our applications. Let ε represent the current value of a vector of "shocks," namely random variables that are partially determined by nature. Let $\varepsilon \in \Psi$ be a finite set.[21] Then, by the notation developed above, the functional equation becomes

$$V(s, \varepsilon) = \max_{s' \in \Gamma(s, \varepsilon)} \sigma(s, s', \varepsilon) + \beta E_{\varepsilon'|\varepsilon} V(s', \varepsilon') \qquad \text{for all } (s, \varepsilon). \qquad (2.13)$$

Further we have assumed that the stochastic process itself is purely exogenous as the distribution of ε' depends on ε but is independent of the current state and control. Note too that the distribution of ε' depends on only the realized value of ε: that is, ε follows a first-order Markov process. This is not restrictive in the sense that if values of shocks from previous periods were relevant for the distribution of ε', then they could simply be added to the state vector.

Finally, note that the distribution of ε' conditional on ε, written as $\varepsilon'|\varepsilon$, is time invariant. This is analogous to the stationarity properties of the payoff and transition equations. In this case the conditional probability of $\varepsilon'|\varepsilon$ are characterized by a transition matrix, Π. The element π_{ij} of this matrix is defined as

$$\pi_{ij} \equiv \text{Prob}(\varepsilon' = \varepsilon_j | \varepsilon = \varepsilon_i),$$

which is just the likelihood that ε_j occurs in the next period, given that ε_i occurs today. Thus this transition matrix is used to compute the transition probabilities in (2.13). Throughout we assume that $\pi_{ij} \in (0, 1)$ and $\sum_j \pi_{ij} = 1$ for each i. By this structure, we have

THEOREM 3   If $\sigma(s, s', \varepsilon)$ is real-valued, continuous, concave, and bounded, $0 < \beta < 1$, and the constraint set is compact and convex, then

1. there exists a unique value function $V(s, \varepsilon)$ that solves (2.13),

2. there exists a stationary policy function, $\phi(s, \varepsilon)$.

---

21. As noted earlier, this structure is stronger than necessary but accords with the approach we will take in our empirical implementation. The results reported in Bertsekas (1976) require that Ψ is countable.

Proof   As in the proof of theorem 2, this is a direct application of Blackwell's theorem. That is, with $\beta < 1$, discounting holds. Likewise monotonicity is immediate as in the discussion above. (See also the proof of proposition 2 in Bertsekas 1976, ch. 6.)

The first-order condition for (2.13) is given by

$$\sigma_{s'}(s,s',\varepsilon) + \beta E_{\varepsilon'|\varepsilon} V_{s'}(s',\varepsilon') = 0. \tag{2.14}$$

Using (2.13) to determine $V_{s'}(s',\varepsilon')$ yields the Euler equation

$$\sigma_{s'}(s,s',\varepsilon) + \beta E_{\varepsilon'|\varepsilon} \sigma_{s'}(s',s'',\varepsilon') = 0. \tag{2.15}$$

This Euler equation has the usual interpretation: the expected sum of the effects of a marginal variation in the control in the current period (s) must be zero. So, if there is a marginal gain in the current period, this gain, in the expectation, is offset by a marginal loss in the next period. Put differently, if a policy is optimal, there should be no variation in the value of the current control that will, in the expectation, make the agent better off. Of course, ex post (after the realization of ε'), there could have been better decisions for the agent and, from the vantage point of hindsight, evidence that mistakes were made. That is to say,

$$\sigma_{s'}(s,s',\varepsilon) + \beta\sigma_{s'}(s',s'',\varepsilon') = 0 \tag{2.16}$$

will surely not hold for all realizations of ε'. Yet, from the ex ante optimization, we know that these ex post errors were not predicable given the information available to the agent. As we will see, this powerful insight underlies the estimation of models based on a stochastic Euler equation such as (2.15).

2.6   Conclusion

This chapter has introduced some of the insights in the vast literature on dynamic programming and some of the results that will be useful in our applications. This chapter has provided a theoretical structure for the dynamic optimization problems we will confront throughout this book. Of course, other versions of the results hold in more general circumstances. The reader is urged to study Bertsekas (1976), Sargent (1987), and Stokey and Lucas (1989) for a more complete treatment of this topic.

3   Numerical Analysis

3.1 Overview

This chapter reviews numerical methods used to solve dynamic programming problems. This discussion provides a key link between the basic theory of dynamic programming and the empirical analysis of dynamic optimization problems. The need for numerical tools arises from the fact that dynamic programming problems generally do not have tractable closed form solutions. Hence techniques must be used to approximate the solutions of these problems. We present a variety of techniques in this chapter that are subsequently used in the macroeconomic applications studied in part II of this book.

The presentation starts by solving a stochastic cake-eating problem using a procedure called **value function iteration**. The same example is then used to illustrate alternative methods that operate on the policy function rather than the value function. Finally, a version of this problem is studied to illustrate the solution to dynamic discrete choice problems.

The appendix and the Web page for this book contain the programs used in this chapter. The applied researcher may find these useful templates for solving other problems. In the appendix we present several tools, such as numerical integration and interpolation techniques, that are useful numerical methods.

A number of articles and books have been devoted to numerical programing. For a more complete description, we refer the reader to Judd (1998), Amman et al. (1996), Press et al. (1986), and Taylor and Uhlig (1990).

3.2   Stochastic Cake-Eating Problem

We start with the stochastic cake-eating problem defined by

$$V(W, y) = \max_{0 \leq c \leq W+y} u(c) + \beta E_{y'|y} V(W', y') \qquad \text{for all } (W, y) \qquad (3.1)$$

with $W' = R(W - c + y)$. Here there are two state variables: W, the size of the cake brought into the current period, and y, the stochastic endowment of additional cake. This is an example of a stochastic dynamic programming problem from the framework in (2.5.2).

We begin by analyzing the simple case where the endowment is iid: the shock today does not give any information on the shock tomorrow. In this case the consumer only cares about the total amount that can be potentially eaten, $X = W + y$, and not the particular origin of any piece of cake. In this problem there is only one state variable X. We can rewrite the problem as

$$V(X) = \max_{0 \leq c \leq X} u(c) + \beta E_{y'} V(X') \qquad \text{for all } X \qquad (3.2)$$

with $X' = R(X - c) + y'$.

If the endowment is serially correlated, then the agent has to keep track of any variables that allow him to forecast future endowment. The state space will include X but also current and maybe past realizations of endowments. We present such a case in section 3.3 where we study a discrete cake eating problem. Chapter 6.1 also presents the continuous cake-eating problem with serially correlated shocks.

The control variable is c, the level of current consumption. The size of the cake evolves from one period to the next according to the transition equation. The goal is to evaluate the value $V(X)$ as well as the policy function for consumption, $c(X)$.

3.2.1   Value Function Iterations

This method works from the Bellman equation to compute the value function by backward iterations on an initial guess. While sometimes slower than competing methods, it is trustworthy in that it reflects the result, stated in chapter 2, that (under certain conditions) the solution of the Bellman equation can be reached by iterating the value function starting from an arbitrary initial value. We illustrate this approach here in solving (3.2).[1]

---

1. We present additional code for this approach in the context of the nonstochastic growth model presented in chapter 5.

In order to program value function iteration, there are several important steps:

1. Choosing a functional form for the utility function.
2. Discretizing the state and control variable.
3. Building a computer code to perform value function iteration
4. Evaluating the value and the policy function.

We discuss each steps in turn. These steps are indicated in the code for the stochastic cake-eating problem.

Functional Form and Parameterization

We need to specify the utility function. This is the only known **primitive** function in (3.2): recall that the value function is what we are solving for! The choice of this function depends on the problem and the data. The consumption literature has often worked with a constant relative risk aversion (CRRA) function:

$$u(c) = \frac{c^{1-\gamma}}{1-\gamma}.$$

The vector θ will represent the parameters. For the cake-eating problem (γ, β) are both included in θ. To solve for the value function, we need to assign particular values to these parameters as well as the exogenous return R. For now we assume that $\beta R = 1$ so that the growth in the cake is exactly offset by the consumers discounting of the future. The specification of the functional form and its parameterization are given in part I of the accompanying Matlab code for the cake-eating problem.

State and Control Space

We have to define the space spanned by the state and the control variables as well as the space for the endowment shocks. For each problem, specification of the state space is important. The computer cannot literally handle a continuous state space, so we have to approximate this continuous space by a discrete one. While the approximation is clearly better if the state space is very fine (i.e., has many points), this can be costly in terms of computation time. Thus there is a trade-off involved.

For the cake-eating problem, suppose that the cake endowment can take two values, low (y_L) and high (y_H). As the endowment is assumed to follow an iid process, denote the probability a shock y_i by π_i for $i = L, H$. The probability of transitions can be stacked in a transition matrix:

$$\pi = \begin{bmatrix} \pi_L & \pi_H \\ \pi_L & \pi_H \end{bmatrix} \quad \text{with } \pi_L + \pi_H = 1.$$

In this discrete setting, the expectation in (3.2) is just a weighted sum, so the Bellman equation can be simply rewritten as

$$V(X) = \max_{0 \leq c \leq X} u(c) + \beta \sum_{i=L,H} \pi_i V(R(X - c) + y_i) \qquad \text{for all } X.$$

For this problem it turns out that the natural state space is given by $[\bar{X}_L, \bar{X}_H]$. This choice of the state space is based on the economics of the problem, which will be understood more completely after studying household consumption choices. Imagine, though, that endowment is constant at a level y_i for $i = L, H$. Then, given the assumption $\beta R = 1$, the cake level of the household will (trust us) eventually settle down to $\bar{X}_i$ for $i = L, H$. Since the endowment is stochastic and not constant, consumption and the size of the future cake will vary with realizations of the state variable X, but it turns out that X will never leave this interval.

The fineness of the grid is simply a matter of choice too. In the program let n_s be the number of elements in the state space. The program simply partitions the interval $[\bar{X}_L, \bar{X}_H]$ into n_s elements. In practice, the grid is usually uniform, with the distance between two consecutive elements being constant.[2]

Call the state space Ψ_S, and let i_s be an index:

$$\Psi_S = \{X^{i_s}\}_{i_s=1}^{n_s} \quad \text{with } X^1 = \bar{X}_L, X^{n_s} = \bar{X}_H.$$

The control variable c takes values in $[\bar{X}_L, \bar{X}_H]$. These are the extreme levels of consumption given the state space for X. We discretize this space into a grid of size n_c, and call the control space $\Psi_C = \{c^{i_c}\}_{i_c=1}^{n_c}$.

Value Function Iteration and Policy Function
Here we must have a loop for the mapping $T(v(X))$, defined as

$$T(v(X)) = \max_c u(c) + \beta \sum_{i=L,H} \pi_i v_j(R(X - c) + y_i). \tag{3.3}$$

---

2. In some applications it can be useful to define a grid that is not uniformally spaced; see the discrete cake-eating problem in section 3.3.

In this expression $v(X)$ represents a candidate value function that is a proposed solution to (3.2). If $T(v(X)) = v(X)$, then indeed $v(X)$ is the unique solution to (3.2). Thus the solution to the dynamic programming problem is reduced to finding a fixed point of the mapping $T(v(X))$.

Starting with an initial guess $v_0(X)$, we compute a sequence of value functions $v_j(X)$:

$$v_{j+1}(X) = T(v_j(X)) = \max_c u(c) + \beta \sum_{i=L,H} \pi_i v_j(R(X - c) + y_i).$$

The iterations are stopped when $|v_{j+1}(X) - v_j(X)| < \varepsilon$ for all i_s, where ε is a small number. As $T(.)$ is a contraction mapping (see chapter 2), the initial guess $v_0(X)$ does not influence the convergence to the fixed point, so one can choose $v_0(X) = 0$, for instance. However, finding a good guess for $v_0(X)$ helps to decrease the computing time. By the contraction mapping property, we know that the convergence rate is geometric, parameterized by the discount rate β.

Let us review in more detail how the iteration is done in practice. At each iteration, the values $v_j(X)$ are stored in a $n_s \times 1$ matrix:

$$\mathbf{V} = \begin{bmatrix} v_j(X^1) \\ \vdots \\ v_j(X^{i_s}) \\ \vdots \\ v_j(X^{n_s}) \end{bmatrix}.$$

To compute v_{j+1}, we start by choosing a particular size for the cake at the start of the period, X^{i_s}. We then search among all the points in the control space Ψ_C for the point where $u(c) + \beta E v_j(X')$ is maximized. We will denote this point $c_c^{i^*}$. Finding next period's value involves calculating $v_j(R(X^{i_s} - c_c^{i^*}) + y_i)$, $i = L, H$. With the assumption of a finite state space, we look for the value $v_j(.)$ at the point nearest to $R(X^{i_s} - c_c^{i^*}) + y_i$. Once we have calculated the new value for $v_{j+1}(X^{i_s})$, we can proceed to compute similarly the value $v_{j+1}(.)$ for other sizes of the cake and other endowment at the start of the period. These new values are then stacked in $\mathbf{V}$. Figure 3.1 gives an example of how this can be programmed on a computer. (Note that the code is not written in a particular computer language, so one has to adapt the code to the appropriate syntax. The code for the value function iteration piece is part III of the Matlab code.)

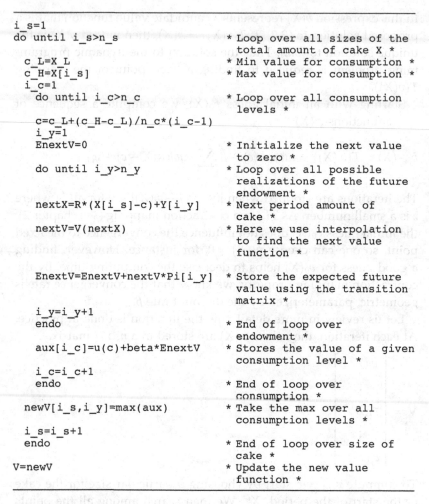

```
i_s=1
do until i_s>n_s                        * Loop over all sizes of the
                                          total amount of cake X *
  c_L=X_L                               * Min value for consumption *
  c_H=X[i_s]                            * Max value for consumption *
  i_c=1
    do until i_c>n_c                    * Loop over all consumption
                                          levels *

    c=c_L+(c_H-c_L)/n_c*(i_c-1)
    i_y=1
    EnextV=0                            * Initialize the next value
                                          to zero *

    do until i_y>n_y                    * Loop over all possible
                                          realizations of the future
                                          endowment *

    nextX=R*(X[i_s]-c)+Y[i_y]           * Next period amount of
                                          cake *

    nextV=V(nextX)                      * Here we use interpolation
                                          to find the next value
                                          function *

    EnextV=EnextV+nextV*Pi[i_y]         * Store the expected future
                                          value using the transition
                                          matrix *

    i_y=i_y+1
    endo                                * End of loop over
                                          endowment *
    aux[i_c]=u(c)+beta*EnextV           * Stores the value of a given
                                          consumption level *

    i_c=i_c+1
    endo                                * End of loop over
                                          consumption *

  newV[i_s,i_y]=max(aux)                * Take the max over all
                                          consumption levels *

  i_s=i_s+1
  endo                                  * End of loop over size of
                                          cake *

V=newV                                  * Update the new value
                                          function *
```

Figure 3.1
Stochastic cake-eating problem

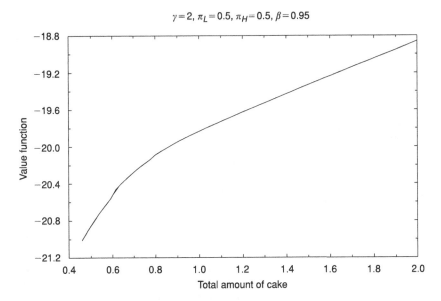

Figure 3.2
Value function, stochastic cake-eating problem

Once the value function iteration piece of the program is com-
pleted, the value function can be used to find the policy function,
$c = c(X)$. This is done by collecting all the optimal consumption
values c^{i_c*} for every value of X^{i_s}. Here again, we only know the
function $c(X)$ at the points of the grid. We can use interpolating
methods to evaluate the policy function at other points. The value
function and the policy function are displayed in figures 3.2 and 3.3
for particular values of the parameters.

As discussed above, approximating the value function and the
policy rules by a finite state space requires a large number of points
on this space (n_s has to be big). These numerical calculations are
often extremely time-consuming. So we can reduce the number of
points on the grid, while keeping a satisfactory accuracy, by using
interpolations on this grid. When we have evaluated the function
$v_j(R(X^{i_s} - c_c^{i^*}) + y_i)$, $i = L, H$, we use the nearest value on the grid to
approximate $R(X^{i_s} - c_c^{i^*}) + y_i$. With a small number of points on the
grid, this can be a very crude approximation. The accuracy of the
computation can be increased by interpolating the function $v_j(.)$ (see
the appendix for more details). The interpolation is based on the
values in **V**.

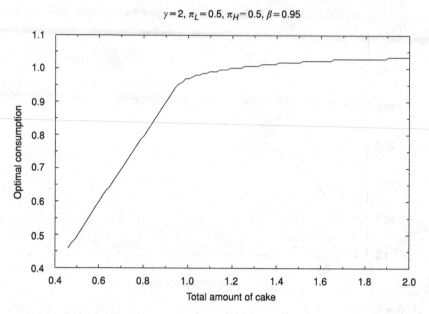

$\gamma = 2, \pi_L = 0.5, \pi_H = 0.5, \beta = 0.95$

Figure 3.3
Policy function, stochastic cake-eating problem

3.2.2 Policy Function Iterations

The value function iteration method can be rather slow, as it converges at a rate β. Researchers have devised other methods that can be faster to compute the solution to the Bellman equation in an infinite horizon. The policy function iteration, also known as Howard's improvement algorithm, is one of these. We refer the reader to Judd (1998) or Ljungqvist and Sargent (2000) for more details.

This method starts with a guess of the policy function, in our case $c_0(X)$. This policy function is then used to evaluate the value of using this rule forever:

$$V_0(X) = u(c_0(X)) + \beta \sum_{i=L,H} \pi_i V_0(R(X - c_0(X)) + y_i) \qquad \text{for all } X.$$

This "policy evaluation step" requires solving a system of linear equations, given that we have approximated $R(X - c^0(X)) + y_i$ by an X on our grid. Next we do a "policy improvement step" to compute $c_1(X)$:

$$c_1(X) = \arg \max_c \left[u(c) + \beta \sum_{i=L,H} \pi_i V_0(R(X - c) + y_i) \right] \quad \text{for all } X.$$

Given this new rule, the iterations are continued to find $V_1(\ )$, $c_2(\ ), \ldots, c_{j+1}(\ )$ until $|c_{j+1}(X) - c_j(X)|$ is small enough. The convergence rate is much faster than the value function iteration method. However, solving the "policy evaluation step" can sometimes be quite time-consuming, especially when the state space is large. Once again, the computation time can be much reduced if the initial guess $c_0(X)$ is close to the true policy rule $c(X)$.

3.2.3 Projection Methods

These methods compute directly the policy function without calculating the value functions. They use the first-order conditions (Euler equation) to back out the policy rules. The continuous cake problem satisfies the first-order Euler equation

$$u'(c_t) = \beta RE_t u'(c_{t+1})$$

if the desired consumption level is less than the total resources $X = W + y$. If there is a corner solution, then the optimal consumption level is $c(X) = X$. Taking into account the corner solution, we can rewrite the Euler equation as

$$u'(c_t) = \max[u'(X_t), \beta RE_t u'(c_{t+1})].$$

We know that by the iid assumption, the problem has only one state variable X, so the consumption function can be written $c = c(X)$. As we consider the stationary solution, we drop the subscript t in the next equation. The Euler equation can then be reformulated as

$$u'(c(X)) - \max[u'(X), \beta RE_{y'} u'(c(R(X - c(X)) + y'))] = 0 \tag{3.4}$$

or

$$F(c(X)) = 0. \tag{3.5}$$

The goal is to find an approximation $\hat{c}(X)$ of $c(X)$, for which (3.5) is approximately satisfied. The problem is thus reduced to find the zero of F, where F is an operator over function spaces. This can be done with a minimizing algorithm. There are two issues to resolve. First, we need to find a good approximation of $c(X)$. Second, we have to define a metric to evaluate the fit of the approximation.

Solving for the Policy Rule

Let $\{p_i(X)\}$ be a base of the space of continuous functions, and let $\Psi = \{\psi_i\}$ be a set of parameters. We can approximate $c(X)$ by

$$\hat{c}(X, \Psi) = \sum_{i=1}^{n} \psi_i p_i(X).$$

There is an infinite number of bases to chose from. A simple one is to consider polynomials in X so that $\hat{c}(X, \Psi) = \psi_0 + \psi_1 X + \psi_2 X^2 + \cdots$. Although this choice is intuitive, it is not usually the best choice. In the function space this base is not an orthogonal base, which means that some elements tend to be collinear.

Orthogonal bases will yield more efficient and precise results.[3] The chosen base should be computationally simple. Its elements should "look like" the function to approximate, so that the function $c(X)$ can be approximated with a small number of base functions. Any knowledge of the shape of the policy function will be to a great help. If, for instance, this policy function has a kink, a method based only on a series of polynomials will have a hard time fitting it. It would require a large number of powers of the state variable to come somewhere close to the solution.

Having chosen a method to approximate the policy rule, we now have to be more precise about what "bringing $F(\hat{c}(X, \Psi))$ close to zero" means. To be more specific, we need to define some operators on the space of continuous functions. For any weighting function $g(x)$, the inner product of two integrable functions f_1 and f_2 on a space A is defined as

$$\langle f_1, f_2 \rangle = \int_A f_1(x) f_2(x) g(x) \, dx. \tag{3.6}$$

Two functions f_1 and f_2 are said to be orthogonal, conditional on a weighting function $g(x)$, if $\langle f_1, f_2 \rangle = 0$. The weighting function indicates where the researcher wants the approximation to be good. We are using the operator $\langle . , . \rangle$ and the weighting function to construct a metric to evaluate how close $F(\hat{c}(X, \Psi))$ is to zero. This will be done

---

3. Popular orthogonal bases are Chebyshev, Legendre, or Hermite polynomials.

by solving for Ψ such that

$$\langle F(\hat{c}(X, \Psi)), f(X) \rangle = 0,$$

where $f(X)$ is some known function. We next review three methods that differ in their choice for this function $f(X)$.

First, a simple choice for $f(X)$ is $F(\hat{c}(X, \Psi))$ itself. This defines the **least square metric** as

$$\min_{\Psi} \langle F(\hat{c}(X, \Psi)), F(\hat{c}(X, \Psi)) \rangle.$$

By the **collocation method**, detailed later in this section, we can choose to find Ψ as

$$\min_{\Psi} \langle F(\hat{c}(X, \Psi)), \delta(X - X_i) \rangle, \qquad i = 1, \ldots, n,$$

where $\delta(X - X_i)$ is the mass point function at point X_i, meaning that $\delta(X) = 1$ if $X = X_i$ and $\delta(X) = 0$ elsewhere. Another possibility is to define

$$\min_{\Psi} \langle F(\hat{c}(X, \Psi)), p_i(X) \rangle, \qquad i = 1, \ldots, n,$$

where $p_i(X)$ is a base of the function space. This is called the **Galerkin method**. An application of this method can be seen below, where the base is taken to be "tent" functions.

Figure 3.4 displays a segment of the computer code that calculates the residual function $F(\hat{c}(X, \Psi))$ when the consumption rule is approximated by a second-order polynomial. This can then be used in one of the proposed methods.

Collocation Methods

Judd (1992) presents in some detail this method applied to the growth model. The function $c(X)$ is approximated using Chebyshev polynomials. These polynomials are defined on the interval $[0, 1]$ and take the form

$$p_i(X) = \cos(i \arccos(X)), \qquad X \in [0, 1], i = 0, 1, 2, \ldots.$$

For $i = 0$, this polynomial is a constant. For $i = 1$, the polynomial is equal to X. As these polynomials are only defined on the $[0, 1]$ interval, one can usually scale the state variables appropriately.[4] The

---

4. The polynomials are also defined recursively by $p_i(X) = 2Xp_{i-1}(X) - p_{i-2}(X)$, $i \geq 2$, with $p_0(0) = 1$ and $p(X, 1) = X$.

```
procedure c(x)
cc=psi_0+psi_1*x+psi_2*x*x
return(cc)
endprocedure


i_s=1
do until i_s>n_s

  utoday=U'(c(X[i_s]))

  ucorner=U'(X[i_s])

  EnextU=0
  i_y=1
  do until i_y>n_y



    nextX=R(X[i_s]-
    c(X[i_s]))+Y[i_y]
    nextU=U'(c(nextX))

    EnextU=EnextU+nextU*Pi[i_y]



  i_y=i_y+1
  endo
F[i_s]=utoday-
max(ucorner,beta*EnextU)
i_s=i_s+1
endo
```

* Here we define an
approximation for the
consumption function based
on a second-order
polynomial *

* Loop over all sizes of the
total amount of cake *
* Marginal utility of
consuming *
* Marginal utility if corner
solution *
* Initialize expected future
marginal utility *
* Loop over all possible
realizations of the future
endowment *
* Next amount of cake *

* Next marginal utility of
consumption *
* Here we compute the expected
future marginal utility of
consumption using the
transition matrix Pi *

* End of loop over endowment *

* End of loop over size of
cake *

Figure 3.4
Stochastic cake-eating problem, projection method

policy function can then be expressed as

$$\hat{c}(X, \Psi) = \sum_{i=1}^{n} \psi_i p_i(X).$$

Next the method finds Ψ, which minimizes

$$\langle F(\hat{c}(X, \Psi)), \delta(X - X_i)\rangle, \qquad i = 1, \ldots, n,$$

where $\delta(\ )$ is the mass point function. Hence the method requires that $F(\hat{c}(X, \Psi))$ is zero at some particular points X_i and not over the whole range $[\overline{X}_L, \overline{X}_H]$. The method is more efficient if these points are chosen to be the zeros of the base elements $p_i(X)$, here $X_i = \cos(\pi/2i)$. This method is referred to as an orthogonal collocation method. Ψ is

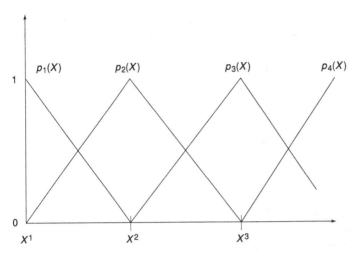

Figure 3.5
Basis functions, finite element method

the solution to a system of nonlinear equations:

$$F(\hat{c}(X_i, \Psi)) = 0, \qquad i = 1, \ldots, n.$$

This method is good at approximating policy functions that are relatively smooth. A drawback is that the Chebyshev polynomials tend to display oscillations at higher orders. The resulting policy function $c(X)$ will also tend to fluctuate. There is no particular rule for choosing n, the highest order of the Chebyshev polynomial. Obviously the higher n is, the better will be the approximation, but this comes at the cost of increased computation.

Finite Element Methods
McGrattan (1996) illustrates the finite element method with the stochastic growth model (see also Reddy 1993 for an in-depth discussion of finite elements).

To start, the state variable X is discretized over a grid $\{X^{i_s}\}_{i_s=1}^{n_s}$. The finite element method is based on the following functions:

$$p_{i_s}(X) = \begin{cases} \dfrac{X - X^{i_s-1}}{X^{i_s} - X^{i_s-1}} & \text{if } X \in [X^{i_s-1}, X^{i_s}], \\[2ex] \dfrac{X^{i_s+1} - X}{X^{i_s+1} - X^{i_s}} & \text{if } X \in [X^{i_s}, X^{i_s+1}], \\[2ex] 0 & \text{elsewhere.} \end{cases}$$

The function $p_{i_s}(X)$ is a simple function in $[0,1]$, as illustrated in figure 3.5. It is in fact a simple linear interpolation (and an order two spline; see the appendix for more on these techniques). On the interval $[X^{i_s}, X^{i_s+1}]$, the function $\hat{c}(X)$ is equal to the weighted sum of $p_{i_s}(X)$ and $p_{i_s+1}(X)$. Here the residual function satisfies

$$\langle F(\hat{c}(X, \Psi)), p_i(X) \rangle = 0, \qquad i = 1, \ldots, n.$$

Equivalently, we could choose a constant weighting function:

$$\int_0^{\bar{X}} p_{i_s}(X) F(\hat{c}(X)) \, dX = 0, \qquad i_s = 1, \ldots, n_s.$$

This gives a system with n_s equations and n_s unknowns, $\{\psi_{i_s}\}_{i_s=1}^{n_s}$. This nonlinear system can be solved to find the weights $\{\psi_{i_s}\}$. To solve the system, the integral can be computed numerically using numerical techniques; see the appendix. As in the collocation method, the choice of n_s is the result of a trade-off between increased precision and a higher computational burden.

3.3   Stochastic Discrete Cake-Eating Problem

We present here another example of a dynamic programming model. It differs from the one presented in section 3.2 in two ways. First, the decision of the agent is not continuous (how much to eat) but discrete (eat or wait). Second, the problem has two state variables as the exogenous shock is serially correlated.

The agent is endowed with a cake of size W. In each period the agent has to decide whether or not to eat the entire cake. Even if not eaten, the cake shrinks by a factor ρ each period. The agent also experiences taste shocks, possibly serially correlated, and which follow an autoregressive process of order one. The agent observes the current taste shock at the beginning of the period, before the decision to eat the cake is taken. However, the future shocks are unobserved by the agent, introducing a stochastic element into the problem. Although the cake is shrinking, the agent might decide to postpone the consumption decision until a period with a better realization of the taste shock. The program of the agent can be written in the form

$$V(W, \varepsilon) = \max[\varepsilon u(W), \beta E_{\varepsilon'|\varepsilon} V(\rho W, \varepsilon')], \tag{3.7}$$

where $V(W, \varepsilon)$ is the intertemporal value of a cake of size W conditional of the realization ε of the taste shock. Here $E_{\varepsilon'}$ denotes the expectation with respect to the future shock ε, conditional on the value of ε. The policy function is a function $d(W, \varepsilon)$ that takes a value of zero if the agent decides to wait or one if the cake is eaten. We can also define a threshold $\varepsilon^*(W)$ such that

$$\begin{cases} d(W, \varepsilon) = 1 & \text{if } \varepsilon > \varepsilon^*(W), \\ d(W, \varepsilon) = 0 & \text{otherwise.} \end{cases}$$

As in section 3.2 the problem can be solved by value function iterations. However, the problem is discrete, so we cannot use the projection technique as the decision rule is not a smooth function but a step function.

3.3.1 Value Function Iterations

As before, we have to define, first, the functional form for the utility function, and we need to discretize the state space. We will consider $\rho < 1$, so the cake shrinks with time and W is naturally bounded between $\overline{W}$, the initial size and 0. In this case the size of the cake takes only values equal to $\rho^t \overline{W}$, $t \geq 0$. Hence $\Psi_S = \{\rho^i \overline{W}\}$ is a judicious choice for the state space. Contrary to an equally spaced grid, this choice ensures that we do not need to interpolate the value function outside of the grid points.

Next, we need to discretize the second state variable, ε. The shock is supposed to come from a continuous distribution, and it follows an autoregressive process of order one. We discretize ε in I points $\{\varepsilon_i\}_{i=1}^{I}$ following a technique presented by Tauchen (1986) and summarized in the appendix. In fact we approximate an autoregressive process by a Markov chain. The method determines the optimal discrete points $\{\varepsilon_i\}_{i=1}^{I}$ and the transition matrix $\pi_{ij} = \text{Prob}(\varepsilon_t = \varepsilon_i | \varepsilon_{t-1} = \varepsilon_j)$ such that the Markov chain mimics the AR(1) process. Of course, the approximation is only good if I is big enough.

In the case where $I = 2$, we have to determine two grid points ε_L and ε_H. The probability that a shock ε_L is followed by a shock ε_H is denoted by π_{LH}. The probability of transitions can be stacked in a transition matrix:

$$\pi = \begin{bmatrix} \pi_{LL} & \pi_{LH} \\ \pi_{HL} & \pi_{HH} \end{bmatrix}$$

with the constraints that the probability of reaching either a low or a high state next period is equal to one: $\pi_{LL} + \pi_{LH} = 1$ and $\pi_{HL} + \pi_{HH} =$

```
i_s=2
do until i_s>n_s                    * Loop over all sizes of the
                                      cake *
  i_e=1
  do until i_e>2                    * Loop over all possible
                                      realizations of the taste shock
                                      *
    ueat=u(W[i_s],e[i_e])           * Utility of doing the eating now
                                      *
    nextV1=V[i_s-1,1]               * Next period value if low taste
                                      shock *
    nextV2=V[i_s-1,2]               * Next period value if high taste
                                      shock *
    EnextV=nextV1*p[i_e,1]+
    nextV2*p[i_e,2]
    newV[i_s,i_e]
    =max(ueat,beta*EnextV)
                                    * Take the max between eating now
                                      or waiting *
    i_e=i_e+1
  endo                             * End of loop over taste shock *
  i_s=i_s+1
endo                               * End of loop over size of cake *
V=newV                             * Update the new value function *
```

Figure 3.6
Discrete cake-eating problem

1. For a given size of the cake $W^{i_s} = \rho^{i_s}\overline{W}$ and a given shock ε_j, $j = L$ or H, it is easy to compute the first term $\varepsilon_j u(\rho^{i_s}\overline{W})$. To compute the second term we need to calculate the expected value of tomorrow's cake. Given a guess for the value function of next period, $v(.,.)$, the expected value is

$$E_{\varepsilon'|\varepsilon_j}v(\rho^{i_s+1}\overline{W}) = \pi_{jL}v(\rho^{i_s+1}\overline{W},\varepsilon_L) + \pi_{jH}v(\rho^{i_s+1}\overline{W},\varepsilon_H).$$

The recursion is started backward with an initial guess for $V(.,.)$. For a given state of the cake W_{i_s} and a given shock ε_j, the new value function is calculated from equation (3.7). The iterations are stopped when two successive value functions are close enough. In numerical computing the value function is stored as a matrix $\mathbf{V}$ of size $n_W \times n_\varepsilon$, where n_W and n_ε are the number of points on the grid for W and ε. At each iteration the matrix is updated with the new guess for the value function. Figure 3.6 gives an example of a computer code that obtains the value function $v_{j+1}(W,\varepsilon)$ given the value $v_j(W,\varepsilon)$.

The way we have computed the grid, the next period value is simple to compute as it is given by $\mathbf{V}[i_s - 1,.]$. This rule is valid if

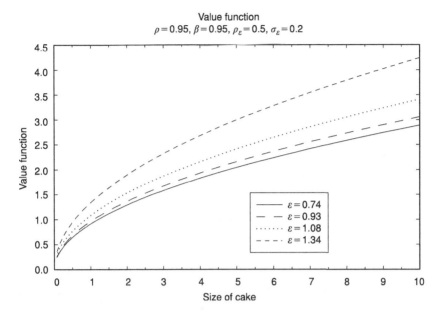

Figure 3.7
Value function, discrete cake-eating problem

$i_s > 1$. Computing $\mathbf{V}[1, .]$ is more of a problem. One way is to use an extrapolation method to approximate the values, given the knowledge of $\mathbf{V}[i_s, .]$, $i_s > 1$.

Figure 3.7 shows the value function for particular parameters. The utility function is taken to be $u(c, \varepsilon) = \ln(\varepsilon c)$, and $\ln(\varepsilon)$ is supposed to follow an AR(1) process with mean zero, autocorrelation $\rho_\varepsilon = 0.5$ and with an unconditional variance of 0.2. We have discretized ε into four grid points.

Figure 3.8 shows the decision rule, and the function $\varepsilon^*(W)$. This threshold was computed as the solution of:

$$u(W, \varepsilon^*(W)) = \beta E_{\varepsilon' | \varepsilon} V(\rho W, \varepsilon'),$$

which is the value of the taste shock that makes the agent indifferent between waiting and eating, given the size of the cake W.

We return later in this book to examples of discrete choice models. In particular, we refer the readers to the models presented in sections 8.5 and 7.3.3.

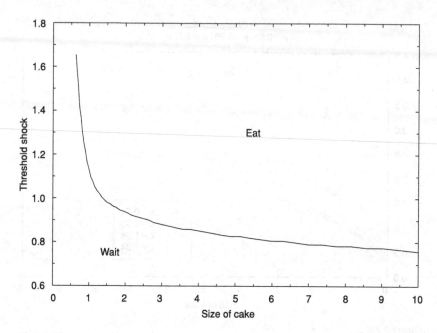

Figure 3.8
Decision rule, discrete cake-eating problem

3.4   Extensions and Conclusion

In this chapter we reviewed the common techniques used to solve
the dynamic programming problems of chapter 2. We applied these
techniques to both deterministic and stochastic problems, to continuous and discrete choice models. These methods can be applied as
well to more complicated problems.

3.4.1   Larger State Spaces

The two examples we have studied in sections 3.2 and 3.3 have small
state spaces. In empirical applications the state space often needs to
be much larger if the model is to confront real data. For instance, the
endowment shocks might be serially correlated or the interest rate R
might also be a stochastic and persistent process.

For the value function iteration method, this means that the successive value functions have to be stacked in a multidimensional
matrix. Also the value function has to be interpolated in several
dimensions. The techniques in the appendix can be extended to deal

with this problem. However, the value function iteration method quickly encounters the "curse of dimensionality." If every state variable is discretized into n_s grid points, the value function has to be evaluated by N^{n_s} points, where N is the number of state variables. This demands an increasing amount of computer memory and so slows down the computation. A solution to this problem is to evaluate the value function for a subset of the points in the state space and then to interpolate the value function elsewhere. This solution was implemented by Keane and Wolpin (1994).

Projection methods are better at handling larger state spaces. Suppose that the problem is characterized by N state variables $\{X_1, \dots, X_N\}$. The approximated policy function can be written as

$$\hat{c}(X_1, \dots, X_N) = \sum_{j=1}^{N} \sum_{i_j=1}^{n_j} \psi_{i_j}^{j} p_{i_j}(X_j).$$

The problem is then characterized by auxiliary parameters $\{\psi_i^j\}$.

EXERCISE 3.1   Suppose that $u(c) = c^{1-\gamma}/(1 - \gamma)$. Construct the code to solve for the stochastic cake-eating problem using the value function iteration method. Plot the policy function as a function of the size of the cake and the stochastic endowment for $\gamma = \{0.5, 1, 2\}$. Compare the level and slope of the policy functions for different values of γ. How do you interpret the results?

EXERCISE 3.2   Consider, again, the discrete cake-eating problem of section 3.3. Construct the code to solve for this problem, with iid taste shocks, using $u(c) = \ln(c)$, $\varepsilon_L = 0.8$, $\varepsilon_H = 1.2$, $\pi_L = 0.3$, and $\pi_H = 0.7$. Map the decision rule as a function of the size of the cake.

EXERCISE 3.3   Consider an extension of the discrete cake-eating problem of section 3.3. The agent can now choose among three actions: eat the cake, store it in fridge 1 or in fridge 2. In fridge 1, the cake shrinks by a factor ρ: $W' = \rho W$. In fridge 2, the cake diminish by a fixed amount: $W' = W - \kappa$. The program of the agent is characterized as

$$V(W, \varepsilon) = \max[V^{\text{Eat}}(W, \varepsilon), V^{\text{Fridge 1}}(W, \varepsilon), V^{\text{Fridge 2}}(W, \varepsilon)]$$

$$\text{with} \begin{cases} V^{\text{Eat}}(W, \varepsilon) = \varepsilon u(W), \\ V^{\text{Fridge 1}}(W, \varepsilon) = \beta E_{\varepsilon'} V(\rho W, \varepsilon'), \\ V^{\text{Fridge 2}}(W, \varepsilon) = \beta E_{\varepsilon'} V(W - \kappa, \varepsilon'). \end{cases}$$

Construct the code to solve for this problem, using $u(c) = \ln(c)$, $\varepsilon_L = 0.8$, $\varepsilon_H = 1.2$, $\pi_L = 0.5$, and $\pi_H = 0.5$. When will the agent switch from one fridge to the other?

EXERCISE 3.4   Consider the stochastic cake-eating problem. Suppose that the discount rate β is a function of the amount of cake consumed: $\beta = \Phi(\beta_1 + \beta_2 c)$, where β_1 and β_2 are known parameters and $\Phi(\ )$ is the normal cumulative distribution function. Construct the code to solve for this new problem using value function iterations. Suppose $\gamma = 2$, $\beta_1 = 1.65$, $\pi_L = \pi_H = 0.5$, $y_L = 0.8$, $y_H = 1.2$, and $\beta_2 = -1$. Plot the policy rule $c = c(X)$. Compare the result with that of the case where the discount rate is independent of the quantity consumed. How would you interpret the fact that the discount rate depends on the amount of cake consumed?

3.5   Appendix: Additional Numerical Tools

In this appendix we provide some useful numerical tools that are often used in solving dynamic problems. We present interpolation methods, numerical integration methods, as well as a method to approximate serially correlated processes by a Markov process. The last subsection is devoted to simulations.

3.5.1   Interpolation Methods

We briefly review three simple interpolation methods. For further readings, see, for instance, Press et al. (1986) or Judd (1996).

When solving the value function or the policy function, we often have to calculate the value of these functions outside of the points of the grid. This requires one to be able to interpolate the function. Using a good interpolation method can also save computer time and space since fewer grid points are needed to approximate the functions. Let us denote $f(x)$ the function to approximate. We assume that we know this function at a number of grid points x_i, $i = 1, \ldots, I$. We denote by $f_i = f(x_i)$ the values of the function at these grid points. We are interested in finding an approximate function $\hat{f}(x)$ such that $\hat{f}(x) \simeq f(x)$, based on the observations $\{x_i, f_i\}$. We present three different methods and use as an example the function $f(x) = x \sin(x)$. Figure 3.9 displays the results for all the methods.

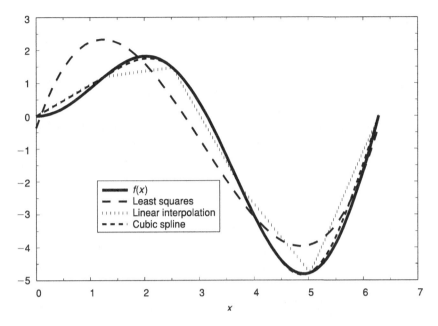

Figure 3.9
Approximation methods

Least Squares Interpolation

A natural way to approximate $f(\ )$ is to use an econometric technique, such as OLS, to "estimate" the function $\hat{f}(.)$. The first step is to assume a functional form for $\hat{f}$. For instance, we can approximate f with a polynomial in x such as

$$\hat{f}(x) = \alpha_0 + \alpha_1 x + \cdots + \alpha_N x^N, \qquad N < I.$$

By regressing f_i on x_i, we can easily recover the parameters α_n. In practice, this method is often not very good, unless the function f is well behaved. Higher-order polynomials tend to fluctuate and can occasionally give an extremely poor fit. This is particularly true when the function is extrapolated outside of the grid points, when $x > x_I$ or $x < x_1$. The least square method is a global approximation method. As such, the fit can be on average satisfactory but mediocre almost everywhere. This can be seen in the example in figure 3.9.

Linear Interpolation

This method fits the function f with piecewise linear functions on the intervals $[x_{i-1}, x_i]$. For any value of x in $[x_{i-1}, x_i]$, an approximation $\hat{f}(x)$ of $f(x)$ can be found as

$$\hat{f}(x) = f_{i-1} + \frac{f_i - f_{i-1}}{x_i - x_{i-1}}(x - x_{i-1}).$$

A finer grid will give a better approximation of $f(x)$. When x is greater than x_I, using this rule can lead to numerical problems as the expression above may not be accurate. Note that the approximation function $\hat{f}$ is continuous but not differentiable at the grid points. This can be an undesirable feature as this nondifferentiability can be translated to the value function or the policy function.

The linear interpolation method can be extended for multivariate functions. For instance, we can approximate the function $f(x, y)$ given data on $\{x_i, y_j, f_{ij}\}$. Denote $d_x = (x - x_i)/(x_{i-1} - x_i)$ and $d_y = (y - y_i)/(y_{i-1} - y_i)$. The approximation can be written as

$$\hat{f}(x, y) = d_x d_y f_{i-1, j-1} + (1 - d_x) d_y f_{i, j-1} + d_x (1 - d_y) f_{i-1, j}$$
$$+ (1 - d_x)(1 - d_y) f_{i, j}.$$

The formula can be extended to higher dimensions as well.

Spline Methods

This method extends the linear interpolation by fitting piecewise polynomials while ensuring that the resulting approximate function $\hat{f}$ is both continuous and differentiable at the grid points x_i. We restrict ourself to cubic splines for simplicity, but the literature on splines is very large (e.g., see De Boor 1978). The approximate function is expressed as

$$\hat{f}_i(x) = f_i + a_i(x - x_{i-1}) + b_i(x - x_{i-1})^2 + c_i(x - x_{i-1})^3, \qquad x \in [x_{i-1}, x_i].$$

Here for each point on the grid, we have to determine three parameters $\{a_i, b_i, c_i\}$, so in total there is $3 \times I$ parameters to compute. However, imposing the continuity of the function and of its derivative up to the second order reduces the number of coefficients:

$$\hat{f}_i(x) = \hat{f}_{i+1}(x),$$
$$\hat{f}_i'(x) = \hat{f}_{i+1}'(x),$$
$$\hat{f}_i''(x) = \hat{f}_{i+1}''(x).$$

It is also common practice to apply $\hat{f}_1''(x_1) = \hat{f}_I''(x_I) = 0$. With these constraints, the number of coefficients to compute is down to I. Some algebra gives

$$
\begin{cases}
a_i = \dfrac{f_i - f_{i-1}}{x_i - x_{i-1}} - b_i(x_i - x_{i-1}) - c_i(x_i - x_{i-1})^2, & i = 1, \ldots, I, \\[3mm]
c_i = \dfrac{b_{i+1} - b_i}{3(x_i - x_{i-1})}, & i = 1, \ldots, I-1, \\[3mm]
c_I = -\dfrac{b_I}{3(x_I - x_{I-1})}, \\[3mm]
a_i + 2b_i(x_i - x_{i-1}) + 3c_i(x_i - x_{i-1})^2 = a_{i+1}.
\end{cases}
$$

Solving this system of equation leads to expressions for the coefficients $\{a_i, b_i, c_i\}$. Figure 3.9 shows that the cubic spline is a very good approximation to the function f.

3.5.2 Numerical Integration

Numerical integration is often required in dynamic programming problems to solve for the expected value function or to "integrate out" an unobserved state variable. For instance, solving the Bellman equation (3.3) requires one to calculate $Ev(X') = \int v(X')\,dF(X')$, where $F(.)$ is the cumulative density of the next period cash-on-hand X. In econometric applications some important state variables might not be observed. For this reason one may need to compute the decision rule unconditional of this state variable. For instance, in the stochastic cake-eating problem of section 3.2, if X is not observed, one could compute $\bar{c} = \int c(X)\,dF(X)$, which is the unconditional mean of consumption, and match it with observed consumption. We present three methods that can be used when numerical integration is needed.

Quadrature Methods
There are a number of quadrature methods. We briefly detail the Gauss-Legendre method (more detailed information can be found in Press et al. 1986). The integral of a function f is approximated as

$$
\int_{-1}^{1} f(x)\,dx \simeq w_1 f(x_1) + \cdots + w_n f(x_n), \tag{3.8}
$$

where w_i and x_i are n weights and nodes to be determined. Integration over a different domain can be easily handled by operating a change of the integration variable. The weights and the nodes are computed such that (3.8) is exactly satisfied for polynomials of degree $2n - 1$ or less. For instance, if $n = 2$, denote $f_i(x) = x^{i-1}$, $i = 1, \ldots, 4$. The weights and nodes satisfy

$$w_1 f_1(x_1) + w_2 f_1(x_2) = \int_{-1}^{1} f_1(x)\, dx,$$

$$w_1 f_2(x_1) + w_2 f_2(x_2) = \int_{-1}^{1} f_2(x)\, dx,$$

$$w_1 f_3(x_1) + w_2 f_3(x_2) = \int_{-1}^{1} f_3(x)\, dx,$$

$$w_1 f_4(x_1) + w_2 f_4(x_2) = \int_{-1}^{1} f_4(x)\, dx.$$

This is a system of four equations with four unknowns. The solutions are $w_1 = w_2 = 1$ and $x_2 = -x_1 = 0.578$. For larger values of n, the computation is similar. By increasing the number of nodes n, the precision increases. Notice that the nodes are not necessarily equally spaced. The weights and the value of the nodes are published in the literature for commonly used values of n.

Approximating an Autoregressive Process with a Markov Chain

In this discussion we follow Tauchen (1986) and Tauchen and Hussey (1991) and show how to approximate an autoregressive process of order one by a first-order Markov process. This way we can simplify the computation of expected values in the value function iteration framework.

To return to the value function in the cake-eating problem, we need to calculate the expected value given ε:

$$V(W, \varepsilon) = \max[\varepsilon u(W), E_{\varepsilon'|\varepsilon} V(\rho W, \varepsilon')].$$

The calculation of an integral at each iteration is cumbersome. So we discretize the process ε_t, into N points ε^i, $i = 1, \ldots, N$. Now we can replace the expected value by

$$V(W, \varepsilon^i) = \max \left[\varepsilon u(W), \sum_{j=1}^{N} \pi_{i,j} V(\rho W, \varepsilon^j) \right], \qquad i = 1, \ldots, N.$$

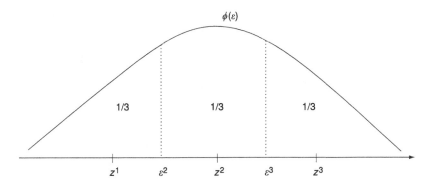

Figure 3.10
Example of discretization, $N = 3$

As in the quadrature method, the method involves finding nodes ε^j and weights $\pi_{i,j}$. As we will see below, the ε^i and the $\pi_{i,j}$ can be computed prior to the iterations.

Suppose that ε_t follows an AR(1) process, with an unconditional mean μ and an autocorrelation ρ:

$$\varepsilon_t = \mu(1 - \rho) + \rho\varepsilon_{t-1} + u_t, \tag{3.9}$$

where u_t is a normally distributed shock with variance σ^2. To discretize this process, we need to determine three different objects. First, we need to discretize the process ε_t into N intervals. Second, we need to compute the conditional mean of ε_t within each intervals, which we denote by z^i, $i, \ldots, N$. Third, we need to compute the probability of transition between any of these intervals, $\pi_{i,j}$. Figure 3.10 shows the plot of the distribution of ε and the cut-off points ε^i as well as the conditional means z^i.

We start by discretizing the real line into N intervals, defined by the limits $\varepsilon^1, \ldots, \varepsilon^{N+1}$. As the process ε_t is unbounded, $\varepsilon^1 = -\infty$ and $\varepsilon^{N+1} = +\infty$. The intervals are constructed such that ε_t has an equal probability of $1/N$ of falling into them. Given the normality assumption, the cut-off points $\{\varepsilon^i\}_{i=1}^{N+1}$ are defined as

$$\Phi\left(\frac{\varepsilon^{i+1} - \mu}{\sigma_\varepsilon}\right) - \Phi\left(\frac{\varepsilon^i - \mu}{\sigma_\varepsilon}\right) = \frac{1}{N}, \qquad i = 1, \ldots, N, \tag{3.10}$$

where $\Phi(\ )$ is the cumulative of the normal density and σ_ε is the standard deviation of ε equal to $\sigma/\sqrt{(1 - \rho^2)}$. Working recursively, we get

$$\varepsilon^i = \sigma_\varepsilon \Phi^{-1}\left(\frac{i-1}{N}\right) + \mu.$$

Now that we have defined the intervals, we want to find the average value of ε within a given interval. We denote this value by z^i, which is computed as the mean of ε_t conditional on $\varepsilon_t \in [\varepsilon^i, \varepsilon^{i+1}]$:

$$z^i = E(\varepsilon_t | \varepsilon_t \in [\varepsilon^i, \varepsilon^{i+1}]) = \sigma_\varepsilon \frac{\phi((\varepsilon^i - \mu)/\sigma_\varepsilon) - \phi((\varepsilon^{i+1} - \mu)/\sigma_\varepsilon)}{\Phi((\varepsilon^{i+1} - \mu)/\sigma_\varepsilon) - \Phi((\varepsilon^i - \mu)/\sigma_\varepsilon)} + \mu.$$

From (3.10), we know that the expression simplifies to

$$z^i = N\sigma_\varepsilon \left(\phi\left(\frac{\varepsilon^i - \mu}{\sigma_\varepsilon}\right) - \phi\left(\frac{\varepsilon^{i+1} - \mu}{\sigma_\varepsilon}\right)\right) + \mu.$$

Next we define the transition probability as

$$\pi_{i,j} = P(\varepsilon_t \in [\varepsilon^j, \varepsilon^{j+1}] \,|\, \varepsilon_{t-1} \in [\varepsilon^i, \varepsilon^{i+1}])$$

$$\pi_{i,j} = \frac{N}{\sqrt{2\pi\sigma_\varepsilon^2}} \int_{\varepsilon^i}^{\varepsilon^{i+1}} e^{-(u-\mu)^2/(2\sigma_\varepsilon^2)} \left[\Phi\left(\frac{\varepsilon^{j+1} - \mu(1-\rho) - \rho u}{\sigma}\right)\right.$$

$$\left. - \Phi\left(\frac{\varepsilon^j - \mu(1-\rho) - \rho u}{\sigma}\right)\right] du.$$

The computation of $\pi_{i,j}$ requires the computation of a nontrivial integral. This can be done numerically. Note that if $\rho = 0$, meaning ε is an iid process, the expression above is simply

$$\pi_{i,j} = \frac{1}{N}.$$

We can now define a Markov process z_t that will mimic an autoregressive process of order one, as defined in (3.9). z_t takes its values in $\{z^i\}_{i=1}^N$ and the transition between period t and $t+1$ is defined as

$$P(z_t = z^j | z_{t-1} = z^i) = \pi_{i,j}.$$

By increasing N, the discretization becomes finer and the Markov process gets closer to the real autoregressive process.

Example For N = 3, $\rho = 0.5$, $\mu = 0$, and $\sigma = 1$, we have

$$z^1 = -1.26, \quad z^2 = 0, \quad z^3 = 1.26,$$

and

$$\pi = \begin{bmatrix} 0.55 & 0.31 & 0.14 \\ 0.31 & 0.38 & 0.31 \\ 0.14 & 0.31 & 0.55 \end{bmatrix}.$$

3.5.3 How to Simulate the Model

Once the value function is computed, the estimation or the evaluation of the model often requires the simulation of the behavior of the agent through time. If the model is stochastic, the first step is to generate a series for the shocks, for $t = 1, \ldots, T$. Then we go from period to period and use the policy function to find out the optimal choice for this period. We also update the state variable and proceed to next period.

How to Program a Markov Process

The Markov process is characterized by grid points, $\{z^i\}$ and by a transition matrix π, with elements $\pi_{ij} = \text{Prob}(y_t = z^j / y_{t-1} = z^i)$. We start in period 1. The process z_t is initialized at, say, z^i. Next, we have to assign a value for z_2. To this end, using the random generator of the computer, we draw a uniform variable u in $[0, 1]$. The state in period 2, j, is defined as

```
t=1
oldind=1                         * Variable to keep track of
                                   state in period t-1 *
y[t]=z[oldind]                   * Initialize first period *
  do until t>T                   * Loop over all time periods *
    u=uniform(0,1)               * Generate a uniform random
                                   variable *

    sum=0                        * Will contain the cumulative
                                   sum of pi *

    ind=1                        * Index over all possible
                                   values for process *

      do until u<=sum            * Loop to find out the state
                                   in period t *

        sum=sum+pi[oldind,ind]   * Cumulative sum of pi *
        ind=ind+1
      endo
    y[t]=z[ind]                  * State in period t *
    oldind=ind                   * Keep track of lagged state *
    t=t+1
  endo
```

Figure 3.11
Simulation of a Markov process

$$\sum_{l=1}^{j} \pi_{i,l} < u \le \sum_{l=1}^{j+1} \pi_{i,l},$$

or $j = 1$ if $u < \pi_{i,1}$. The values for the periods ahead are constructed in a similar way. Figure 3.11 presents a computer code that will construct iteratively the values for T periods.

How to Simulate the Model

For the model we need to initialize all stochastic processes that are the exogenous shock and the state variables. The state variables can be initialized to their long-run values or to some other value. Often the model is simulated over a long number of periods and the first periods are discarded to get rid of initial condition problems.

The value of the state variables and the shock in period 1 are used to determine the choice variable in period 1. In the case of the continuous stochastic cake-eating problem of section 3.2, we would construct $c_1 = c(X_1)$. Next we can generate the values of the state variable in period 2, $X_2 = R(X_1 - c_1) + y_2$, where y_2 is calculated using the method described in section 3.5.3 above. This procedure would be repeated over T periods to successively construct all the values for the choice variables and the state variables.

4   Econometrics

4.1 Overview

In this chapter we review the techniques for estimating parameters
of models based on dynamic programming. This chapter is orga-
nized in two sections. In section 4.2 we present two simple examples
that illustrate the different estimation methodologies. We analyze a
simple coin-flipping experiment and the classic problem of supply
and demand. We review standard techniques such as maximum
likelihood and the method of moments as well as simulated estimation techniques. The reader who is already familiar with econometric
techniques could go to section 4.3, which gives more details on these
techniques and studies the asymptotic properties of the estimators. A
more elaborate dynamic programming model of cake eating is used
to illustrate these different techniques.

4.2 Some Illustrative Examples

4.2.1 Coin Flipping

In this simple coin-flipping example the coin is not necessarily fair,
and the outcome of the draw is either heads with a probability P_1
or tails with a probability $P_2 = 1 - P_1$, with $\{P_1, P_2\} \in [0, 1] \times [0, 1]$.
We are interested in estimating the probability of each outcome. We
observe a series of T draws from the coin. Denote the realization of
the tth draw by x_t, which is equal either to 1 (if heads) or 2 (if tails).
The data set at hand is thus a series of observations $\{x_1, x_2, \ldots, x_T\}$.
This section will describe a number of methods to uncover the
probabilities $\{P_1, P_2\}$ from observed data.

The simple coin-flipping example can be extended in two directions. First, we can try to imagine a coin with more than two sides (a dice). We are then able to consider more than two outcomes per draw. In this case we denote $P = \{P_1, \ldots, P_I\}$ a vector with I elements where $P_i = P(x_t = i)$ is the probability of outcome i. We are interested in estimating the probabilities $\{P_i\}_{i=1,\ldots,I}$. For simplicity we sometimes state results for the case where $I = 2$, but the generalization to a larger number of outcomes is straightforward.

Second, it may be possible that the draws are serially correlated. The probability of obtaining a head might depend on the outcome of the previous draw. In this case we want to estimate $P(x_t = j \mid x_{t-1} = i)$. We also consider the generalized example below.

Of course, a researcher might not be interested in these probabilities alone but rather, as in many economic examples, in the parameters that underlie P. To be more specific, suppose a model parameterized by $\theta \in \Theta \subset R^K$ that determines P. That is, associated with each θ is a vector of probabilities P. Denote by $M(\theta)$ the mapping from parameters to probabilities: $M : \Theta \to [0,1]^I$.

In the case where $I = 2$, we could consider a fair coin, namely $\theta = (1/2, 1/2)$ and $P = (P_1, P_2) = (1/2, 1/2)$. Alternatively we could consider a coin that is biased toward heads, with $\theta = (2/3, 1/3)$ and $P = (P_1, P_2) = (2/3, 1/3)$. In these examples the model M is the identity, $M(\theta) = \theta$. In practice, we would have to impose $\theta \in [0,1]$ in the estimation algorithm. Another way of specifying the model is to chose a function $M(.)$ that is naturally bounded between 0 and 1. In this case we can let θ to belong to R. For instance, the cumulative distribution of the normal density, noted $\Phi(.)$ satisfies this condition. In the fair coin example we would have $\theta = (0,0)$ and $P = (\Phi(0), \Phi(0)) = (1/2, 1/2)$. With the biased coin we would have $\theta = (0.43, -0.43)$, as $\Phi(0.43) = 2/3$ and $\Phi(-0.43) = 1/3$.

Maximum Likelihood

IID CASE   We start with the case where the draws from the coin are identically and independently distributed. The likelihood of observing the sample $\{x_1, x_2, \ldots, x_T\}$ is given by

$$\mathcal{L}(x, P) = \prod_{i=1}^{I} P_i^{N_i},$$

where N_i is the number of observations for which event i occurs. Thus $\mathscr{L}$ represents the probability of observing $\{x_t\}_{t=1}^{T}$ given P. The maximum likelihood estimator of P is given by

$$P = \arg\max \mathscr{L}. \tag{4.1}$$

After we derive the first-order condition for a maximum of $\mathscr{L}(x, P)$, the maximum likelihood estimate of P_i, $i = 1, 2, \ldots, I$ becomes

$$P_i^* = \frac{N_i}{\sum_j N_j}. \tag{4.2}$$

In words, the maximum likelihood estimator of P_i is the fraction of occurrences of event i.

Suppose that one has a model $M(.)$ for the probabilities parameterized by θ. So, indirectly, the likelihood of the sample depends on this vector of parameters, denote it $\tilde{\mathscr{L}}(x, \theta) = \mathscr{L}(x, M(\theta))$. In that case the maximum likelihood estimator of the parameter vector (θ^*) is given by

$$\theta^* = \arg\max_{\theta} \tilde{\mathscr{L}}(x, \theta).$$

In effect, by a judicious choice of θ, we choose the elements of P to maximize the likelihood of observing the sample. In fact, by maximizing this function we would end up at the same set of first-order conditions, (4.2), that we obtained in solving (4.1).

Example 4.1 Suppose $I = 2$ and that $M(\theta) = \Phi(\theta)$, where $\Phi(.)$ is the cumulative distribution function of the standardized normal density.[1] In this case $p_1 = P(x_t = 1) = \Phi(\theta)$ and $p_2 = 1 - \Phi(\theta)$. The parameter is estimated by maximizing the likelihood of observing the data

$$\theta^* = \arg\max_{\theta} \Phi(\theta)^{N_1}(1 - \Phi(\theta))^{N_2},$$

where N_1 and N_2 are the number of observations that fall into categories 1 and 2. Straightforward derivation gives

$$\theta^* = \Phi^{-1}\left(\frac{N_1}{N_1 + N_2}\right).$$

---

1. This is in fact the structure of a probit model.

MARKOV STRUCTURE   Similar issues arise in a model that exhibits more dynamics, as when the outcomes are serially correlated. Let P_{ij} denote the probability of observing event j in period $t+1$ conditional on observing event i in period t:

$$P_{ij} = \text{Prob}(x_{t+1} = j \mid x_t = i).$$

These conditional probabilities satisfy: $P_{ij} \in (0,1)$ and $\sum_j P_{ij} = 1$ for $i = 1, 2, \ldots, I$. Intuitively, the former condition says that given the current state is i, in period $t+1$ all $j \in I$ will occur with positive probability and the latter condition requires that these probabilities sum to one. The probability of observing the sample of data is

$$\mathscr{L}(x, P) = P(x_1, \ldots, x_T) = \prod_{l=2}^{T} P(x_l \mid x_{l-1}) P(x_1).$$

Let N_{ij} denote the number of observations in which state j occurred in the period following state i. Then the likelihood function is

$$\mathscr{L}(x, P) = \left(\prod_{ij} P_{ij}^{N_{ij}} \right) * P(x_1).$$

We can express the probability of the first observation as a function of the P_{ij} probabilities:

$$P(x_1) = \sum_{j=1}^{I} P(x_1 \mid x_0 = j) = \sum_{j=1}^{I} P_{j1}.$$

As before, the conditional probabilities and this initial probability can, in principle, depend on θ. Thus the maximum likelihood estimator of θ would be the one that maximizes $\mathscr{L}(x, P)$. Note that there are now a large number of probabilities that are estimated through maximum likelihood: $I(I - 1)$. Thus a richer set of parameters can be estimated with this structure.

Method of Moments

Continuing with our examples, we consider an alternative way to estimate the parameters. Consider again the iid case, and suppose that there are only two possible outcomes, $I = 2$, such that we have a repeated Bernoulli trial. Given a sample of observations, let μ denote a moment computed from the data. For example, μ might simply be the fraction of times event $i = 1$ occurred in the sample. In this case $\mu = P_1$.

Let $\mu(\theta)$ denote the same moment calculated from the model when the data-generating process (the model M) is parameterized by θ. For now, assume that the number of parameters, κ, is equal to one so that the number of parameters is equal to the number of moments (the problem is then said to be just identified). Consider the following optimization problem:

$$\min_{\theta}(\mu(\theta) - \mu)^2.$$

Here we are choosing the parameters to bring the moment from the model as close as possible to that from the actual data. The θ that emerges from this optimization is a **method of moments estimator**, and we denote this estimate by $\hat{\theta}$.

Example 4.2 Suppose that we chose as a moment the fraction of times event $i = 1$ occurs in the sample. From our model of coin flipping, this fraction is equal to $\Phi(\theta)$. The parameter is estimated by minimizing the distance between the fraction predicted by the model and the observed one:

$$\theta^* = \arg\min_{\theta}\left(\Phi(\theta) - \frac{N_1}{N_1 + N_2}\right)^2.$$

Solving the minimization problem gives

$$\theta^* = \Phi^{-1}\left(\frac{N_1}{N_1 + N_2}\right).$$

Hence, with this choice of moment, the method of moment estimator is the same as that of the maximum likelihood seen in example 4.1.

In example 4.2 the particular moment we chose was the fraction of heads in the sample. Often in a data set there is a large set of moments to chose from. The method of moments does not guide us in the choice of a particular moment. So which moment should we consider? Econometric theory has not come out with a clear indication of "optimal" moments. However, the moments should be informative of the parameters to be estimated. This means that the moments under consideration should depend on the parameters in such a way that slight variations in their values results in different values for the moments.

With the choice of moment different from the one in example 4.2, the method of moments estimator would be different from the maximum likelihood estimator. However, asymptotically, when the size of the data set increases, both estimators converge to the true value.

More generally, let μ be a $m \times 1$ column vector of moments from the data. If $\kappa < m$, the model is said to be over identified, as there are more moments than parameters to estimate. If $\kappa = m$, the model is said to be just identified, and if $\kappa > m$, the model is under identified. In the latter case estimation cannot be achieved as there are too many unknown parameters.

So, if $\kappa \leq m$, the estimator of θ comes from

$$\min_{\theta}((\mu(\theta) - \mu)'W^{-1}(\mu(\theta) - \mu)).$$

In this quadratic form, W is a weighting matrix. As explained below, the choice of W is important for obtaining an efficient estimator of θ when the model is overidentified.

Using Simulations
In many applications the procedures outlined above are difficult to implement, either because the likelihood of observing the data or the moments is difficult to compute analytically or because it involves solving too many integrals. Put differently, the researcher does not have an analytic representation of $M(\theta)$. If this is the case, then estimation can still be carried out numerically using simulations.

Consider again the iid case, where $I = 2$. The simulation approach proceeds in the following way: First, we fix θ, the parameter of $M(\theta)$. Second, using the random number generator of a computer, we generate S draws $\{u_s\}$ from a uniform distribution over $[0, 1]$. We classify each draw as heads (denoted $i = 1$) if $u_s < M(\theta)$ or tails (denoted $i = 2$) otherwise. The fractions of the two events in the simulated data are used to approximate $P_i^S(\theta)$ by counting the number of simulated observations that take value i, denoted by S_i. So, $P_i^S(\theta) = S_i/S$. The **simulated maximum likelihood** estimator is defined as

$$\theta_S^* = \arg \max_{\theta} \prod_i P_i^S(\theta)^{N_i},$$

where, as before, N_i refers to the fraction of observations in which i occurs. The estimator is indexed by S, the number of simulations.

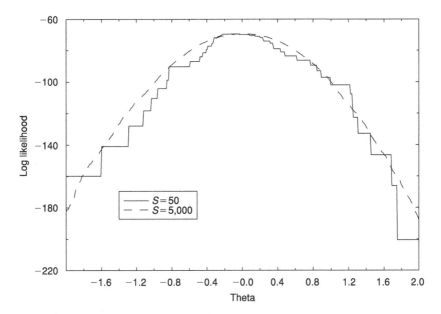

Figure 4.1
Log likelihood, true $\theta_0 = 0$

Obviously, a larger number of simulation draws will yield more precise estimates. Figure 4.1 shows the log-likelihood for the coin-flipping example based on two series of simulation with respectively 50 and 5,000 draws. The observed data set is for a series of 100 draws. The log-likelihood has a maximum at the true value of the parameter, although the likelihood is very flat around the true value when the number of simulations is small.

EXERCISE 4.1 Build a computer program that computes the likelihood function using simulations of a sample of T draws for the case where $I = 3$.

For the method of moments estimator, the procedure is the same. Once an artificial data set has been generated, we can compute moments both on the artificial data and on the observed data. Denote by $\mu^S(\theta)$ a moment derived from the simulated data. For instance, μ and $\mu^S(\theta)$ could be the fraction of heads in the observed sample and in the simulated one. The **simulated method of moments** estimator is defined as

$$\theta_S^* = \arg \min_\theta (\mu^S(\theta) - \mu)' W^{-1} (\mu^S(\theta) - \mu).$$

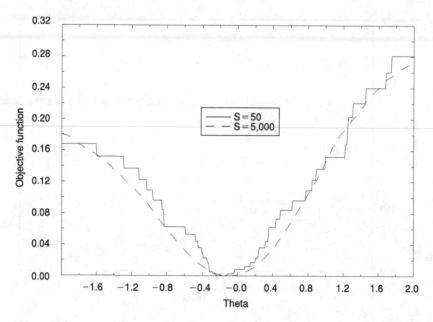

Figure 4.2
Objective function, simulated method of moments, true $\theta_0 = 0$

Figure 4.2 shows the objective function for the simulated method of moments. The function has a minimum at the true value of the parameter. Once again, using more simulation draws obtains a smoother function, which is easier to minimize.

EXERCISE 4.2   Build a computer program that computes the objective function using simulations of a sample of T draws for the case where $I = 3$.

In both methods the estimation requires two steps. First, given a value of θ, one needs to simulate artificial data and compute either a likelihood or a moment from this data set. Second, using these objects, the likelihood or the objective function has to be evaluated and a new value for the parameters, closer to the true one, found. These two steps are repeated until convergence occurs to the true value.

To compute the simulated data, we need to draw random shocks using the random number generator of a computer. Note that the random draws have to be computed once and for all at the start of the estimation process. If the draws change between iterations, it would be unclear whether the change in the criterion function comes from a change in the parameter or from a change in the random draws.

The ability to simulate data opens the way to yet another estimation method: **indirect inference**. This method depends on an auxiliary model chosen by the researcher. The model should be easy to estimate by standard techniques and should capture enough of the interesting variation in the data. Let us denote it by $\tilde{M}(\psi)$, where ψ is a vector of auxiliary parameters describing this new model. Given a guess for the vector of structural parameters θ, the true (structural) model can be simulated to create a new data set. The auxiliary model is estimated both on the real data and on the simulated one, providing two sets of auxiliary parameters. The vector θ is chosen such that the two sets of auxiliary parameters are close to each other.

Note that the vector of auxiliary parameters ψ is of no particular interest as it describes a misspecified model ($\tilde{M}$). Within the context of the original model, it has no clear interpretation. However, it serves as a mean to identify and estimate the structural parameters θ.

Example 4.3   If, for instance, $M(\theta) = \Phi(\theta)$, the model has no closed-form solution as the cumulative of the normal density has no analytical form. Instead of approximating it numerically, we can use the indirect inference method to estimate parameters of interest without computing this function. We might turn to an auxiliary model that is easier to estimate. For instance, the logit model has closed forms for the probabilities. Denote by ψ the auxiliary parameter of the logit model. With such a model, the probability of observing $x_t = 1$ is equal to

$$P(x_t = 1) = \frac{\exp(\psi)}{1 + \exp(\psi)}.$$

Denote by N_1 and N_2 the number of cases that fall into categories 1 and 2. The log-likelihood of observing some data is

$$\mathcal{L} = N_1 \ln \frac{\exp(\psi)}{1 + \exp(\psi)} + N_2 \ln \frac{1}{1 + \exp(\psi)}$$

$$= N_1 \psi - (N_1 + N_2) \ln(1 + \exp(\psi)).$$

Maximization of this log-likelihood and some rearranging gives a simple formula for the ML estimator of the auxiliary parameter: $\psi =$

$\ln(N_1/N_2)$. We can compute this estimator of the auxiliary parameter both for our observed data and for the simulated data by observing in each case the empirical frequencies. Denote the former by $\hat{\psi}$ and the latter by $\hat{\psi}^S(\theta)$. The indirect inference estimator is then

$$\theta_S^* = \arg\min_\theta(\hat{\psi}^S(\theta) - \hat{\psi})^2 = \arg\min_\theta\left(\ln\frac{S_1(\theta)}{S_2(\theta)} - \ln\frac{N_1}{N_2}\right)^2.$$

In this example, as the probit model is difficult to estimate by maximum likelihood directly, we have replaced it with a logit model that is easier to estimate. Although we are not interested in ψ, this parameter is a means to estimate the parameter of importance θ.

So far we have not discussed the size of the simulated data set. Obviously one expects that the estimation will be more efficient if S is large, as the moments, the likelihood, or the auxiliary model will be pinned down with greater accuracy. Using simulations instead of analytical forms introduces randomness into the estimation method. For short samples this randomness can lead to biased estimates. For instance, with the simulated maximum likelihood, we need the number of simulation draws to go to infinity to get rid of the bias. This is not the case for the simulated method of moment or the indirect inference, although the results are more precise for a large S. We discuss this issue later on in this chapter.

Identification Issues

We conclude this section on coin flipping with an informal discussion of identification issues. Up to here, we implicitly assumed that the problem was identified, that the estimation method and the data set allowed us to get a unique estimate of the true vector of parameters θ.

A key issue is the dimensionality of the parameter space κ relative to I, the dimensionality of P. First, suppose that $\kappa = I - 1$ so that the dimensionality of θ is the same as the number of free elements of P.[2] Second, assume that $M(\theta)$ is one to one. This means that M is a function and that for every P there exists only one value of θ such that $P = M(\theta)$. In this case we effectively estimate θ from P^* by using the inverse of the model: $\theta^* = M^{-1}(P^*)$.

This is the most favorable case of identification, and we would say the parameters of the model are **just identified**. It is illustrated in

---

2. This is not I since we have the restriction $\sum_i P_i = 1$.

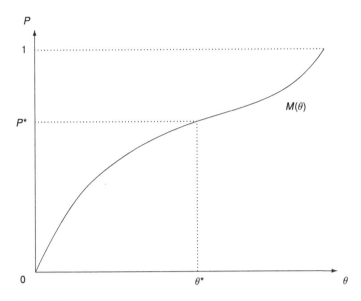

Figure 4.3
Just identification

figure 4.3 for $I = 2$ and $\kappa = 1$. There is a unique value of the parameter θ^* for which the probability predicted by the model $M(\theta^*)$ is equal to the true probability.

A number of problems can arise even for the special case of $\kappa = I - 1$. First, it might be that the model $M(\theta)$ is not invertible. Thus, for a given maximum likelihood estimate of P^*, there could be multiple values of θ that generate this vector of probabilities. In this case the model is not identified. This is shown in figure 4.4. Example 4.4 shows a method of moments estimation where a particular choice of moment leads to nonidentification.

Example 4.4   Let us label heads 1 and tails 2. Suppose that instead of focusing on the mean of the sample (i.e., the fraction of heads), we chose the variance of the sample. The variance can be expressed as

$$V(x) = Ex^2 - (Ex)^2$$

$$= \frac{N_1}{N_1 + N_2} + 4\frac{N_2}{N_1 + N_2} - \left(\frac{N_1}{N_1 + N_2} + 2\frac{N_2}{N_1 + N_2}\right)^2$$

$$= \frac{N_1}{N_1 + N_2}\left(1 - \frac{N_1}{N_1 + N_2}\right).$$

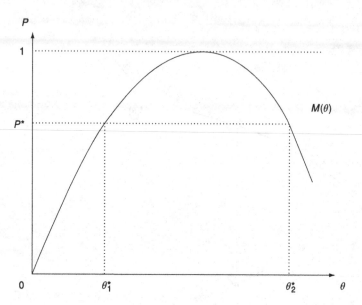

Figure 4.4
Nonidentification

The theoretical and the empirical moments then are

$$\mu(\theta) = \Phi(\theta)(1 - \Phi(\theta)),$$

$$\mu = \frac{N_1}{N_1 + N_2}\left(1 - \frac{N_1}{N_1 + N_2}\right).$$

This might appear as a perfectly valid choice of moment, but in fact it is not. The reason is that the function $\Phi(\theta)(1 - \Phi(\theta))$ is not a monotone function but a hump-shaped one and thus is not invertible. For both low and high values of θ, the function is close to 0. The variance is maximal when the probability of obtaining a head is equal to that of obtaining a tail. If either tails or heads are likely, the variance is going to be low. So a low variance indicates that either heads or tails are more frequent but does not tell us which occurrence is more likely. Hence, in this case, the variance is not a valid moment to consider for identification purposes.

Second, it might be that for a given value of P^*, there does not exist a value of θ such that $M(\theta) = P^*$. In this case the model is simply not rich enough to fit the data. This is a situation of **misspecifi-**

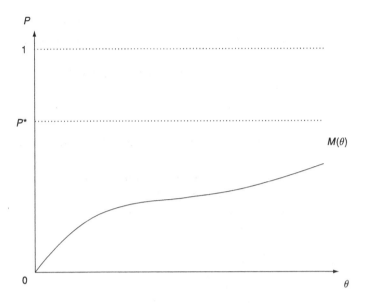

Figure 4.5
Zero likelihood

cation. Put differently, there is a **zero-likelihood problem** here as the model, however parameterized, is unable to match the observations. This is illustrated in figure 4.5.

So, returning to the simple coin-flipping example, if there is a single parameter characterizing the probability of a head occurring and the mapping from this parameter to the likelihood of heads is one to one, then this parameter can be directly estimated from the fraction of heads. But it might be that there are multiple values of this parameter that can generate the same fraction of heads in a sample. In this case the researcher needs to bring additional information to the problem. If there is no value of this parameter that can generate the observed frequency of heads, the model needs to be re-specified.

If, instead of $\kappa = I - 1$, we have more dimensions to θ than information in P ($\kappa > I - 1$), we have a situation where the model is again **underidentified**. Given the maximum likelihood estimate of P^*, there are multiple combinations of the parameters that, through the model, can generate P^*. Again, the researcher needs to bring additional information to the problem to overcome the indeterminacy of the parameters. So in the coin-flipping example a physical theory that involves more than a single parameter cannot be used to estimate from data that yield a single probability of heads.

Alternatively, if $\kappa < I - 1$, then the parameters are **overidentified**. In this case there may not be any θ that is consistent with all the components of P. In many applications, such as those studied in this book, this situation allows the researcher a more powerful test of a model. If a model is just identified, then essentially there exists a θ such that P^* can be generated by the model. But when a model is overidentified, matching the model to the data is a much more demanding task. Thus a model that succeeds in matching the data characterized by P^* when the parameters are overidentified is considered a more compelling model.

4.2.2 Supply and Demand Revisited

The classic problem of supply and demand will serve as an illustration of the previous estimation methods and to elucidate the problem of identification. Suppose that supply depends on prices p and the weather z. Demand depends on prices and income y:

$$q^S = \alpha_p p + \alpha_z z + \varepsilon_S \quad \text{(supply),}$$

$$q^D = \beta_p p + \beta_y y + \varepsilon_D \quad \text{(demand).} \tag{4.3}$$

Both the demand and supply shocks are iid, normally distributed, with mean zero, variances σ_S^2 and σ_D^2, and covariance ρ_{SD}. In total, this model has seven parameters. We solve for the reduced form by expressing the equilibrium variables as function of the exogenous variables y and z:

$$p^* = \frac{\beta_y}{\alpha_p - \beta_p} y - \frac{\alpha_z}{\alpha_p - \beta_p} z + \frac{\varepsilon_D - \varepsilon_S}{\alpha_p - \beta_p} = A_1 y + A_2 z + U_1,$$

$$q^* = \frac{\alpha_p \beta_y}{\alpha_p - \beta_p} y - \frac{\alpha_z \beta_p}{\alpha_p - \beta_p} z + \frac{\alpha_p \varepsilon_D - \beta_p \varepsilon_S}{\alpha_p - \beta_p} = B_1 y + B_2 z + U_2, \tag{4.4}$$

where A_1, A_2, B_1, and B_2 are the reduced-form parameters. These parameters can be consistently estimated from regressions using the reduced form. If the system is identified, we are able to recover all the structural parameters from the reduced-form coefficients using

$$\alpha_p = \frac{B_1}{A_1}, \quad \beta_p = \frac{B_2}{A_2},$$

$$\beta_y = A_1 \left(\frac{B_1}{A_1} - \frac{B_2}{A_2} \right), \quad \alpha_z = -A_2 \left(\frac{B_1}{A_1} - \frac{B_2}{A_2} \right). \tag{4.5}$$

With these four parameters it is straightforward to back out the variance of the demand and supply shocks. We can compute $\varepsilon_S = q - \alpha_p p + \alpha_z z$ and calculate the empirical variance. The same procedure can be applied to recover ε_D.

The estimation in two steps is essentially an instrumental variable estimation where y and z are used as instruments for the endogenous variables p and q. Instead of two-step OLS, we can use a number of alternative methods including the method of moments, maximum likelihood, and indirect inference. We review these methods in turn.

Method of Moments

Denote by θ the vector of parameters describing the model

$$\theta = (\alpha_p, \alpha_z, \beta_p, \beta_y).$$

For simplicity assume that σ_D, σ_S, and ρ_{SD} are known to the researcher. From the data compute a list of empirical moments, for example, of the variance of prices and quantities and the covariances between prices, quantities, income, and the weather. Denote $\mu = \{\mu_1, \mu_2, \mu_3, \mu_4\}'$ a 4×1 vector of empirical moments with[3]

$$\mu_1 = \frac{\text{cov}(p, y)}{V(y)}, \quad \mu_3 = \frac{\text{cov}(p, z)}{V(z)},$$

$$\mu_2 = \frac{\text{cov}(q, y)}{V(y)}, \quad \mu_4 = \frac{\text{cov}(q, z)}{V(z)}. \tag{4.6}$$

These moments can be computed directly from the data. For instance, μ_1 can be expressed as

$$\mu_1 = \frac{\sum_{t=1}^{T}(p_t - \bar{p})(y_t - \bar{y})}{\sum_{t=1}^{T}(y_t - \bar{y})^2}.$$

---

3. If we also want to estimate σ_D, σ_S, and ρ_{SD}, we can include additional moments such as $E(p)$, $E(q)$, $V(p)$, $V(q)$, or $\text{cov}(p, q)$.

From the model we can derive the theoretical counterpart of these moments, expressed as functions of the structural parameters. We denote these theoretical moments by $\mu(\theta) = \{\mu_1(\theta), \mu_2(\theta), \mu_3(\theta), \mu_4(\theta)\}$. Starting with the expressions in (4.4), some straightforward algebra gives

$$\mu_1(\theta) = \frac{\beta_y}{\alpha_p - \beta_p}, \quad \mu_3(\theta) = -\frac{\alpha_z}{\alpha_p - \beta_p},$$

$$\mu_2(\theta) = \frac{\alpha_p \beta_y}{\alpha_p - \beta_p}, \quad \mu_4(\theta) = -\frac{\alpha_z \beta_p}{\alpha_p - \beta_p}. \tag{4.7}$$

The basis of the method of moments estimation is that at the true value of the vector of parameters,

$$E(\mu_i(\theta) - \mu_i) = 0, \qquad i = \{1, \ldots, 4\}.$$

This is called an orthogonality condition. In practical terms, we can bring the moments from the model as close as possible to the empirical ones by solving

$$\theta^* = \arg \min_\theta L(\theta) = \arg \min_\theta (\mu - \mu(\theta))' \Omega (\mu - \mu(\theta)). \tag{4.8}$$

The ergodicity condition on the sample is the assumption used to make the empirical and the theoretical moments the same as the sample size goes to infinity. Note that this assumption is easily violated in many macroeconomic samples, as the data are nonstationary. In practice, most of the macro data are first made stationary by removing trends.

How do the results of (4.8) compare to the results in (4.5)? Note that by our choice of moments, $\mu_1(\theta) = A_1$, $\mu_2(\theta) = B_1$, $\mu_3(\theta) = A_2$, and $\mu_4(\theta) = B_2$. At the optimal value of the parameters we solve the same problem as in (4.4). This leads to exactly the same values for the parameters as in (4.5). The method of moments approach collapses the two steps of the previous section into a single one. The reduced form is estimated and the nonlinear system of equations solved in a single procedure.

Could we chose other moments to estimate the structural parameters? As in example 4.4, the answer is both yes and no. The moments must be informative of the parameters of the model.

For instance, if we chose $\mu_1 = E(z)$, the average value of weather, this moment is independent of the parameterization of the model, since z is an exogenous variable. Hence we are left to estimate four parameters with only three identifying equations. Any moment involving an endogenous variable (p or q in our example) can be used in the estimation and would asymptotically produce the same results. With a finite number of observations, higher-order moments cannot be precisely computed, so an estimation based on $\text{cov}(p^4, y)$, say, would not be very efficient.

Finally, note that in computing the moments of (4.7), we have not used the assumption that the error terms ε_D and ε_S are normally distributed. Whatever their joint distribution, (4.8) would give a consistent estimate of the four parameters of interest. The next section presents the maximum likelihood estimation, which assumes the normality of the residuals.

Maximum Likelihood

The likelihood of observing jointly a given price p and a quantity q conditional on income and weather can be derived from the reduced form (4.4) as $f(p - A_1 y - A_2 z, q - B_1 y - B_2 z)$, where $f(.,.)$ is the joint density of the disturbances U_1 and U_2 and where A_1, A_2, B_1, B_2 are defined as in (4.4). The likelihood of the entire sample is thus

$$\mathscr{L}(\theta) = \prod_{t=1}^{T} f(p_t - A_1 y_t - A_2 z_t, q_t - B_1 y_t - B_2 z_t). \tag{4.9}$$

We assume here that ε_D and ε_S are normally distributed, so U_1 and U_2 are also normally distributed with zero mean.[4] The maximization of the likelihood function with respect to the reduced form coefficients is a straightforward exercise. It will give asymptotically consistent estimates of A_1, A_2, B_1, and B_2. Since there is a one-to-one

---

4. The variance of U_1 and U_2 are defined as

$$\sigma_1^2 = \frac{\sigma_D^2 + \sigma_S^2 - 2\rho_{DS}}{(\alpha_p - \beta_p)^2}, \quad \sigma_2^2 = \frac{\alpha_p^2 \sigma_D^2 + \beta_p^2 \sigma_S^2 - 2\alpha_p \beta_p \rho_{DS}}{(\alpha_p - \beta_p)^2},$$

and the covariance between U_1 and U_2 is

$$\rho_{12} = \frac{\alpha_p \sigma_D^2 + \beta_p \sigma_S^2 - \rho_{DS}(\alpha_p + \beta_p)}{(\alpha_p - \beta_p)^2}.$$

The joint density of U_1 and U_2 can be expressed as

$$f(u_1, u_2) = \frac{1}{2\pi\sigma_1\sigma_2\sqrt{1-\rho^2}} \exp - \frac{1}{2(1-\rho^2)} \left(\frac{u_1^2}{\sigma_1^2} + \frac{u_2^2}{\sigma_2^2} + 2\rho u_1 u_2 \right)$$

with $\rho = \rho_{12}/(\sigma_1\sigma_2)$.

mapping between the reduced form and the structural parameters, the estimation will also provide consistent estimates of the parameters α_p, β_p, α_z, and β_y as in the method of moment case.

Indirect Inference

For a given value of the parameters we are able to draw supply and demand shocks from their distribution and to simulate artificial data for prices and demand conditional on observed weather and income. This is done using expression (4.4). Denote the observed data as $\{q_t, p_t, y_t, z_t\}_{t=1}^{T}$. Denote the simulated data as $\{q_i^s, p_i^s\}_{t=1\ldots,T,s=1,\ldots,S}$. Denote the set of parameters of the structural system (4.3) as $\theta = \{\alpha_p, \alpha_z, \beta_p, \beta_z\}$. For simplicity we assume that the parameters σ_D, σ_S, and ρ_{DS} are known.

Next, we need an auxiliary model that is simple to estimate. We could use the system (4.3) as this auxiliary model. For both the observed and the simulated data, we can regress the quantities on the prices and the income or the weather. Denote the first set of auxiliary estimate $\hat{\psi}_T$ and the second one $\tilde{\psi}_T^s$, $s = 1, \ldots, S$. These vectors contains an estimate for the effect of prices on quantities and the effect of weather and income on quantity from both the supply and the demand equations. These estimates will undoubtedly be biased given the simultaneous nature of the system. However, we are interested in these auxiliary parameters only to get to the structural ones (θ). The next step is to find θ that brings the vector $\tilde{\psi}_T^S = 1/S \sum_{s=1}^{S} \tilde{\psi}(\theta)_T^s$ as close as possible to $\hat{\psi}_T$. Econometric theory tells us that this will produce a consistent estimate of the parameters of interest, α_p, α_z, β_q, β_y. Again, we rely here on the assumption of ergodicity. As will become apparent in section 4.3.3, the estimator will be less efficient than maximum likelihood or the method of moments, unless one relies on a very large number of simulations.

Nonidentification

If the weather has no influence on supply, meaning $\alpha_z = 0$, then the reduced form equations only expresses p^* and q^* as a function of income and shocks only. In this case the system is underidentified. We can only recover part of the original parameters:

$$\alpha_p = \frac{B_1}{A_1}, \quad \sigma_p^2 = V\left(\frac{q - B_1}{A_1 p}\right).$$

Further manipulation gives

$$\beta_y = B_1 - A_1\beta_p. \tag{4.10}$$

There is an infinity of pairs $\{\beta_y, \beta_p\}$ that satisfies the equality above. Hence we cannot recover the true values for these two parameters. From (4.10) it is easy to see that there is an identification problem.

When the estimation involves moment matching or minimization of a likelihood function, nonidentification may not be as straightforward to spot. Some estimation routines will provide an estimate for the parameters whether the system is identified or not. There is no reason to think that these estimates will coincide with the true values, as many sets of parameter values will satisfy the first-order conditions (4.8). If the estimation routine is based on a gradient calculation, finding the minimum of a function requires one to calculate and to find the inverse Hessian of the criterion function $L(\theta)$. If $\alpha_z = 0$, the Hessian will not be of full rank, as the cross derivatives of L with respect to α_z and the other parameters will be zero. Hence one should be suspicious about the results when numerical problems occur such as invertibility problems. As the Hessian matrix enters the calculation of the standard errors, a common sign is also abnormally imprecise coefficients. If the estimation routine is not based on gradients (e.g., the simplex algorithm), the problem will be more difficult to spot, as the estimation routine will come up with an estimate. However, these results will usually look strange, with some coefficients taking absurdly large values. Moreover the estimation results will be sensible to the choice of initial values.

EXERCISE 4.3   Build a computer program that creates a data set of prices and quantities using (4.4) for given values z and y. Use this program to create a data set of size T, the "true data set," and then to construct a simulated data set of size S. Next construct the objective function for the indirect inference case as suggested in section 4.3.3. What happens when you set α_z to zero?

4.3   Estimation Methods and Asymptotic Properties

In this section we present in more detail the asymptotic properties of each estimator discussed in the previous section. First, we review the generalized method of moments, which encompasses most of the classic estimation methods such as maximum likelihood or nonlinear least squares. Then, we present methods using simulations. All the methods are illustrated using simple dynamic programming models as we did in the cake-eating problem of chapters 2 and 3.

In the following discussion we assume that there is a "true" model, $x(u_t, \theta)$, parameterized by a vector θ of dimension κ. u_t is a shock that makes the model probabilistic. For instance, the shock u_t can be a taste shock, a productivity shock, or a measurement error. We observe a sequence of data generated by this model at the "true" value of the parameters, which we denote by θ_0, and at the "true" value of the shocks u_t^0. Let $\{x(u_t^0, \theta_0)\}_{t=1}^{T}$ be the observed data, which we also denote as $\{x_t\}_{t=1}^{T}$ for simplicity.[5] We are interested in recovering an estimate of θ_0 from the observed data and making statistical inferences.

4.3.1 Generalized Method of Moments

In the method of moments presented in section 4.2 we minimized the distance between an empirical moment and the predicted one. This way we could exploit the fact that on average, the difference between the predicted and the observed series (or a function of these series) should be close to zero at the true value of the parameter θ_0. Let is denote this difference as $h(\theta, x_t)$, so that

$$E(h(\theta_0, x_t)) = 0. \tag{4.11}$$

This identifying equality is called an orthogonality restriction. We denote the sample average of $h(\theta, x_t)$ as

$$g(\theta) = \frac{1}{T} \sum_{t=1}^{T} h(\theta, x_t).$$

Then an estimate of θ can be found as

$$\hat{\theta} = \arg \min_{\theta} Q(\theta) = \arg \min_{\theta} g(\theta)' W_T^{-1} g(\theta).$$

In the expression above W_T^{-1} is a weighting matrix, which might depend on the data, and hence the T subscript. If $g(\theta)$ is of size $q \times 1$, then W_T^{-1} is of size $q \times q$. For instance, if we want to match the first two moments of the process $\{x_t\}$, the function $h(\cdot)$ can be written as

---

5. Here we view T as the length of the data for time series applications and as the number of observations in a cross section.

$$h(\theta, x_t) = \begin{pmatrix} x_t(\theta) - x_t \\ x_t(\theta)^2 - x_t^2 \end{pmatrix}.$$

Averaging this vector over the sample will yield $g(\theta) = (\bar{x}(\theta) - \bar{x}, \bar{x}(\theta)^2 - \bar{x}^2)$.

Economic theory often provides more restrictions that can be used in the estimation method. They often take the form of first-order conditions, such as Euler equations, that can be used as an orthogonality restriction as in (4.11). This is the intuition that guided the Hansen and Singleton (1982) study of consumption, as we will see in chapter 6 (section 6.3.3). Here we summarize that approach with an example.

Example 4.5 In a standard intertemporal model of consumption with stochastic income and no borrowing constraints, the first-order condition gives

$$u'(c_t) = \beta R E_t u'(c_{t+1}).$$

One can use this restriction to form $h(\theta, c_t, c_{t+1}) = [u'(c_t) - \beta R u'(c_{t+1})]$, where θ is parameterizing the utility function. On average, $h(\theta, c_t, c_{t+1})$ should be close to zero at the true value of the parameter. The Euler equation above brings actually more information than we have used so far. Not only should the differences between the marginal utility in period t and $t + 1$ be close to zero, but it should also be orthogonal to information dated t. Suppose that z_t is a variable that belongs to the information set at date t. Then the first-order condition also implies that on average, $h(\theta, c_t,) = z_t.[u'(c_t) - \beta R u'(c_{t+1})]$ should be close to zero at the true value of the parameter. If we have more than one z_t variable, then we can exploit as many orthogonality restrictions.

For further examples, we refer the reader to section 8.4.3.

Asymptotic Distribution
Let $\hat{\theta}_T$ be the GMM estimate, that is, the solution to (4.3.1). Under regularity conditions (see Hansen 1982):

• $\hat{\theta}_T$ is a consistent estimator of the true value θ_0.

• The GMM estimator is asymptotically normal:

$$\sqrt{T}(\hat{\theta}_T - \theta_0) \xrightarrow{d} N(0, \Sigma),$$

where $\Sigma = (DW_\infty^{-1}D')^{-1}$ and where

$$D' = \plim_T \left\{ \frac{\partial g(\theta, Y_T)}{\partial \theta'} \bigg|_{\theta=\theta_0} \right\}.$$

The empirical counterpart of D is

$$\hat{D}'_T = \frac{\partial g(\theta, Y_T)}{\partial \theta'} \bigg|_{\theta=\hat{\theta}_T}.$$

This means that asymptotically, one can treat the GMM estimate $\hat{\theta}_T$ as a normal variable with mean θ_0 and variance $\hat{\Sigma}/T$:

$$\hat{\theta}_T \sim N\left(\theta_0, \frac{\hat{\Sigma}}{T}\right).$$

Note that the asymptotic properties of the GMM estimator are independent of the distribution of the error term in the model. In particular, one does not have to assume normality.

Optimal Weighting Matrix
We have not yet discussed the choice of the weighting matrix W_T^{-1}. The choice of the weighting matrix does not have any bearing on the convergence of the GMM estimator to the true value. However, a judiciously chosen weighting matrix can minimize the asymptotic variance of the estimator. It can be shown that the optimal weighting matrix W_T^* produces the estimator with the smallest variance. It is defined as

$$W_\infty^* = \lim_{T\to\infty} \frac{1}{T} \sum_{t=1}^{T} \sum_{l=-\infty}^{\infty} h(\theta_0, y_t)h(\theta_0, y_{t-l})'.$$

Empirically one can replace W_∞^* by a consistent estimator of this matrix $\hat{W}_T^*$:

$$\hat{W}_T^* = \Gamma_{0,T} + \sum_{v=1}^{q} \left(1 - \left[\frac{v}{q+1}\right]\right)(\Gamma_{v,T} + \Gamma_{v,T}')$$

with

$$\Gamma_{v,T} = \frac{1}{T} \sum_{t=v+1}^{T} h(\hat{\theta}, y_t)h(\hat{\theta}, y_{t-v})',$$

which is the Newey-West estimator (see Newey and West 1987 for a more detailed exposition).

Overidentifying Restrictions

If the number of moments q is larger than the number of parameters to estimate κ, then the system is overidentified. One would only need κ restrictions to estimate θ. The remaining restrictions can be used to evaluate the model. Under the null hypothesis that the model is the true one, these additional moments should be empirically close to zero at the true value of the parameters. This forms the basis of a specification test:

$$T g(\hat{\theta}_T)' \hat{W}_T^{-1} g(\hat{\theta}_T) \xrightarrow{L} \chi^2(q - \kappa).$$

In practice, this test is easy to compute, as one has to compare T times the criterion function evaluated at the estimated parameter vector to a chi-square critical value.

Link with Other Estimation Methods

The generalized method of moments actually encompasses most estimation methods such as OLS, nonlinear least squares, instrumental variables, and maximum likelihood because it involves choosing an adequate moment restriction. For instance, the OLS estimator is defined such that the right-hand side variables are not correlated with the error term, and this provides a set of orthogonal restrictions that can be used in a GMM framework. In a linear model the GMM estimator defined in this way is also an OLS estimator. The instrumental variable method exploits the fact that an instrument is orthogonal to the residual.

4.3.2 Maximum Likelihood

In contrast to the GMM approach, the maximum likelihood strategy requires an assumption on the distribution of the random variables. Denote by $f(x_t, \theta)$ the probability of observing x_t given a parameter θ. The estimation method is designed to maximize the likelihood of observing a sequence of data $X = \{x_1, \ldots, x_T\}$. Assuming iid shocks, the likelihood for the entire sample is

$$L(X, \theta) = \prod_{t=1}^{T} f(x_t, \theta).$$

It is easier to maximize the log of the likelihood:

$$l(X, \theta) = \sum_{t=1}^{T} \log f(x_t, \theta).$$

Example 4.6 Consider the cake-eating problem, defined by the Bellman equation below, where W is the size of the cake, ρ is a shrink factor, and ε is an iid shock to preferences:

$$V(W, \varepsilon) = \max[\varepsilon u(W), EV(\rho W, \varepsilon')].$$

$V(.)$ represents the value of having a cake of size W, given the realization of the taste shock ε. The equation above states that the individual is indifferent between consuming the cake and waiting if the shock is $\varepsilon^*(W, \theta) = EV(\rho W, \varepsilon')/u(W)$, where θ is a vector of parameters describing preferences, the distribution of ε, and the shrink factor ρ. If $\varepsilon > \varepsilon^*(W, \theta)$, then the individual will consume the cake. $\varepsilon^*(W, \theta)$ has no analytical expression but can be solved numerically with the tools developed in chapter 3. The probability of not consuming a cake of size W in a given period is then

$$P(\varepsilon < \varepsilon^*(W, \theta)) = F(\varepsilon^*(W, \theta)),$$

where F is the cumulative density of the shock ε. The likelihood of observing an individual i consuming a cake after t periods is then

$$l_i(\theta) = (1 - F(\varepsilon^*(\rho^t W_1, \theta))) \prod_{l=1}^{t-1} F(\varepsilon^*(\rho^l W_1, \theta)).$$

Suppose that we observe the stopping time for N individuals. Then the likelihood of the sample is

$$L(\theta) = \prod_{i=1}^{N} l_i(\theta).$$

The maximization of the likelihood with respect to θ gives the estimate, $\hat{\theta}$.

For additional examples, we refer the reader to the second part of the book, and in particular, section 5.5.4.

EXERCISE 4.4 Use the stochastic cake-eating problem to simulate some data. Construct the likelihood of the sample and plot it against different possible values for ρ.

Asymptotic Properties

To derive the asymptotic properties of the maximum likelihood estimator, it is convenient to regard the maximum likelihood as a GMM procedure. The first-order condition for the maximum of the log-likelihood function is

$$\sum_{t=1}^{T} \frac{\partial \log f(x_t, \theta)}{\partial \theta} = 0.$$

This orthogonality condition can be used as a basis for a GMM estimation, where $h(\theta, x_t) = \partial \log f(x_t, \theta)/\partial \theta$. The first derivative of the log-likelihood function is also called the score function.

From the GMM formula the covariance matrix is $\hat{D}_T \hat{S}_T^{-1} \hat{D}_T'$, with

$$\hat{D}_T' = \frac{\partial g(\theta)}{\partial \theta'}\bigg|_{\theta=\hat{\theta}_T} = \frac{1}{T} \sum_{t=1}^{T} \frac{\partial^2 \log f(x_t, \theta)}{\partial \theta \partial \theta'} = -I,$$

where I is also known as the information matrix, namely minus the second derivative of the log-likelihood function:

$$\hat{S}_T = \frac{1}{T} \sum_{t=1}^{T} h(x_t, \hat{\theta}_T) h(x_t, \hat{\theta}_T)' = I.$$

So we get

$$\sqrt{T}(\hat{\theta}_T - \theta_0) \xrightarrow{L} N(0, I^{-1}).$$

The maximum likelihood estimator is asymptotically normal, with mean zero and a variance equal to I^{-1}/T.

4.3.3 Simulation-Based Methods

We review here estimation methods based on simulation. This field is growing, so we will concentrate on only a few methods. For a more in-depth discussions of these methods, we refer the reader to Gourieroux and Monfort (1996) and Pakes and Pollard (1989), McFadden (1989), Laroque and Salanié (1989), and McFadden and Ruud (1994) (see also Lerman and Manski 1981 for an early presentation).

These methods are often used because the calculation of the moments are too difficult to construct (e.g., multiple integrals in multinomial probits as in McFadden 1989 or Hajivassiliou and Ruud

1994, or because the model includes a latent (unobserved) variable as in Laroque and Salanié 1993). Or, it might be that the model $M(\theta)$ has no simple analytic representation so that the mapping from the parameters to moments must be simulated.

Example 4.7 Consider the cake-eating problem studied in section 4.3.2, but where the taste shocks ε are serially correlated. The Bellman equation is expressed as

$$V(W, \varepsilon) = \max[\varepsilon u(W), E_{\varepsilon' \mid \varepsilon} V(\rho W, \varepsilon')].$$

Here the expectations operator indicates that the expectation of next period's shock depends on the realization of the current shock. We can still define the threshold shock $\varepsilon^*(W) = E_{\varepsilon' \mid \varepsilon^*} V(\rho W, \varepsilon') / u(W)$, for which the individual is indifferent between eating and waiting. The probability of waiting t periods to consume the cake can be written as

$$P_t = P(\varepsilon_1 < \varepsilon^*(W_1), \varepsilon_2 < \varepsilon^*(\rho W_1), \ldots, \varepsilon_t > \varepsilon^*(\rho^t W_1)).$$

In section 4.3.2 the shocks were iid, and this probability could easily be decomposed into a product of t terms. If ε is serially correlated, then this probability is extremely difficult to write as ε_t is correlated with all the previous shocks.[6] For t periods we have to solve a multiple integral of order t, which conventional numerical methods of integration cannot handle. In this section we will show how simulated methods can overcome this problem to provide an estimate of θ.

The different simulation methods can be classified into two groups. The first group of methods compares a function of the observed data to a function of the simulated data. Here the average is taken both on the simulated draws and on all observation in the original data set at once. This approach is called moment calibration. It includes the simulated method of moments and indirect inference.

---

6. For instance, if $\varepsilon_t = \rho \varepsilon_{t-1} + u_t$ with $u_t \sim N(0, \sigma^2)$, the probability that the cake is eaten in period 2 is

$$p_2 = P(\varepsilon_1 < \varepsilon^*(W_1), \varepsilon_2 > \varepsilon^*(W_2))$$

$$= P(\varepsilon_1 < \varepsilon^*(W_1)) P(\varepsilon_2 > \varepsilon^*(W_2) \mid \varepsilon_1 < \varepsilon^*(W_1))$$

$$= \Phi\left(\frac{\varepsilon_1^*(W_1)}{\sigma / \sqrt{1 - \rho^2}}\right) \frac{1}{\sqrt{2\pi}\sigma} \int_{\varepsilon_2^*}^{+\infty} \int_{-\infty}^{\varepsilon_1^*} \exp\left(-\frac{1}{2\sigma^2}(u - \rho v)^2\right) du\, dv.$$

If $\rho = 0$, then the double integral resumes to a simple integral of the normal distribution.

The second set of methods compare the observed data, observation by observation, to an average of the simulated predicted data, where the average is taken over the simulated shocks. This is called path calibration. Simulated nonlinear least squares or maximum likelihood fall into this category.

The general result is that path calibration methods require the number of simulations to go to infinity to achieve consistency. In contrast, moment calibration methods are consistent for a fixed number of simulations.

Simulated Method of Moments

DEFINITION   This method was developed by McFadden (1989), Lee and Ingram (1991), and Duffie and Singleton (1993). Let $\{x(u_t, \theta_0)\}_{t=1}^{T}$ be a sequence of observed data. Let $\{x(u_t^s, \theta)\}$, $t = 1, \ldots, T$, $s = 1, \ldots,$ S, or $x_t^s(\theta)$ for short, be a set of S series of simulated data, each of length T conditional on a vector of parameters θ. The simulations are done by fixing θ and by using the TS draws of the shocks u_t^s (drawn once and for all). Denote by $\mu(x_t)$ a vector of functions of the observed data.[7] The estimator for the SMM is defined as

$$\hat{\theta}_{S,T}(W) = \arg \min_{\theta} \left[\sum_{t=1}^{T} \left(\mu(x_t) - \frac{1}{S} \sum_{s=1}^{S} \mu(x(u_t^s, \theta)) \right) \right]'$$

$$\cdot W_T^{-1} \left[\sum_{t=1}^{T} \left(\mu(x_t) - \frac{1}{S} \sum_{s=1}^{S} \mu(x(u_t^s, \theta)) \right) \right].$$

This criterion is similar to the one presented for the method of moments in section 4.2.1. The difference is that we can avoid the calculation of the theoretical moments $\mu(x_t(\theta))$ directly. Instead, we are approximating them numerically with simulations.

Example 4.8 Say the cake example has serially correlated shocks. Suppose that we have a data set of T cake eaters for which we observe the duration of their cake D_t, $t = 1, \ldots, T$.

Given a vector of parameter θ that describes preferences and the process of ε, we can solve numerically the model and compute the thresholds $\varepsilon^*(W)$. Next we can simulate a series of shocks and

---

7. For instance, $\mu(x) = [x, x^2]$ if one wants to focus on matching the mean and the variance of the process.

determine the duration for this particular draws of the shock. We can repeat this step in order to construct S data sets each containing T simulated durations.

To identify the parameters of the model, we can, for instance, use the mean duration and the variance of the duration. Both of these moments would be calculated from the observed data set and the simulated data. If we want to identify more than two parameters, we can try to characterize the distribution of the duration better and include the fraction of cake eaten at the end of the first, second, and third periods.

For further examples, we refer the reader to the second part of the book, and in particular, to sections 6.3.6 and 7.3.3.

EXERCISE 4.5 Construct a computer program to implement the approach outlined in example 4.8. First, use as moments the mean and the variance of the duration. Increase then the number of moments for the fraction of cakes eaten after the first and second period. As the model is overidentified, test the overidentification restrictions.

PROPERTIES   When the number of simulation S is fixed and $T \to \infty$,

- $\hat{\theta}_{ST}(W)$ is consistent.
- $\sqrt{T}(\hat{\theta}_{ST} - \theta_0) \to N(0, Q_S(W))$, where

$$
Q_S(W) = \left(1 + \frac{1}{S}\right) \left[E_0 \frac{\partial \mu'}{\partial \theta} W_T^{-1} \frac{\partial \mu}{\partial \theta'} \right]^{-1} E_0 \frac{\partial \mu'}{\partial \theta} W_T^{-1} \Sigma(\theta_0) W_T^{-1} \frac{\partial \mu}{\partial \theta'}
$$

$$
\times \left[E_0 \frac{\partial \mu'}{\partial \theta} W_T^{-1} \frac{\partial \mu}{\partial \theta'} \right]^{-1}.
$$

In the expression above $\Sigma(\theta_0)$ is the covariance matrix of $1/\sqrt{T} \left(\frac{1}{T} \sum_{t=1}^{T} (\mu(x_t) - E_0 \mu(x_t^s(\theta))) \right)$.

The optimal SMM is obtained when $\hat{W}_T = \hat{\Sigma}_T$. In this case

$$
Q_S(W^*) = \left(1 + \frac{1}{S}\right) \left[E_0 \frac{\partial \mu'}{\partial \theta} W^{*-1} \frac{\partial \mu}{\partial \theta'} \right]^{-1}.
$$

When S increases to infinity, the variance of the SMM estimator is the same as the variance of the GMM estimator. Note that when S tends to infinity, the covariance matrix of the estimator converges to the covariance matrix of the standard GMM estimator.

In practice, the optimal weighting matrix can be estimated by

$$\hat{W}_T^* = \frac{1}{T} \sum_{t=1}^{T} \left[\mu(x_t) - \frac{1}{S} \sum_{s=1}^{S} \mu(x_t^s(\hat{\theta}_{ST})) \right] \cdot \left[\mu(x_t) - \frac{1}{S} \sum_{s=1}^{S} \mu(x_t^s(\hat{\theta}_{ST})) \right]'$$

$$+ \frac{1}{S} \frac{1}{T} \sum_{s=1}^{S} \sum_{t=1}^{T} \left[\mu(x_t^s(\hat{\theta}_{ST})) - \frac{1}{L} \sum_{l=1}^{L} \mu(x_t^l(\hat{\theta}_{ST})) \right]$$

$$\cdot \left[\mu(x_t^s(\hat{\theta}_{ST})) - \frac{1}{L} \sum_{l=1}^{L} \mu(x_t^l(\hat{\theta}_{ST})) \right]',$$

where $x_t^s(\theta)$ and $x_t^l(\theta)$ are simulations generated by independent draws from the density of the underlying shock. $\hat{W}_T^*$ is a consistent estimate of W_∞^* for $T \to \infty$ and $L \to \infty$. Note that the SMM requires a large number of simulations to compute the standard errors of the estimator, even if the estimator is consistent for a fixed number of simulation.

Simulated Nonlinear Least Squares

DEFINITION   We could estimate the parameters θ by matching, at each period, the observation x_t with the prediction of the model $x(u_t^s, \theta)$, where u_t^s is a particular draw for the shock. There are two reasons why the predicted data would not match the observed one. First, we might evaluate the model at an incorrect parameter point (i.e., $\theta \neq \theta_0$). Second, the "true" shock u_t^0 is unobserved, so replacing it with a random draw u_t^s would lead to a discrepancy. In trying to minimize the distance between these two objects, we would not know whether to change θ or u_t^s. To alleviate the problem, we could use S simulated shocks and compare x_t with $\bar{x}_t^S(\theta) = 1/S \sum_{s=1}^{S} x(u_t^s, \theta)$. A natural method of estimation would be to minimize the distance between the observed data and the average predicted variable:

$$\min \frac{1}{T} \sum_{t=1}^{T} (x_t - \bar{x}_t^S(\theta))^2.$$

Unfortunately, this criterion does not provide a consistent estimator of θ, for a fixed number of simulation S, as the sample size T
increases to infinity.[8]

Laffont et al. (1995) proposes to correct the nonlinear least square
objective function by minimizing the following criterion:

$$\min_{\theta} \frac{1}{T} \sum_{t=1}^{T} \left[(x_t - \bar{x}_t^S(\theta))^2 - \frac{1}{S(S-1)} \sum_{s=1}^{S} (x(u_t^s, \theta) - \bar{x}_t^S(\theta))^2 \right]. \qquad (4.12)$$

The first term is the same as the one discussed above, the distance
between the observed variable and the average predicted one. The
second term is a second-order correction term that takes into account
the bias introduced by the simulation for a fixed S.

Example 4.9 Consider a continuous cake-eating problem defined as

$$V(W, \varepsilon) = \max_{c} \varepsilon u(c) + \beta E_{\varepsilon' | \varepsilon} V(W - c, \varepsilon'),$$

where W is the size of the cake, c is the amount consumed, and ε is a
taste shock. The optimal policy rule for this program is of the form
$c = c(W, \varepsilon)$. Suppose that we can observe over time both an individual's consumption level and the size of the cake, $\{\hat{c}_t, \hat{W}_t\}_{t=1,\dots,T}$. The

---

8. To see this, define θ_∞, the solution to the minimization of the criterion above, when
the sample size T goes to infinity:

$$\theta_\infty = \arg \min_{\theta} \lim_{T} \frac{1}{T} \sum_{t=1}^{T} (x(u_t, \theta_0) - \bar{x}(\theta))^2$$

$$= \arg \min_{\theta} E(x(u, \theta_0) - \bar{x}(\theta))^2$$

$$= \arg \min_{\theta} E(x(u, \theta_0)^2 + \bar{x}(\theta)^2 - 2x(u, \theta_0)\bar{x}(\theta))$$

$$= \arg \min_{\theta} V(x(u, \theta_0)) + V(\bar{x}(\theta)) + (Ex(u, \theta_0) - E\bar{x}(\theta))^2.$$

This result holds as $Ex\bar{x} = ExE\bar{x}$, meaning the covariance between u_t and u_t^s is zero.
Differentiating the last line with respect to θ, we obtain the first-order conditions satisfied by θ_∞:

$$\frac{\partial}{\partial \theta} V(\bar{x}(\theta_\infty)) + 2 \frac{\partial}{\partial \theta} E\bar{x}(\theta_\infty)[E\bar{x}(\theta_\infty) - Ex(u, \theta_0)] = 0.$$

If $\theta_\infty = \theta_0$, this first-order condition is only satisfied if $\partial V(\bar{x}(\theta_0))/\partial \theta = 0$, which is not
guaranteed. Hence θ_∞ is not necessarily a consistent estimator. This term depends on
the (gradient of) variance of the variable, where the stochastic element is the simulated
shocks. Using simulated paths instead of the true realization of the shock leads to this
inconsistency.

taste shock remains unobserved. To estimate the vector of parameter θ that describes preferences, we can use the simulated nonlinear least square method. We simulate S paths for the taste shock, $\{\varepsilon_t^s\}_{t=1,\ldots,T,s=1,\ldots,S}$ which are used to construct simulated predictions for the model $\{x(W_t, \varepsilon_t^s)\}_{t=1,\ldots,T,s=1,\ldots,S}$. At each period we construct the average consumption conditional on the observed size of the cake, $\bar{c}(\hat{W}_t)$, by averaging out over the S simulated taste shocks. This average is then compared with that of the observed consumption level $\hat{c}_t$, using formula (4.12).

For further examples on the simulated nonlinear least square method, we refer the reader to section 7.3.3.

ASYMPTOTIC PROPERTIES   For any fixed number of simulation S,

- $\hat{\theta}_{ST}$ is consistent.
- $\sqrt{T}(\hat{\theta}_{ST} - \theta_0) \xrightarrow{d} N(0, \Sigma_{S,T})$.

A consistent estimate of the covariance matrix $\Sigma_{S,T}$ can be obtained by computing

$$\hat{\Sigma}_{S,T} = \hat{A}_{S,T}^{-1} \hat{B}_{S,T} \hat{A}_{S,T}^{-1},$$

where $\hat{A}_{S,T}$ and $\hat{B}_{S,T}$ are defined below. To this end, denote $\nabla x_t^s = \partial x(u_t^s, \theta) / \partial \theta$, the gradient of the variable with respect to the vector of parameters, and $\overline{\nabla x}_t = \frac{1}{S} \sum_{s=1}^{S} \nabla x_t^s$, its average across all simulations:

$$\hat{A}_{S,T} = \frac{1}{T} \sum_{t=1}^{T} \left[\overline{\nabla x}_t \overline{\nabla x}_t' - \frac{1}{S(S-1)} \sum_{s=1}^{S} (\nabla x_t^s - \overline{\nabla x}_t)(\nabla x_t^s - \overline{\nabla x}_t)' \right],$$

$$\hat{B}_{S,T} = \frac{1}{T} \sum_{t=1}^{T} d_{S,t}(\theta) \, d_{S,t}(\theta)',$$

with $d_{S,t}$ a k-dimensional vector

$$d_{S,t}(\theta) = (x_t - \bar{x}_t(\theta)) \overline{\nabla x}_t(\theta) + \frac{1}{S(S-1)} \sum_{s=1}^{S} [x(u_t^s, \theta) - \bar{x}(\theta)] \nabla x_t^s(\theta).$$

Simulated Maximum Likelihood

DEFINITION   We write the model as $x(u_t, \theta)$, where θ is a vector of parameters and u_t is an unobserved error. The distribution of u_t

implies a distribution for $x(u_t, \theta)$; call it $\phi(x_t, \theta)$. This can be used to evaluate the likelihood of observing a particular realization x_t. In many cases the exact distribution of $x(\theta, u_t)$ is not easily determined, as the model may be nonlinear or might not even have an explicit analytical form. In this case we can evaluate the likelihood using simulations.

We use the simulated maximum likelihood (SML) method to approximate this likelihood. Let $\tilde{\phi}(x_t, u, \theta)$ be an unbiased simulator of $\phi(x_t, \theta)$:

$$E_u \tilde{\phi}(x_t, u, \theta) = \lim_S \frac{1}{S} \sum_{s=1}^{S} \tilde{\phi}(x_t, u^s, \theta) = \phi(x_t, \theta).$$

The SML estimator is defined as

$$\hat{\theta}_{ST} = \arg \max_{\theta} \sum_{t=1}^{T} \log \left[\frac{1}{S} \sum_{s=1}^{S} \tilde{\phi}(x_t, u_t^s; \theta) \right].$$

ASYMPTOTIC PROPERTIES

• The SML estimator is consistent if T *and* S tend to infinity. When both T and S go to infinity and when $\sqrt{T}/S \to 0$, then

$$\sqrt{T}(\hat{\theta}_{ST} - \theta_0) \xrightarrow{d} N(0, I^{-1}(\theta_0)).$$

The matrix $I(\theta_0)$ can be approximated by

$$-\frac{1}{T} \sum_{t=1}^{T} \frac{\partial^2 \log((1/S) \sum_{s=1}^{S} \tilde{\phi}(x_t, u_t^s, \theta))}{\partial \theta \partial \theta'}.$$

• It is inconsistent if S is fixed.

The bias is then

$$E\hat{\theta}_{ST} - \theta_0 \sim \frac{1}{S} I^{-1}(\theta_0) E a(x_t, \theta),$$

where

$$a(x_t, \theta) = \frac{E_u(\partial \tilde{\phi}/\partial \theta) V_u \tilde{\phi}}{(E_u \tilde{\phi})^3} - \frac{\text{cov}_u(\partial \tilde{\phi}/\partial \theta, \tilde{\phi})}{(E_u \tilde{\phi})^2}.$$

The bias decreases in the number of simulations and with the precision of the estimated parameters, as captured by the information matrix. The bias also depends on the choice of the simulator, through the function a. Gourieroux and Monfort (1996) propose a first-order correction for the bias. Fermanian and Salanié (2001) extend these results and propose a nonparametric estimator of the unknown likelihood function based on simulations.

Indirect Inference
When the model is complex, the likelihood is sometimes intractable. The indirect inference method works around it by using a simpler *auxiliary model*, which is estimated instead. This auxiliary model is estimated both on the observed data and on simulated data. The indirect inference method tries to find the vector of structural parameters that brings the auxiliary parameters from the simulated data as close as possible to the one obtained on observed data. A complete description can be found in Gourieroux et al. (1993; see also Smith 1993).

Consider the likelihood of the auxiliary model $\tilde{\phi}(x_t, \beta)$, where β is a vector of auxiliary parameters. The estimator $\hat{\beta}_T$, computed from the observed data is defined by

$$\hat{\beta}_T = \arg \max_{\beta} \prod_{t=1}^{T} \tilde{\phi}(x_t, \beta).$$

Under the null the observed data are generated by the model at the true value of the parameter θ_0. There is thus a link between the auxiliary parameter β_0 (the true value of the auxiliary parameter) and the structural parameters θ. Following Gourieroux et al. (1993), we denote this relationship by the binding function $b(\theta)$. Were this function known, we could invert it to directly compute θ from the value of the auxiliary parameter. Unfortunately, this function usually has no known analytical form, so the method relies on simulations to characterize it.

The model is then simulated by taking independent draws for the shock u_t^s. This gives S artificial data sets of length T: $\{x_1^s(\theta), \ldots, x_T^s(\theta)\}$, $s = 1, \ldots, S$. The auxiliary model is then estimated out of the simulated data, to get $\hat{\beta}_{sT}$:

$$\hat{\beta}_{sT}(\theta) = \arg \max_{\beta} \prod_{t=1}^{T} \tilde{\phi}(x_t^s(\theta), \beta).$$

Define $\hat{\beta}_{ST}$ the average value of the auxiliary parameters, over all simulations:

$$\hat{\beta}_{ST} = \frac{1}{S}\sum_{s=1}^{S}\hat{\beta}_{sT}(\theta).$$

The indirect inference estimator $\hat{\theta}_{ST}$ is the solution to

$$\hat{\theta}_{ST} = \arg\min_{\theta}[\hat{\beta}_T - \hat{\beta}_{ST}(\theta)]'\Omega_T[\hat{\beta}_T - \hat{\beta}_{ST}(\theta)],$$

where Ω_T is a positive definite weight matrix which converges to a deterministic positive definite matrix Ω.

Example 4.10 Consider the cake problem with serially correlated shocks. The likelihood of the structural model is intractable, but we can find an auxiliary model that is easier to estimate. As the data set consists of durations, a natural auxiliary model is the standard duration model. Suppose that we chose an exponential model, which is a simple and standard model of duration characterized by a constant hazard equal to β. The probability of observing a particular duration is $\beta e^{-\beta D_t}$. The log-likelihood of observing a set of durations $D_t, t = 1, \ldots, T$ is

$$\ln L = \sum_{t=1}^{T}\ln(\beta e^{-(\beta D_t)}).$$

This likelihood can be maximized with respect to β. Straightforward maximization gives $\hat{\beta}_T = \sum_{t=1}^{T} D_t/T$. In this case the auxiliary parameter is estimated as the average duration in the data set. Given a value for the structural parameters of our model of interest θ, we can construct by simulation S data sets containing T observations. For each artificial data set s, we can estimate the auxiliary duration model to obtain $\hat{\beta}_{sT}$. Using the procedure above, we are then able to obtain an estimate of θ, such that the auxiliary parameters on both observed and simulated data are as close as possible. Note that with the simple auxiliary model we use, the indirect inference procedure turns out to be the same as the simulated method of moments because we are matching the average duration.

We used the exponential duration model for simplicity of exposition. This model is parameterized by only one parameter, so we can identify at best only one structural parameter. For more parameters we would estimate a duration model with a more flexible hazard.

For other examples on the indirect inference method, we refer the reader to the second part of the book, in particular, to sections 5.5.3 and 8.6.1.

Gallant and Tauchen (1996) develop an efficient method of moments based on the use of an auxiliary method. Instead of matching on a set of auxiliary parameters, they propose to minimize the score of the auxiliary model, meaning the first derivative of the likelihood of the auxiliary model:

$$m(\theta, \beta_T) = \frac{1}{S}\sum_{s=1}^{S}\frac{1}{T}\sum_{t=1}^{T}\frac{\partial}{\partial\beta}\ln\tilde{\phi}(x_t^s(\theta), \hat{\beta}_T).$$

The structural parameter are obtained from

$$\theta^* = \arg\min_{\theta}\ m(\theta, \hat{\beta}_T)'\Omega m(\theta, \hat{\beta}_T),$$

where Ω is a weighting matrix. Gourieroux et al. (1993) show that the EMM and the indirect inference estimators are asymptotically equivalent.

PROPERTIES   For a fixed number of simulations S as T goes to infinity, the indirect inference estimator is consistent and normally distributed:

$$\sqrt{T}(\hat{\theta}_{ST} - \theta_0) \to N(0, Q_S(\Omega)),$$

where

$$Q_S(\Omega) = \left(1 + \frac{1}{S}\right)\left[\frac{\partial b'(\theta_0)}{\partial\theta}\Omega\frac{\partial b(\theta_0)}{\partial\theta'}\right]^{-1}\frac{\partial b'(\theta_0)}{\partial\theta}\Omega J_0^{-1}(I_0 - K_0)J_0^{-1}\Omega\frac{\partial b(\theta_0)}{\partial\theta'}$$

$$\times\left[\frac{\partial b'(\theta_0)}{\partial\theta}\Omega\frac{\partial b(\theta_0)}{\partial\theta'}\right]^{-1}.$$

Denote $\psi_T(\theta, \beta) = \sum_{t=1}^{T}\log\tilde{\phi}(x_t^s(\theta), \beta)$. The matrices I_0, J_0, and K_0 are defined as

$$J_0 = \operatorname*{plim}_{T} -\frac{\partial^2\psi_T(\theta, \beta)}{\partial\beta\partial\beta'},$$

$$I_0 = \lim_{T} V\left[\sqrt{T}\frac{\partial\psi_T(\theta, \beta)}{\partial\beta}\right],$$

$$K_0 = \lim_T V\left[E\left(\sqrt{T}\frac{\partial}{\partial\beta'}\sum_{t=1}^{T}\tilde{\phi}(x_t,\beta)\right)\right],$$

$$\frac{\partial b'(\theta_0)}{\partial\theta} = J_0^{-1}\lim_T\frac{\partial^2\psi_T(\theta_0,b(\theta_0))}{\partial\beta\partial\theta'}.$$

The last formula is useful for computing the asymptotic covariance matrix without calculating directly the binding function. As in the GMM case there exists an optimal weighting matrix such that the variance of the estimator is minimized. The optimal choice denoted Ω^* is

$$\Omega^* = J_0(I_0 - K_0)^{-1}J_0.$$

In this case the variance of the estimator simplifies to

$$Q_S(\Omega^*) = \left(1+\frac{1}{S}\right)\left(\frac{\partial b'(\theta_0)}{\partial\theta}J_0(I_0 - K_0)^{-1}J_0\frac{\partial b(\theta_0)}{\partial\theta'}\right)^{-1},$$

or equivalently

$$Q_S(\Omega^*) = \left(1+\frac{1}{S}\right)\left(\frac{\partial^2\psi_\infty(\theta_0,b(\theta_0))}{\partial\theta\partial\beta'}(I_0 - K_0)^{-1}\frac{\partial^2\psi_\infty(\theta_0,b(\theta_0))}{\partial\beta\partial\theta'}\right)^{-1}.$$

The formula above does not require us to compute explicitly the binding function. Note that the choice of the auxiliary model matters for the efficiency of the estimator. Clearly, one would want an auxiliary model such that $\partial b'(\theta)/\partial\theta$ is large in absolute values. If not, the model would poorly identify the structural parameters.

In practice, $b(\theta_0)$ can be approximated by $\hat{\beta}_{ST}(\hat{\theta}_{ST})$. A consistent estimator of $I_0 - K_0$ can be obtained by computing

$$(\widehat{I_0 - K_0}) = \frac{T}{S}\sum_{s=1}^{S}(W_s - \overline{W})(W_s - \overline{W})'$$

with

$$W_s = \frac{\partial\psi_T(\hat{\theta},\hat{\beta})}{\partial\beta},$$

$$\overline{W} = \frac{1}{S}\sum_{s=1}^{S}W_s;$$

see Gourieroux et al. (1993, app. 2). Now, if the number of parameters to be estimated in the structural model is equal to the number of parameters in the auxiliary parameters, the weighting matrix Ω plays no role, and the variance $Q_S(\Omega)$ simplifies to

$$Q_S(\Omega) = \left(1 + \frac{1}{S}\right)\left[\frac{\partial b'(\theta_0)}{\partial \theta}\Omega^*\frac{\partial b(\theta_0)}{\partial \theta'}\right]^{-1}.$$

SPECIFICATION TESTS A global specification test can be carried out using the minimized

$$\zeta_T = \frac{TS}{1+S}\min_{\theta}[\hat{\beta}_T - \hat{\beta}_{ST}(\theta)]'\Omega_T[\hat{\beta}_T - \hat{\beta}_{ST}(\theta)],$$

which follows asymptotically a chi-square distribution with $q - p$ degrees of freedom.

4.4 Conclusion

In this chapter we considered methods to use in estimating the parameters of a model. We reviewed classical methods such as maximum likelihood and the generalized method of moments as well as simulation-based methods. In general, in dynamic programming models the likelihood function or the analytical form of the moments is difficult to write out, so simulated methods are of great help. However, they come at a cost, for simulated methods are quite time-consuming. The computation of the value function and the optimal policy rules often requires the use of numerical techniques. If, in addition, simulation estimation methods are used, the estimation of a full fledged structural model can take hours, and even days.

The choice of method depends on the problem and the data set. Path calibration methods such as nonlinear least squares and maximum likelihood use all the information available in the data, as each observation is needed in the estimation procedure. The drawback is that one has to specify the entire model up to the distribution of the unobserved shock. To have tractable likelihood functions, one must often impose a normal distribution for the shocks, and this might impose too much structure on the data. On the other hand, moment calibration methods such as the method of moments use only part of the information provided by the data. These methods concentrate on particular functions of the data, as the mean or the variance, for instance. In contrast to maximum likelihood, the method does not necessarily requires the specification of the whole model.

Both methods can be justified. The researcher might be interested in only a subset of the parameters, such as the intertemporal elasticity of consumption. As in example 4.5, the GMM method allows one to estimate this parameter, without specifying the distribution of the income shock. However, calibration methods require the choice of moments that identify the parameters of the model. When the model is simple, this is not very difficult. When the models are more complex, for instance, when unobserved heterogeneity is present, it is not that straightforward to find informative moments. In such cases the maximum likelihood may be more desirable. Finally, if the data are subject to measurement errors, taking moments of the data can reduce the problem. When using simulation methods, calibration methods also present the advantage of requiring only a fixed number of simulations to get consistent estimates, so the computation time is shorter.

Overview of Methodology

In the first three chapters we presented theoretical tools to model, solve, and estimate economic models. Ideally, to investigate a particular economic topic, a research agenda would include all three parts, building on economic theory and confronting it with the data to assess its validity.

Figure 4.6 summarizes this approach and points to the relevant chapters. The figure starts with an economic model, described by a set of parameters and some choice structure. It is important at this stage to characterize the properties of that model and the first-order conditions or to write it as a recursive problem. The model under consideration might be difficult to solve analytically. It is sometime necessary to use numerical methods as developed in chapter 3. One can then derive the optimal policy rules, namely the optimal behavior given a number of predetermined variables.

From the policy rules[9] the parameters can be estimated. This is usually done by comparing some statistics built both from the observed data and from the model. The estimated parameters are

---

9. The specification of the model should also be rich enough so that the estimation makes sense. In particular, the model must contain a stochastic element that explains why the model is not fitting the data exactly. This can be the case if some characteristics, such as taste shocks, are unobserved.

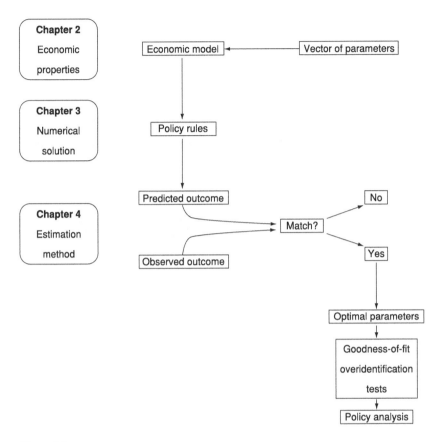

Figure 4.6
Overview of methodology

produced by minimizing the distance between the observed and the predicted outcome of the model. Once the optimal parameters are found, the econometric task is not over. One has to evaluate the fit of the model. There are various ways of doing this. First, although the models are often nonlinear, one can construct a measure such as the R^2 to evaluate the percentage of the variance explained by the model. A higher value is seen as a better fit. However, the model may be very good at reproducing some aspects of the data but fail miserably in other important dimensions. For instance, in the discrete cake-eating problem, the fit of the model could be considerably increased in the first T periods if one were to construct time dependent utility functions with T dummy variables for each time period.

Such a model would generate a perfect fit when it comes to predict the fraction of cakes eaten in the first periods. However, the model could do very poorly for the remaining periods. A second way to evaluate the estimated model is to use overidentification restrictions if the model is overidentified. Finally, one can also perform out of sample forecasts.

Once one is confident that the estimated model is a convincing representation of reality, the model can be used to evaluate different scenarios. The next chapters present examples of this strategy using a number of relevant topics.

II

Applications

5   Stochastic Growth

5.1   Overview

We begin our exploration of applications of dynamic programming problems in macroeconomics with the stochastic growth model. This is a natural starting point. This framework has been used for understanding fluctuations in the aggregate economy since it was introduced by Kydland and Prescott (1982). In order to do so, the researcher must understand the mapping from the parameters of preferences and technology to observations, perhaps summarized by pertinent moments of the data. The model also provides an analytic structure for policy evaluation.[1]

The stochastic growth model provides our first opportunity to review the techniques of dynamic programming, numerical methods and estimation methodology. We begin with a review of the non-stochastic model to get some basic concepts straight, and then we enrich the model to include shocks and other relevant features.

5.2   Nonstochastic Growth Model

Consider the dynamic optimization problem of a very special household. This household is endowed with *one* unit of leisure each period and supplies this inelastically to a production process. The household consumes an amount c_t each period that it evaluates using a utility function $u(c_t)$. Assume that $u(\cdot)$ is strictly increasing and strictly concave. The household's lifetime utility is given by

---

1. In the standard real business cycle model, however, there is no rationale for such intervention.

$$\sum_{1}^{\infty} \beta^{t-1} u(c_t). \tag{5.1}$$

The household has access to a technology that produces output (y) from capital (k), given its inelastically supplied labor services. Let $y = f(k)$ be the production function. Assume that $f(k)$ is strictly increasing and strictly concave.

The capital input into the production process is accumulated from forgone consumption. That is, the household faces a resource constraint that decomposes output into consumption and investment (i_t):

$$y_t = c_t + i_t.$$

The capital stock accumulates according to

$$k_{t+1} = k_t(1 - \delta) + i_t,$$

where $\delta \in (0, 1)$ is the rate of physical depreciation.

Essentially the household's problem is to determine an optimal savings plan by splitting output between these two competing uses. Note that we have assumed that the household maintains a concave production function rather than simply renting labor and capital in a market for factors of production. This way the model of the household is very special, and often it is referred to as a Robinson Crusoe economy as the household is entirely self-sufficient. Nonetheless, one could argue (see below) that the model is informative about market economies as the resulting allocation can be decentralized as a competitive equilibrium. For now, our focus is on solving for this allocation as a dynamic optimization problem.

To do so, we use the dynamic programming approach and consider the following functional equation:

$$V(k) = \max_{k'} \ u(f(k) + (1 - \delta)k - k') + \beta V(k') \qquad \text{for all } k. \tag{5.2}$$

Here the state variable is the stock of capital at the start of the period and the control variable is the capital stock for the next period.[2]

With $f(k)$ strictly concave, there will exist a maximal level of capital achievable by this economy given by $\bar{k}$ where

$$\bar{k} = (1 - \delta)\bar{k} + f(\bar{k}).$$

---

2. Equivalently we could have specified the problem with k as the state, c as the control, and then used a transition equation of $k' = f(k) + (1 - \delta)k - c$.

This provides a bound on the capital stock for this economy and thus guarantees that our objective function, $u(c)$, is bounded on the set of feasible consumption levels, $[0, f(\bar{k}) + (1 - \delta)\bar{k}]$. We assume that both $u(c)$ and $f(k)$ are continuous and real-valued so that there exists a $V(k)$ that solves (5.2).[3]

The first-order condition is given by

$$u'(c) = \beta V'(k').\tag{5.3}$$

Of course, we don't know $V(k)$ directly, so we need to use (5.2) to determine $V'(k)$. As (5.2) holds for all $k \in [0, \bar{k}]$, we can take a derivative and obtain

$$V'(k) = u'(c)(f'(k) + (1 - \delta)).$$

Updating this one period and inserting this into the first-order condition yields

$$u'(c) = \beta u'(c')(f'(k') + (1 - \delta)).$$

This is an Euler condition that is not unlike the one we encountered in the cake eating problem. Here the left-hand side is the cost of reducing consumption by ε today. The right-hand side is then the increase in utility in the next period from the extra capital created by investment of the ε. As in the cake-eating example, if the Euler equation holds, then no single period deviations will increase the utility of the household. As in that example, this is a necessary but not a sufficient condition for optimality.[4]

From the discussion in chapter 2, $V(k)$ is strictly concave. Consequently, from (5.3), k' must be increasing in k. To see why, suppose that current capital increases but future capital falls. Then current consumption will certainly increase so that the left-hand side of (5.3) decreases. Yet with k' falling and $V(k)$ strictly concave, the right-hand side of (5.3) increases. This is a contradiction.

5.2.1 An Example

Suppose that $u(c) = \ln(c)$, $f(k) = k^\alpha$, and $\delta = 1$. With this special structure, we can set up the nonstochastic growth model. As in Sargent (1987) we choose a value function (a guess)

$$V(k) = A + B \ln k \qquad \text{for all } k.$$

We want to show that this function satisfies (5.2). If it does, then the first-order condition, (5.3), can be written as

$$\frac{1}{c} = \frac{\beta B}{k'}.$$

We use the resource constraint ($k^\alpha = c + k'$) to obtain

$$\beta B(k^\alpha - k') = k'$$

or

$$k' = \left(\frac{\beta B}{1 + \beta B} \right) k^\alpha. \qquad (5.4)$$

So, if our choice of $V(k)$ is correct, then (5.4) is the policy function.

From this policy function we can verify whether or not our choice of $V(k)$ satisfies the functional equation (5.2). Substitution of (5.4) into (5.2) yields

$$A + B \ln k = \ln \left[\left(\frac{1}{1 + \beta B} \right) k^\alpha \right] + \beta \left[A + B \ln \left(\left(\frac{\beta B}{1 + \beta B} \right) k^\alpha \right) \right] \qquad \text{for all } k.$$

$$(5.5)$$

Here we can use $c = y - k'$ so that

$$c = \left(\frac{1}{1 + \beta B} \right) k^\alpha.$$

Grouping constant terms yields

$$A = \ln \left(\frac{1}{1 + \beta B} \right) + \beta \left[A + B \ln \left(\frac{\beta B}{1 + \beta B} \right) \right].$$

Next we group terms that multiply $\ln k$:

$$B = \alpha + \beta B \alpha.$$

Hence $B = \alpha/(1 - \beta \alpha)$. Now A can be determined. So we have a solution to the functional equation. As for the policy functions, using B, we find that

$$k' = \beta \alpha k^\alpha$$

and

$$c = (1 - \beta\alpha)k^{\alpha}.$$

It is important to understand how this type of argument works. We started by choosing (guessing) the value function. Then we derived a policy function. Substituting this policy function into the functional equation gave us an expression (5.5) that depends only on the current state k. As this expression must hold for all k, we grouped terms and solved for the unknown coefficients of the proposed value function.

EXERCISE 5.1 To see how this approach to finding a solution to the nonstochastic growth model could "fail," argue that the following cannot be solutions to the functional equation:

1. $V(k) = A$
2. $V(k) = B \ln k$
3. $V(k) = A + Bk^{\alpha}$

5.2.2 Numerical Analysis

The nonstochastic growth model is too simple to seriously take to the data. Still it provides us with a starting point for applying the contraction mapping theorem and finding a numerical solution to a dynamic programming problem. These techniques are quite valuable since the set of economies for which we can obtain an analytic solution to (5.2) is too small. These techniques will be used again to study versions of the stochastic growth model that can be taken to the data.

The Matlab code grow.m solves (5.2) for certain functional forms by a value function iteration routine.[5] The code has four main sections, which we discuss in turn below.

Functional Forms

There are two primitive functions that must be specified for the nonstochastic growth model. The first is the production function and the second is the utility function of the household. The grow.m code assumes that the production function is given by

$$f(k) = k^{\alpha}.$$

---

5. That code and explanations for its use are available on the Web site for this book.

Here α is restricted to lie in the interval $(0,1)$ so that $f(k)$ is strictly increasing and strictly concave.

The household's utility function is given by

$$u(c) = \frac{c^{1-\sigma}}{1 - \sigma}.$$

With this utility function the curvature of the utility function,

$$-\frac{u''(c)c}{u'(c)}$$

is equal to σ.[6] We assume that σ is positive so that $u(c)$ is strictly increasing and strictly concave. When $\sigma = 1$, $u(c)$ is given by $\ln(c)$.

Parameter Values
The second component of the program specifies parameter values. The code is written so that the user can either accept some baseline parameters (which you can edit) or change these values in the execution of the program. Let

$$\Theta = (\alpha, \beta, \delta, \sigma)$$

denote the vector of parameters that are inputs to the program. In an estimation exercise, Θ would be chosen so that the model's quantitative implications match data counterparts. Here we are simply interested in the anatomy of the program, and thus Θ is set at somewhat arbitrary values.

Spaces
As noted earlier, the value function iteration approach does require an approximation to the state space of the problem. That is, we need to make the capital state space discrete. Let κ represent the capital state space. We solve the functional equation for all $k \in \kappa$ with the requirement that k' lie in κ as well. So the code for the nonstochastic growth model does not interpolate between the points in this grid but rather solves the problem on the grid.

The choice of κ is important. For the nonstochastic growth model we might be interested in transition dynamics: if the economy is not at the steady state, how does it return to the steady state? Let k^* be

---

6. In the discussion of King et al. (1988), this term is often called the elasticity of the marginal utility of consumption with respect to consumption.

the steady state value of the capital stock. From (5.2), it solves

$$1 = \beta[\alpha k^{*(\alpha-1)} + (1 - \delta)].$$

This is the value of steady state computed in grow.m. The state space is built in the neighborhood of the steady state through the definitions of the highest and lowest values of the capital stock, which are *khi* and *klow* in the code.[7] A grid is then set up between these two extreme values. The user specifies the fineness of the grid with the consideration that a finer grid provides a better approximation but is "expensive" in terms of computer time.[8]

Value Function Iteration
The fourth section of the program solves (5.2) by a value function iteration routine. We initiate the routine by supplying a guess on the value function. The program uses the value of the one-period problem in which the household optimally consumes all output as well as the undepreciated capital stock (termed ytot in grow.m) as the initial guess.[9]

From our initial guess, a loop is set up to perform the value function iteration, as described in chapter 3. Here the program requires two additional inputs. The first is the total number of iterations that is allowed, termed T. The second is the tolerance to use in determining whether the value function iteration routine has "converged." This tolerance is called *toler*, and this scalar figure is compared against the largest percent difference between the last two calculations of the value function V and v in the grow.m program.

Evaluating the Results
Once the program has converged, aspects of the policy function can be explored. The program produces two plots. The first plot (figure 5.1) is the policy function: k' as a function of k. The policy function is

---

7. One must take care that the state space is not binding. For the growth model we know that k' is increasing in k and that k' exceeds (is less than) k when k is less than (exceeds) k^*. Thus the state space is not binding.
8. This trade-off can be seen by varying the size of the state space in grow.m. In many empirical applications, there is a limit to the size of the state space in that a finer grid doesn't influence the moments obtained from a given parameter vector.
9. A useful exercise is to alter this initial guess and determine whether the solution of the problem is independent of it. Making good initial guesses helps solve the functional equation quickly and is often valuable for estimation routines involving many loops over parameters.

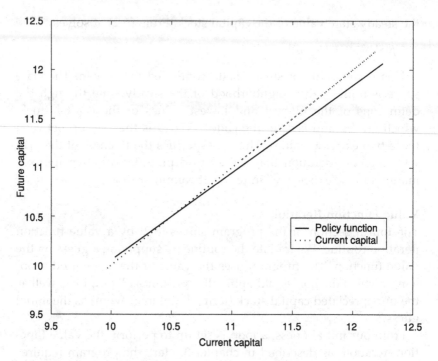

Figure 5.1
Policy function

upward sloping as argued earlier. The second plot (figure 5.2) is the level of net investment $(k' - k)$ for each level of k in the state space. This line crosses zero at the steady state and is downward sloping. So, for value of k below the steady state, the capital stock is increasing (net investment is positive), while for k above k^*, net investment is negative.

The program also allows one to calculate transition dynamics starting from an (arbitrary) initial capital stock. There are two useful exercises that help one practice this piece of code.

EXERCISE 5.2

1. Show how other variables (output, consumption, the real interest rate) behave along the transition path. Explain the patterns of these variables.

2. Show how variations in the parameters in Θ influence the speed and other properties of the transitional dynamics.

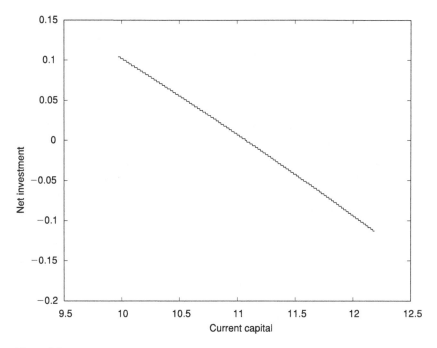

Figure 5.2
Net investment

5.3   Stochastic Growth Model

We build on the discussion of the nonstochastic growth model
to introduce randomness into the environment. We start from a
specification of the basic economic environment. Our intention is
to make clear the nature of the intertemporal choice problem and
the assumptions underlying the specification of preferences and
technology.

We then turn to the planners' optimization problem. We take
the approach of a planner with an objective of maximizing the expected lifetime utility of a representative agent.[10] This way we can
characterize allocations as the results of a single optimization problem rather than through the solution of a competitive equilibrium.
Since there are no distortions in the economy, it is straightforward
to determine the prices that support the allocation as a competitive

---

10. Later in this chapter we move away from this framework to discuss economies
with distortions and heterogeneity.

equilibrium. We do this later in a discussion of the recursive equilibrium concept.

5.3.1 Environment

The stochastic growth model we study here is based on an economy with infinitely lived households. Each household consumes some of the single good (c_t) and invests the remainder (i_t). Investment augments the capital stock (k_t) with a one-period lag: investment today creates more capital in the next period. There is an exogenous rate of capital depreciation denoted by $\delta \in (0,1)$. For now, we assume there is a single good which is produced each period from capital and labor inputs.[11] The capital input is predetermined from past investment decisions and the labor input is determined by the household.

Fluctuations in the economy are created by shocks to the process of producing goods. Thus "good times" represent higher productivity of both labor and capital inputs. The planner will optimally respond to these variations in productivity by adjusting household labor supply and savings (capital accumulation) decisions. Of course, investment is a forward-looking decision, since the new capital is durable and is not productive until the next period. Further the extent to which the labor decision responds to the productivity variation depends, in part, on whether capital and labor are likely to be more productive in the future. Consequently the serial correlation properties of the shocks are critical for understanding the responses of employment and investment.

More formally, the households preferences over consumption (c_t) and leisure (l_t) are given by

$$\sum_{t=0}^{\infty} \beta^t u(c_t, l_t),$$

where the discount factor $\beta \in (0,1)$. We will assume that the function $u(c,l)$ is continuously differentiable and strictly concave. The households face a constraint on their time allocation:

$$1 = l_t + n_t,$$

where the unit time endowment must be allocated between leisure and work (n_t).

---

11. Later in this chapter we discuss extensions that include multiple sectors.

The production side of the economy is represented by a constant returns to scale production function over the two inputs. Since scale is not determined, we model the economy as if there is a single competitive firm that hires the labor services of the households (N_t) and uses the households' capital in the production process. The production function is expressed as

$$Y_t = A_t F(K_t, N_t),$$

where $F(K, N)$ is increasing in both inputs, exhibits constant returns to scale, and is strictly concave. Variations in total factor productivity, A_t, are the source of fluctuations in this economy. Here uppercase letters refer to economywide aggregates and lowercase letters to household (per capita) variables.

Finally, there is a resource constraint: the sum of consumption and investment cannot exceed output in each period. That is,

$$Y_t = C_t + I_t.$$

For characterizing the solution to the planner's problem, this is all the information that is necessary. The planner's problem can be specified from the statement of preferences, the production function, and the time and resource constraints. A natural approach might be to allow the planner to choose a sequence of history-dependent functions that describe the choices of consumption, investment, and employment for all time periods conditional on the state of the economy at that point in time. The description of the state would then include all productivity shocks and the value of the capital stock.

Instead of solving a planner's problem in which the choice is a sequence of state-contingent functions, the tools of dynamic programming can be used. We turn to that approach now.

5.3.2 Bellman's Equation

To begin the analysis, we assume that labor is inelastically supplied at one unit per household. Thus we consider preferences represented by $u(c)$. This allows us to focus on the dynamics of the problem. Of course, we will want to include a labor supply decision before confronting the data, else we would be unable to match any moments with labor variations. Hence we turn to the more general endogenous labor supply formulation later.

In this case we use the constant returns to scale assumption on $F(K, N)$ to write per capita output (y_t) as a strictly concave function of the per capita capital stock (k_t):

$$y_t \equiv A_t F\left(\frac{Kt}{N}, 1\right) \equiv A_t f(k_t).$$

As $F(K, N)$ exhibits constant returns to scale, $f(k)$ will be strictly concave. Bellman's equation for the infinite horizon stochastic growth model is specified as

$$V(A, k) = \max_{k'} \ u(Af(k) + (1 - \delta)k - k') + \beta E_{A'|A} V(A', k')$$

$$\text{for all } (A, k). \tag{5.6}$$

Here the transition equation used to construct (5.6) is $k' = Af(k) + (1 - \delta)k - c$.

An important element of this model is the multiplicative productivity shock. Through the introduction of this shock, the model is constructed to capture procyclical fluctuations in productivity. An important question is whether the fluctuations in output, employment, consumption, investment, and so forth, induced by these shocks match relevant features of the data.

For the quantitative analysis, we assume that A is a bounded, discrete random variable that follows a first-order Markov process. The transition matrix is given by Π, and this is implicitly used in the conditional expectation in (5.6).[12]

As in the general discussion of chapter 2, one important question is whether there exists a solution to the function equation. A second is characterizing the optimal policy function.

For the growth model it is important to be sure that the problem is bounded. For this, let $\bar{k}$ solve

$$k = A^+ f(k) + (1 - \delta)k, \tag{5.7}$$

where A^+ is the largest productivity shock. Since consumption must be nonnegative, the k that solves this expression from the transition equation is the largest amount of capital that this economy could

---

12. Some of these restrictions are stronger than necessary to obtain a solution. As we are going to literally compute the solution to (5.6), we will eventually have to create a discrete representation anyways. So we have imposed some of these features at the start of the formulation of the problem. The assumptions on the shocks parallel those made in the presentation of the stochastic dynamic programming problem in chapter 2.

accumulate. Since $f(k)$ is strictly concave, there will exist a unique finite value of $\bar{k}$ that satisfies (5.7). This implies that the largest level of consumption is also $\bar{k}$: the largest feasible consumption occurs when the largest capital stock is consumed in a single period. Thus we can bound utility by $u(\bar{k})$.

Since we have bounded the problem, the results from chapter 2 will apply provided that the discount factor is less than one and that the shocks follow a bounded, first-order Markow process. Thus we know that there exists a unique value function $V(A,k)$ that solves (5.6). Further we know that there is a policy function given by $k' = \phi(A,k)$.

Our goal is to learn more about the properties of this solution. An important characteristic of the policy function is that it provides a bridge from the optimization problem to the data. The policy function itself depends on the underlying structural parameters and generates relationships between variables, some of which are observable. So the inference problem is: What can be determined about the structural parameters from observations on output, capital, consumption, productivity, and the like?

5.3.3   Solution Methods

Linearization
We could formulate a solution to the stochastic growth model above through analysis of the resource constraints and the intertemporal Euler equation. The latter is a necessary condition for optimality, and it can be obtained directly from the sequence problem representation of the planners problem. Alternatively, from Bellman's equation, the first-order condition for the planner is written as

$$u'(Af(k) + (1 - \delta)k - k') = \beta E_{A' \mid A} V_{k'}(A', k') \qquad \text{for all } (A,k). \qquad (5.8)$$

Though we do not know $V(A,k)$, we can solve for its derivative. From (5.6), we have

$$V_k(A,k) = u'(c)[Af'(k) + (1 - \delta)].$$

Substituting this into (5.8) and evaluating it at (A', k') yields

$$u'(c) = \beta E_{A' \mid A} u'(c')[A' f'(k') + (1 - \delta)], \qquad (5.9)$$

where

$$c = Af(k) + (1 - \delta)k - k' \qquad (5.10)$$

and c' is defined accordingly. These two expressions, along with
the evolution of A (specified below), defines a system of equations.
So one can represent the optimal growth model as a system of first-
order stochastic difference equations in (c, k, A).

An approximate solution is obtained by linearizing this condition
and the resource constraints around the steady state, (c^*, k^*).[13] In
this approach we fix A at the mean value, $\bar{A}$. The steady state value
of the capital stock will then satisfy

$$1 = \beta[\bar{A}f'(k^*) + (1 - \delta)]. \tag{5.11}$$

Further in steady state $k' = k = k^*$, so the steady state level of consumption satisfies $c^* = \bar{A}f(k^*) - \delta k^*$.

Following King et al. (1988), we let $\hat{c}_t$, $\hat{k}_t$ and $\hat{A}_t$ denote percent
deviations from their steady state values respectively. For example,
$\hat{x}_t \equiv (x_t - x^*)/x^*$. Assume that in terms of deviations from mean, the
shocks follow a first-order autoregressive process, $\hat{A}_{t+1} = \rho \hat{A}_t + \varepsilon_{t+1}$
with $\rho \in (0, 1)$.

Then we can rewrite the Euler condition, (5.9), as

$$\xi \hat{c}_t = \xi \hat{c}_{t+1} + \nu \rho \hat{A}_t + \nu \chi \hat{k}_{t+1}, \tag{5.12}$$

where ξ is the elasticity of the marginal utility of consump-
tion, $\xi \equiv u''(c^*)c^*/(u'(c^*))$. The parameter $\nu \equiv \beta \bar{A}f'(k^*)$, which equals
$1 - \beta(1 - \delta)$ in the steady state. The parameter ρ is the serial correlation of the deviation of the shock from steady state, and $\chi \equiv$
$f''(k^*)k^*/(f'(k^*))$ is the elasticity of the marginal product of capital
with respect to capital.

The resource condition (5.10) can be approximated by

$$\hat{k}_{t+1} = \frac{1}{\beta}\hat{k}_t + \frac{\delta}{(1 - s_c)}\hat{A}_t - \frac{s_c}{(1 - s_c)}\delta \hat{c}_t. \tag{5.13}$$

Here s_c is consumption's steady state share of output.

If the researcher specifies a problem such that preferences and the
production function exhibit constant elasticities, then ξ and χ are
fixed parameters, and one does not have to ever solve explicitly for
a steady state. For example, if the production function is Cobb-
Douglas where α is capital's share, then χ is simply $(\alpha - 1)$. Likewise
ν just depends on the discount factor and the rate of physical capital

---

13. The problem is similar to that described by King et al. (1988), though here we have
not yet introduced employment.

depreciation. The consumption share s_c is just a function of the parameters of the economy as well.

For example, in the Cobb-Douglas case, (5.11) can be written as

$$1 = \beta\left[\alpha\left(\frac{y^*}{k^*}\right) + (1 - \delta)\right],$$

where y^* is the steady state level of output. Since the steady state level of investment $i^* = \delta k^*$, this can be rewritten as

$$1 = \beta[\alpha\delta/(1 - s_c) + (1 - \delta)].$$

Solving this, we obtain

$$(1 - s_c) = \frac{\beta\alpha\delta}{1 - \beta(1 - \delta)},$$

so s_c can be calculated directly from the underlying parameters.

This approach delivers a log-linearized system whose parameter are determined by the underlying specification of preferences, technology, and the driving processes of the economy. This system can be simplified by solving out for $\hat{c}_t$ yielding a stochastic system characterizing the evolution of the state variables; put differently, the system can be written solely in terms of $(\hat{A}_t, \hat{k}_t)$. At this point the response of the system to productivity innovations can be evaluated using the data.[14]

Value Function Iteration
Instead of obtaining an approximate solution by log-linearization, we could pursue the dynamic programming solution more directly. First we need to more fully characterize the solution. For this we often resort to specific examples or numerical analysis.

As a lead example, suppose that $u(c) = \ln(c)$ and that the rate of depreciation of capital is 100 percent. Assume that the process for the shocks is given by

$$\ln A' = \rho \ln A + \varepsilon,$$

where $\rho \in (-1, 1)$ so that the process is stationary. Now suppose that the production function has the form $f(k) = Ak^\alpha$.

---

14. The discussion in the appendix of King et al. (1988) is recommended for those who want to study this linearization approach in some detail.

With these restrictions the Euler equation (5.9) reduces to

$$\frac{1}{c} = \beta E_{A'|A}\left[\frac{A'\alpha k'^{(\alpha-1)}}{c'}\right]. \tag{5.14}$$

Note that here we take the expectation, over A' given A, of the ratio since future consumption c' will presumably depend on the realized value of the productivity shock next period.

To solve for the policy function, we make a guess and attempt to verify it.[15] We claim that the policy function $k' = \phi(A, k)$ is given by

$$\phi(A, k) = \lambda A k^\alpha,$$

where λ is an unknown constant. That is, our guess is that the future capital is proportional to output, which is similar to the policy function we deduced for the example of the nonstochastic growth model. The resource constraint then is

$$c = (1 - \lambda)Ak^\alpha.$$

To verify this guess and determine λ, we substitute this in the proposed policy function (5.14). This yields

$$\frac{1}{(1 - \lambda)Ak^\alpha} = \beta E_{A'|A}\left[\frac{A'\alpha k'^{(\alpha-1)}}{(1 - \lambda)A'k'^\alpha}\right].$$

Solving for the policy function yields

$$k' = \beta\alpha Ak^\alpha. \tag{5.15}$$

Hence our guess is verified and $\lambda = \alpha\beta$. This implies that consumption is proportional to income:

$$c = (1 - \beta\alpha)Ak^\alpha. \tag{5.16}$$

We could also show that the value function that solves (5.6) is given by

$$V(A, k) = G + B\ln(k) + D\ln(A) \qquad \text{for all } (A, k),$$

where G, B, and D are the unknown constants that we need to solve for.

Then using (5.15) and (5.16), we would write the functional equation as

---

15. Here we formulate the guess of the policy function rather than the value function. In either case the key is to check that the functional equation is satisfied.

$$G + B \ln(k) + D \ln(A) = \ln((1 - \beta\alpha)Ak^{\alpha}) + \beta[G + B \ln(\beta\alpha Ak^{\alpha})]$$

$$+ DE_{A' \mid A} \ln(A') \qquad \text{for all } (A, k). \tag{5.17}$$

Note that there is no maximization here as we have substituted the policy function into the functional equation.[16] Since $E_{A' \mid A} \ln(A') = \rho \ln A$, we make use of the fact that this relationship holds for all (A, k) and group terms together as we did in the analysis of the nonstochastic growth model. So the constants must be the same on both sides of (5.17):

$$G = \ln(1 - \beta\alpha) + \beta G + \beta B \ln(\beta\alpha).$$

Similarly, for the coefficients multiplying $\ln(k)$, we must have

$$B = \alpha + \beta B\alpha.$$

Finally, with respect to $\ln(A)$,

$$D = 1 + \beta B + \beta D\rho.$$

As we solve for G, B, and D in this system of equations, we solve the functional equation. The solution is unique, so we verify our guess. Although tedious, we could solve this as

$$G = \frac{\ln(1 - \beta\alpha) + \beta(\alpha/(1 - \beta\alpha)) \ln(\beta\alpha)}{1 - \beta},$$

$$B = \frac{\alpha}{1 - \beta\alpha},$$

$$D = \frac{1}{(1 - \beta\rho)(1 - \beta\alpha)}.$$

Here we see the importance of discounting: if $\beta = 1$, then G is infinity. However, this is a very special case. We will use discounting again when we discuss the empirical implications of the stochastic growth model.

EXERCISE 5.3 Show that if there is less than 100 percent depreciation, the solution given by $\phi(A, k) = \lambda Ak^{\alpha}$ fails.

Outside of the special examples, we are left with a direct analysis of (5.6). It is straightforward to apply the analysis of chapter 2 to the

---

16. Alternatively, one could start from this guess of the value function and then use it to deduce the policy function.

nonstochastic problem and solve the functional equation.[17] We could even show that the value function is a strictly concave function of k. Consequently the policy function would be increasing in k. To see this, we refer to (5.8). An increase in k will increase the left-hand side of the equation. If k' does not rise, then (5.8) will not hold since the right-hand side, because of the concavity of $V(A, k)$, is a decreasing function of k'.

Further details about the policy function require numerical analysis. A stochastic version of the program, termed grow.m, could be built as discussed above. This is a good exercise for the reader who knows and how to write a value function iteration program.[18] We return to the value function iteration program in the next section after we introduce to the model a labor supply decision.

EXERCISE 5.4   Write a value function iteration program that draws on grow.m to find the solution to (5.6).

5.3.4 Decentralization

To study the decentralized economy, the household's problem must be supplemented by a budget constraint, and the sources of income (labor income, capital income, profits) would have to be specified along with the uses of these funds (consumption, savings). Likewise the firm's demands for labor and capital inputs would have to be specified as well. We discuss these in turn using the recursive equilibrium concept.[19]

The firm's problem is static as we assume that the households hold the capital. Thus the firm rents capital from the household at a price of r per unit and hires labor at a wage of ω per hour. The wage and rental rates are all in terms of current period output. Taking these prices as given, the representative firm will maximize profits by choosing inputs (K, N) such that

$$A f_N(K, N) = \omega \quad \text{and} \quad A f_K(K, N) + (1 - \delta) = r.$$

17. Given that $u(c)$ and $f(k)$ are both strictly concave, it is straightforward to see that the value function for the one-period problem is strictly concave in k. As we argued in chapter 2, this property is preserved by the $T(V)$ mapping used to construct a solution to the functional equation.

18. See Tauchen (1990) for a discussion of this economy and a comparison of the value function iteration solution relative to other solution methods.

19. See also the presentation of various decentralizations in Stokey and Lucas (1989).

Here we stipulate that the capital rental agreement allows the firm to use the capital and to retain the undepreciated capital, which it then sells for the same price as output in the one-sector model. Due to the constant returns to scale assumption, the number and size of the firms is not determined. We assume, for simplicity, that there is a single firm (though it acts competitively) that employs all the capital and labor in the economy, denoted by uppercase letters.

For the households, their problem is

$$V(A, k, K) = \max_{k'} u(r(K)k + \omega(K) + \Pi - k') + \beta E_{A'|A} V(A', k', K'),$$
(5.18)

where Π is the flow of profits from the firms to the households. This is a different expression than (5.6) as there is an additional state variable, K. Here k is the household's own stock of capital while K is the per capita capital stock economywide. The household needs to know the current value of K, since factor prices depend on this aggregate state variable through the factor demand equations. This is indicated in (5.18) by the dependence of $r(K)$ and $\omega(K)$ on K.

Let $K' = H(A, K)$ represent the evolution of the aggregate capital stock. As the household is competitive, it takes the evolution of the aggregate state variable as given. Thus the household takes current and future factor prices as given.

The first-order condition for the household's capital decision is

$$u'(c) = \beta E V_k(A', k', K').$$
(5.19)

Here the household uses the law of motion for K. From (5.18) we know that $V_k = r(K)u'(c)$, so the first-order condition can be written as

$$u'(c) = \beta E r' u'(c').$$
(5.20)

A **recursive equilibrium** is comprised of

- factor price functions: $r(K)$ and $\omega(K)$
- individual policy functions: $h(A, k, K)$ from (5.18)
- a law for motion for K: $H(A, K)$

such that

- households and firms optimize
- markets clear
- $H(A, k) = h(A, k, k)$

From these first-order conditions for factor demand of the operating firm, it is easy to see that the solution to the planner's problem is a recursive equilibrium.

5.4 A Stochastic Growth Model with Endogenous Labor Supply

We now supplement our version of the stochastic growth model with an endogenous labor supply decision. For now, we retain the perspective of the planner's problem and discuss decentralization later in this section.

5.4.1 Planner's Dynamic Programming Problem

We can supplement preferences and technology with a labor input and thus modify the planner's problem as

$$V(A,k) = \max_{k',n} \ u(Af(k,n) + (1-\delta)k - k', 1-n) + \beta E_{A'|A} V(A',k')$$

$$\text{for all } (A,k). \tag{5.21}$$

Here the variables are measured in per capita terms: k and n are the capital and labor inputs per capita.

The optimization problem entails dynamic choice between consumption and investment. Recall that this was the key to the stochastic growth model with fixed labor input. In addition **given** k', (5.21) has a "static" choice of n.[20] This distinction is important when we turn to a discussion of programming the solution to this functional equation.

For given (A,k,k'), define $\sigma(A,k,k')$ from

$$\sigma(A,k,k') = \max_{n} \ u(Af(k,n) + (1-\delta)k - k', 1-n), \tag{5.22}$$

and let $n = \hat{\phi}(A,k,k')$ denote the solution to the optimization problem. The first-order condition for this problem is given by

$$u_c(c, 1-n)Af_n(k,n) = u_l(c, 1-n). \tag{5.23}$$

This condition equates the marginal gain from increasing employment and consuming the extra output with the marginal cost in terms of the reduction in leisure time. This is clearly a necessary

---

20. Of course, this is static for a given k'. The point is that the choice of n does not influence the evolution of the state variable.

condition for optimality: in an optimal solution this type of static variation should not increase welfare.

Thus, for the current productivity shock and current capital stock and for a level of future capital, $\hat{\phi}(A, k, k')$ characterizes the employment decision. We can think of $\sigma(A, k, k')$ as a return function given the current state (A, k) and control (k').

The return function from this choice of the labor input can then be used to rewrite the functional equation as

$$V(A, k) = \max_{k'} \, \sigma(A, k, k') + \beta E_{A' \mid A} V(A', k') \qquad \text{for all } (A, k). \qquad (5.24)$$

This has the same structure as the stochastic growth model with a fixed labor supply, though the return function, $\sigma(A, k, k')$, is not a primitive object. Instead, it is derived from a maximization problem and thus inherits its properties from the more primitive $u(c, 1 - n)$ and $f(k, n)$ functions. Referring to the results in chapter 2, we know there is a solution to this problem and that a stationary policy function will exist. Denote the policy function by $k' = h(A, k)$.

The first-order condition for the choice of the future capital stock is given by

$$\sigma_{k'}(A, k, k') + \beta E_{A' \mid A} V_{k'}(A', k') = 0,$$

where the subscripts denote partial derivatives. Using (5.24), we can solve for $E_{A' \mid A} V_k(A', k')$. The result is a Euler equation

$$-\sigma_{k'}(A, k, k') = \beta E_{A' \mid A} \sigma_{k'}(A', k', k'').$$

Using (5.22), we can rewrite this in more familiar terms as

$$u_c(c, 1 - n) = \beta E_{A' \mid A}[u_c(c', 1 - n')[A' f_k(k', n') + (1 - \delta)], \qquad (5.25)$$

where $c = Af(k, n) + (1 - \delta)k - k'$ and c' is defined similarly. This Euler equation is another necessary condition for an optimum: else a variation in the level of savings would increase lifetime expected utility.

The policy functions will exhibit a couple of key properties revolving around the themes of intertemporal substitution and consumption smoothing. The issue is essentially understanding the response of consumption and employment to a productivity shock. By intertemporal substitution, the household will be induced to work more when productivity is high. But, due to potentially offsetting income and substitution effects, the response to a productivity shocks will be lower the more permanent are these shocks.[21] By consumption smoothing, a household will optimally adjust consumption in all periods to an increase in productivity. The more persistent is the shock to productivity, the more responsive will consumption be to it.[22]

5.4.2 Numerical Analysis

A discussion along the same lines as that for the stochastic growth model with fixed labor input applies here as well. As in King et al. (1988) one can attack the set of necessary conditions—(5.23), (5.25), and the resource constraint—through a log-linearization procedure. The reader is urged to study that approach from their paper.

Alternatively, one can again simply solve the functional equation directly. This is just an extension of the programming exercise given at the end of the previous section on the stochastic growth model with fixed labor supply. The outline of the program will be discussed here leaving the details as an additional exercise.

The program should be structured to focus on solving (5.24) through the value function iteration. The problem is that the return function is derived and thus must be solved for inside of the program. The researcher can obtain an approximate solution to the employment policy function, given previously as $\hat{\phi}(A, k, k')$. This is achieved by specifying grids for the shocks, the capital state space and the employment space.[23] As noted earlier, this is the point of approximation in the value function iteration routine: finer grids yield better approximations but are costly in terms of computer time. Once $\hat{\phi}(A, k, k')$ is obtained, then

$$\sigma(A, k, k') = u(Af(k, \hat{\phi}(A, k, k')) + (1 - \delta)k - k', 1 - \hat{\phi}(A, k, k'))$$

can be calculated and stored. This should all be done prior to start-

---

21. Preferences are actually often specified so that there is no response in hours worked to permanent shocks. Another specification of preferences, pursued by Hansen (1985), arises from the assumption that employment is a discrete variable at the individual level. Rogerson (1988) provides the basic framework for the "indivisible labor model."
22. We will see this in more detail in the following chapter on household savings and consumption where there is stochastic income.
23. For some specifications of the utility function, $\hat{\phi}(A, k, k')$ can be solved analytically and inserted into the program. For example, suppose that $u(c, 1 - n) = U(c + \xi(1 - n))$, where ξ is a parameter. Then the first-order condition is $Af_n(k, n) = \xi$, which can be solved to obtain $\hat{\phi}(A, k, k')$ given the production function. To verify this, assume that $Af(k, n)$ is a Cobb-Douglas function.

ing the value function iteration phase of the program. So, given $\sigma(A,k,k')$, the program would then proceed to solve (5.24) through the usual value function iteration routine.

The output of the program is then the policy function for capital accumulation, $k' = h(A,k)$, and a policy function for employment, $n = \phi(A,k)$, where

$$\phi(A,k) = \hat{\phi}(A,k,h(A,k)).$$

Hence both of these policy functions ultimately depend only on the state variables, (A,k). These policy functions provide a link between the primitive functions (and their parameters) and observables. We turn now to a discussion of exploiting that link as the stochastic growth model confronts the data.

5.5   Confronting the Data

Since its presentation by Kydland and Prescott (1982), macro-economists have debated the empirical success of the stochastic growth model. This debate is of interest both because of its importance for the study of business cycles and for its influence on empirical methodology. Our focus here is on the latter point as we use the stochastic growth model as a vehicle for exploring alternative approaches to the quantitative analysis of dynamic equilibrium models.

Regardless of the methodology the link between theory and data is provided by the policy functions. To set notation, let Θ denote a vector of unknown parameters. We will assume that the production function is Cobb-Douglas and is constant returns to scale. Let α denote capital's share. Further assume

$$u(c, 1 - n) = \ln(c) + \xi(1 - n)$$

as the utility function.[24] The parameter vector then is

$$\Theta = (\alpha, \delta, \beta, \xi, \rho, \sigma),$$

where α characterizes the technology, δ determines the rate of depreciation of the capital stock, β is the discount factor, and ξ

---

24. The interested reader can go beyond this structure, though the arguments put forth by King et al. (1988) on restrictions necessary for balanced growth should be kept in mind. Here the function $\xi(1 - n)$ is left unspecified for the moment, though we assume it has a constant elasticity given by η.

parameterizes preferences. The technology shock process is parameterized by a serial correlation (ρ) and a variance (σ). To make clear that the properties of this model economy depend on these parameters, we index the policy functions by Θ: $k' = h_\Theta(A,k)$ and $n = \phi_\Theta(A,k)$. At this point we assume that for a given Θ these policy functions have been obtained from a value function iteration program. The question is then how to estimate Θ.

5.5.1 Moments

One common approach to estimation of Θ is based on matching moments. The researcher specifies a set of moments from the data and then finds the value of Θ to match (as closely as possible) these moments. A key element, of course, is determining the set of moments to match.

Kydland and Prescott (1982) give one version of this approach, termed **calibration**. Kydland and Prescott consider a much richer model than that presented in the previous section as they include a sophisticated time to build model of capital accumulation, nonseparable preferences, and a signal extraction problem associated with the technology shock. They pick the parameters for their economy using moments obtained from applied studies and from low frequency observations of the U.S. economy. In their words, "Our approach is to focus on certain statistics for which the noise introduced by approximations and measurement errors is likely to be small relative to the statistic."

Since the model we have studied thus far is much closer to that analyzed by King, Plosser, and Rebelo (1988), we return to a discussion of that paper for an illustration of this calibration approach.[25] King, Plosser, and Rebelo calibrate their parameters from a variety of sources. As do Kydland and Prescott, the technology parameter is chosen to match factor shares. The Cobb-Douglas specification implies that labor's share in the National Income and Product Accounts should equal $1 - \alpha$. The rate of physical depreciation is set at 10 percent annually, and the discount rate is chosen to match a 6.5 percent average annual return on capital. The value of ξ is set so that, on average, hours worked are 20 percent of total hours corre-

---

25. King, Plosser, and Rebelo, however, build a deterministic trend into their analysis, which they remove to render the model stationary. As noted in section 3.2.1 of their paper, this has implications for selecting a discount factor.

Table 5.1
Observed and predicted moments

Moments	U.S. data	KPR calibrated model
Std relative to output		
Consumption	0.69	0.64
Investment	1.35	2.31
Hours	0.52	0.48
Wages	1.14	0.69
Cross correlation with output		
Consumption	0.85	0.82
Investment	0.60	0.92
Hours	0.07	0.79
Wages	0.76	0.90

sponding to the average hours worked between 1948 and 1986. King, Plosser, and Rebelo use variations in the parameters of the stochastic process (principally ρ) as a tool for understanding the response of economic behavior as the permanence of shocks is varied. In other studies, such as Kydland and Prescott (1982), the parameters of the technology shock process is inferred from the residual of the production function.

Note that for these calibration exercises the model does not have to be solved in order to pick the parameters. That is, the policy functions are not actually used in the calibration of the parameters. Instead, the parameters are chosen by looking at evidence that is outside of business cycle properties, such as time series averages. Comparing the model's predictions against actual business cycle moments is thus an informal overidentification exercise.

Table 5.1 shows moments from U.S. data as well as the predictions of these moments from the King, Plosser, and Rebelo model parameterized as described above.[26] The first set of moment is the standard deviation of key macroeconomic variables relative to output. The second set of moments is the correlation of these variables with output.

In the literature this is a common set of moments to study. Note that the stochastic growth model, as parameterized by King, Plosser,

---

26. Specifically the moments from the KPR model are taken from their table 4, using the panel data labor supply elasticity and $\rho = 0.9$. The standard deviation of the technology shock (deviation from steady state) is set at 2.29.

and Rebelo exhibits many important features of the data. In particular, the model produces consumption smoothing as the standard deviation of consumption is less than that of output. Further, as in U.S. data, the variability of investment exceeds that of output. The cross correlations are all positive in the model as they are in the data. One apparent puzzle is the low correlation of hours and output in the data relative to the model.[27] Still, based on casual observation, the model "does well." However, these papers do not provide "tests" of how close the moments produced by the model actually are to the data.

Of course, one can go a lot further with this moment-matching approach. Letting Ψ^D be the list of eight moments from U.S. data shown in table 5.1, one could solve the problem of

$$\min_{\Theta}(\Psi^D - \Psi^S(\Theta))W(\Psi^D - \Psi^S(\Theta))', \tag{5.26}$$

where $\Psi^S(\Theta)$ is a vector of simulated moments that depend on the vector Θ which parameterizes the stochastic growth model. As discussed in chapter 4, W is a weighting matrix. So, for their parameterization, the $\Psi^S(\Theta)$ produced by the King, Plosser, and Rebelo model is simply the column of moments reported in table 5.1. But, as noted earlier, the parameter vector was chosen based on other moments and evidence from other studies.

EXERCISE 5.5   Solve (5.26), using a version of the stochastic growth model to create the mapping Ψ^D.

5.5.2   GMM

Another approach, closer to the use of orthogonality conditions in the GMM approach, is that of Christiano and Eichenbaum (1992). Their intent is to enrich the RBC model to encompass the observations that the correlation between the labor input (hours worked) and the return to working (the wage and/or the average product of labor). In doing so, they add shocks to government purchases, financed by lump-sum taxes. Thus government shocks influence the labor choice of households through income effects. For their exercise, this is important as this shift in labor supply interacts with variations in labor demand, thereby reducing the excessively high correlation

---

27. See King et al. (1988) for a discussion of this.

between hours and the return to work induced by technology shocks alone.

While the economics here is, of course, of interest, we explore the estimation methodology employed by Christiano and Eichenbaum. They estimate eight parameters: the rate of physical depreciation (δ), the labor share of the Cobb-Douglas technology (α), a preference parameter for household's marginal rate of substitution between consumption and leisure (γ), as well as the parameters characterizing the distributions of the shocks to technology and government spending.

Their estimation routine has two phases. In the first, they estimate the parameters, and in the second they look at additional implications of the model.

For the first phase they use unconditional moments to estimate these parameters. For example, using the capital accumulation equation, they solve for the rate of depreciation as

$$\delta = 1 - \frac{k_{t+1} - i_t}{k_t}.$$

An estimate of δ can be obtained as the time series average of this expression with data on the capital stock and on investment.[28] Note that since there is just a single parameter in this condition, δ is estimated independently of the other parameters of the model. Building on this estimate, Christiano and Eichenbaum use the intertemporal optimality condition—on the assumption that $u(c) = \ln(c)$—to determine capital's share in the production function. They proceed in this fashion of using unconditional movements to identify each of the structural parameters.

Christiano and Eichenbaum then construct a larger parameter vector, termed Φ, which consists of the parameters described above from their version of the stochastic growth model and a vector of second moments from the data. They place these moments within the GMM framework. With this structure, they use GMM to estimate the parameters and obtain a variance covariance matrix that they then use to produce standard errors for their parameter estimates.[29]

---

28. As the authors indicate, this procedure may only uncover the depreciation rate used to construct the capital series from observations on investment.

29. In contrast to many studies in the calibration tradition, this is truly an estimation exercise, complete with standard errors.

The point of their study is to confront observations on the correlation of hours and the average product of labor, $\text{corr}(y/n, n)$, and the relative standard deviations of the labor input and the average productivity of labor, $\sigma_n/\sigma_{y/n}$. They test whether their model, at the estimated parameters, is able to match the values of these moments in the data. Note that this is in the spirit of an overidentification test, although the model they estimate is just identified. They find that the stochastic growth model with the addition of government spending shocks is unable (with one exception) to match the observations for these two labor market statistics. The most successful version of the model is estimated with establishment data. In this specification they assume that the labor input is indivisible and government spending is not valued at all by the households.[30]

5.5.3 Indirect Inference

Smith (1993) illustrates the indirect inference methodology by a version of the simple stochastic growth model with fixed employment, as in (5.6). There is one important modification: Smith considers an accumulation equation of the form

$$k' = k(1 - \delta) + Z_t i_t,$$

where Z_t is a second shock in the model. Greenwood et al. (1988) interpret this as a shock to next investment goods, and Cooper and Ejarque (2000) view this as an "intermediation shock."

With this additional shock, the dynamic programming problem for the representative household becomes

$$V(A, Z, k) = \max_{k', n} u\left(Af(k, n) + \frac{(1 - \delta)k - k'}{Z}, 1 - n\right)$$

$$+ \beta E_{A'|A} V(A', Z', k'). \tag{5.27}$$

Note the timing here: the realized value of Z is known prior to the accumulation decision. As with the stochastic growth model, this dynamic programming problem can be solved by a value function iteration or by linearization around the steady state.

From the perspective of the econometrics, by introducing this second source of uncertainty, the model has enough randomness to

---

30. The model cannot be rejected at a 15 percent level based on the J-statistic computed from the match of these two moments.

avoid zero likelihood observations.[31] As with the technology shock, there is a variance and a serial correlation parameter used to characterize this normally distributed shock. Smith assumes that the innovations to these shocks are uncorrelated.

To take the model to the data, Smith estimates a VAR(2) on log detrended quarterly U.S. time series for the period 1947:1–1988:4. The vector used for the analysis is

$$x_t = [y_t \quad i_t]',$$

where y_t is the detrended log of output and i_t is the detrended log of investment expenditures. With two lags of each variable, two constants and three elements of the variance-covariance matrix, Smith generates thirteen coefficients.

He estimates nine parameters using the SQML procedure. As outlined in his paper and in chapter 3, this procedure finds the structural parameters that maximize the likelihood of observing the data when the likelihood function is evaluated at the coefficients produced by running the VARs on simulated data created from the model at the estimated structural parameters. Alternatively, one could directly choose the structural parameters to minimize the difference between the VAR(2) coefficients on the actual and simulated data.

5.5.4 Maximum Likelihood Estimation

Last, but certainly not least, is a version of the stochastic growth model estimated using the maximum likelihood approach. As in the indirect inference approach, it is necessary to supplement the basic model with additional sources of randomness to avoid the zero likelihood problem. This point is developed in the discussion of maximum likelihood estimation in Kocherlakota et al. (1994). Their goal is to evaluate the contribution of technology shocks to aggregate fluctuations.

Kocherlakota et al. (1994) construct a model economy that includes shocks to the production function and stochastic depreciation. In particular, the production function is given by $Y_t = A_t K_t^\alpha (N_t X_t)^{1-\alpha} + Q_t$. Here X_t is exogenous technological progress, Y_t is the output of the single good, K_t is the capital stock, and N_t is the labor input. The

---

31. The reason is that the empirical analysis focuses on output and investment fluctuations.

transition equation for capital accumulation is $K_{t+1} = (1 - \delta_t)K_t + I_t$, where δ_t is the rate of depreciation and I_t is the level of investment.

The authors first consider a version of the stochastic growth model without a labor input. They show that the linearized decision rules imply that consumption and the future capital stock are proportional to the current stock of capital.[32]

They then proceed to the estimation of their model economy with these three sources of uncertainty. They assume that the shocks follow an AR(1) process. Kocherlakota et al. (1994) construct a representation of the equilibrium process for consumption, employment, and output as a function of current and lagged values of the shocks. This relationship can then be used to construct a likelihood function, conditional on initial values of the shocks.

Kocherlakota et al. (1994) fix a number of the parameters that one might ultimately be interested in estimating and focus attention on Σ, the variance-covariance matrix of the shocks. This is particularly relevant to their exercise of determining the contribution of technology shocks to fluctuations in aggregate output. In this regard they argue that without additional assumptions about the stochastic process of the shocks, they are unable to identify the relative variances of the shocks.

There are a number of other papers that have taken the maximum likelihood approach.[33] Altug (1989) estimates a version of the Kydland and Prescott (1982) model with a single fundamental shock to technology and measurement error elsewhere. Altug (1989) finds some difficulty matching the joint behavior of labor and other series.

Hall (1996) studies a version of a labor-hoarding model, which is then compared to the overtime labor model of Hansen and Sargent (1988). While the Hall (1996) paper is too complex to present here, it is particularly noteworthy for the comparison of results from estimating parameters using GMM and maximum likelihood.

5.6 Some Extensions

In the final section of this chapter we consider extensions of the basic models. These are provided here partly as exercises for readers

---

32. When employment is variable and wages are observed, then (5.23) has no error term either. So researchers include taste shocks. This way they find that current consumption can be written as a function of current output and lagged consumption *without* any error term. This prediction is surely inconsistent with the data.

33. See Hansen et al. (1994) for a general formulation of this approach.

interested in going beyond the models presented here.[34] One of the compelling aspects of the stochastic growth model is its flexibility in terms of admitting a multitude of extensions.

5.6.1 Technological Complementarities

As initially formulated in a team production context by Bryant (1983) and explored subsequently in the stochastic growth model by Baxter and King (1991), supplementing the individual agent's production function with a measure of the level of activity by other agents is a convenient way to introduce interactions across agents.[35] The idea is to introduce a complementarity into the production process so that high levels of activity in other firms implies that a single firm is more productive as well.

Let y represent the output at a given firm, Y be aggregate output, k and n the firm's input of capital and labor respectively. Consider a production function of

$$y = Ak^{\alpha}n^{\phi}Y^{\gamma}Y^{\varepsilon}_{-1}, \tag{5.28}$$

where A is a productivity shock that is common across producers. Here γ parameterizes the contemporaneous interaction between producers. If γ is positive, then there is a complementarity at work: as other agents produce more, the productivity of the individual agent increases as well. In addition this specification allows for a dynamic interaction parameterized by ε. As discussed in Cooper and Johri (1997), this may be interpreted as a dynamic technological complementarity or even a learning by doing effect. This production function can be embedded into a stochastic growth model.

Consider the problem of a representative household with access to a production technology given by (5.28). This is essentially a version of (5.21) with a different technology.

There are two ways to solve this problem. The first is to write the dynamic programming problem, carefully distinguishing between

---

34. Each of these extensions creates an environment that the interested reader can use in specifying, solving, and estimating parameters of a dynamic programming problem.

35. Cooper (1999) explores a wide variety of ways to model complementarities. Enriching the neoclassical production function is the one closest to existing models. See the discussion in Benhabib and Farmer (1994) and Farmer and Guo (1994) on the use of these models to study indeterminacy. Manski (1993) and Cooper (2002) discuss issues associated with the estimation of models with complementarities and multiple equilibria.

individual and aggregate variables. As in our discussion of the recursive equilibrium concept, a law of motion must be specified for the evolution of the aggregate variables. Given this law of motion, the individual household's problem is solved and the resulting policy function compared to the one that governs the economywide variables. If these policy functions match, then there is an equilibrium. Else, another law of motion for the aggregate variables is specified and the search continues.[36]

Alternatively, one can use the first-order conditions for the individuals' optimization problem. As all agents are identical and all shocks are common, the representative household will accumulate its own capital, supply its own labor, and interact with other agents only because of the technological complementarity. In a symmetric equilibrium, $y_t = Y_t$. As in Baxter and King (1991), this equilibrium condition is neatly imposed through the first-order conditions when the marginal products of labor and capital are calculated. From the set of first-order conditions, the symmetric equilibrium can be analyzed through by approximation around a steady state.

The distinguishing feature of this economy from the traditional RBC model is the presence of the technological complementarity parameters, γ and ε. It is possible to estimate these parameters directly from the production function or to infer them from the equilibrium relationships.[37]

5.6.2   Multiple Sectors

The stochastic growth model explored so far has a single sector of production. Of course this is just an abstraction that allows the research to focus on intertemporal allocations without being very precise about the multitude of activities arising contemporaneously.

As an example, suppose that there are two sectors in the economy. Sector one produces consumption goods and second two produces investment goods.[38] Let the production function for sector $j = 1, 2$ be given by

---

36. In contrast to the contraction mapping theorem, there is no guarantee that this process will converge. In some cases the household's response to an aggregate law of motion can be used as the next guess on the aggregate law of motion. Iteration of this may lead to a recursive equilibrium.

37. See Cooper (1999) and the references therein.

38. For now think of these are producer durables, though one could also add consumer durables to this sector or create another sector.

$y_j = A^j f(k^j, n^j).$

Here there are sector-specific total factor productivity shocks. An important issue for this model is the degree of correlation across the sectors of activity.

Assuming that both capital and labor can be costlessly shifted across sectors of production, the state vector contains the aggregate stock of capital rather than its use in the previous period. Further there is only a single accumulation equation for capital. The dynamic programming problem for the planner becomes

$$V(A^1, A^2, k) = \max_{\{k^j, n^j\}} u(c, 1 - n) + \beta E_{A^{1\prime}, A^{2\prime} | A^1, A^2} V(A^{1\prime}, A^{2\prime}, k') \qquad (5.29)$$

subject to

$$c = A^1 f(k^1, n^1), \qquad (5.30)$$

$$k' = k(1 - \delta) + A^2 f(k^2, n^2), \qquad (5.31)$$

$$n = n^1 + n^2, \qquad (5.32)$$

$$k = k^1 + k^2. \qquad (5.33)$$

This optimization problem can be solved using value function iteration, and the properties of the simulated economy can, in principle, be compared to data. For this economy the policy functions will specify the state contingent allocation of capital and labor across sectors.

Economies generally exhibit positive comovement of employment and output across sectors. This type of correlation may be difficult for a multisector economy to match unless there is sufficient correlation in the shocks across sectors.[39]

This problem can be enriched by introducing costs of reallocating capital and/or labor across the sectors. At the extreme, capital may be entirely sector specific. In that case the state space for the dynamic programming problem must include the allocation of capital across sectors inherited from the past. By adding this friction to the model, we reduce the flow of factors across the sectors.

EXERCISE 5.6   Extend the code for the one sector stochastic growth model to solve (5.29). Use the resulting policy functions to simulate

---

39. Similar problems of matching positive comovements arise in multiple-country real business cycle models.

the model, and compute moments as a function of key parameters, such as the correlation of the shocks across the sectors. Relate these to observed correlations across sectors.

5.6.3 Taste Shocks

Another source of uncertainty that is considered within the stochastic growth model allows for randomness in tastes. This may be a proxy for variations in the value of leisure brought about by technology changes in a home production function. Here we specify a model with shocks to the marginal rate of substitution between consumption and work. Formally, we consider

$$V(A, S, k) = \max_{\{k', n\}} u(c, 1 - n, S) + \beta E_{A', S' \mid A, S} V(A', S', k') \tag{5.34}$$

subject to the usual production function and capital accumulation equations. Here S represents the shocks to tastes. This problem may be interpreted as a two-sector model where the second sector produces leisure from time and a shock (S). Empirically this type of specification is useful as there is a shock, internal to the model, that allows the intratemporal first-order condition to be violated provided that S is not observable to the econometrician.

As usual, the policy functions will specify state-contingent employment and capital accumulation. Again, the model can be solved, for example, through value function iteration, and then parameters selected to match moments of the data.

EXERCISE 5.7   Extend the code for the one sector stochastic growth model to solve (5.34). Use the resulting policy functions to simulate the model, and compute moments as a function of key parameters, including the variance/covariance matrix for the shocks. Relate these to observed correlations from U.S. data. Does the existence of taste shocks "help" the model fit the data better?

5.6.4 Taxes

One important extension of the stochastic growth model introduces taxes and government spending. These exercises are partly motivated as attempts to determine the sources of fluctuations. Further, from a policy perspective, the models are used to evaluate the impacts of taxes and spending on economic variables. Further, because the models are based on optimizing households, one can evaluate the welfare implications of various policies.

McGrattan (1994) and Braun (1994) study these issues. We summarize the results and approach of McGrattan as we elaborate on the maximum likelihood estimation of these models.

McGrattan specifies a version of the stochastic growth model with four sources of fluctuations: productivity shocks, government-spending shocks, capital taxes, and labor taxes. The government's budget is balanced each period by the use of lump-sum taxes/transfers to the households. So household preferences are given by $U(c, g, n)$, where c is private consumption, g is public consumption, and n is the labor input.[40] The budget constraint for the household in any period t is given by

$$c_t + i_t = (1 - \tau_t^k)r_t k_t + (1 - \tau_t^n)w_t n_t + \delta \tau_t^k k_t + T_t, \tag{5.35}$$

where i_t is investment by the household and the right side is represents income from capital rentals, labor supply, depreciation allowances, and a lump-sum transfer. Here τ_t^k and τ_t^n are the period t tax rates on capital and labor respectively. Because of the presence of these distortionary taxes, McGrattan cannot use a planner's optimization problem to characterize optimal decision rules, and thus must work directly with a decentralized allocation.

As in the preceding discussion of recursive equilibrium, the idea is to specify state-contingent transitions for the aggregate variables and thus, in equilibrium, for relative prices. These prices are, of course, relevant to the individual through the sequence of budget constraints, (5.35). Individual households take these aggregate variables as given rules and optimize. In equilibrium the representative households's choices and the evolution of the aggregate variables coincide.[41]

McGrattan estimates the model using maximum likelihood techniques. Here the fundamental shocks are supplemented by measurement errors through the specification of a measurement equation. McGrattan assumes that innovations are normally distributed, and so writes down a likelihood function for the model economy. The parameters of the model are estimated using quarterly observations

---

40. McGrattan (1994) allows for past labor to enter current utility as well.
41. See McGrattan (1994) and the references therein for a discussion of computing such equilibria.

on output, investment, government purchases, hours, capital, and the tax rates on capital and labor. Included are parameters that characterize the utility function, the production function, and the stochastic processes for the shocks in the system. McGrattan finds a capital share of 0.397, a discount factor of 0.9927, and a capital depreciation rate of about 0.02. Interestingly government purchases do not appear to enter directly into the household's utility function. Further the log utility specification cannot be rejected.

5.7 Conclusion

The models in this chapter are some of the simpler versions of the stochastic growth model. This is one of the most useful models of macroeconomics. There is an enormous literature on it and its solution techniques. The intention here was more to provide insights into the solutions and estimations of these models using the dynamic programming approach than to provide a case for or against the applications of these models in the evaluation of aggregate fluctuations.

There are almost endless ways to extend this basic framework. The approach of this chapter allows the researcher to solve stochastic growth models numerically and to begin the task of confronting the models with data.

6   Consumption

6.1   Overview and Motivation

In the next two chapters we study consumption. We devote a number of chapters to this topic because of its importance in macroeconomics and also because of the common (though unfortunate) separation of consumption into a study of (1) nondurables and services and (2) durables.

From the perspective of business cycle theory, consumption is the largest component of total expenditures. One of the main aspects of consumption theory is the theme of consumption smoothing (defined below). This is evident in the data as the consumption of nondurables and services is not as volatile as income. In the GDP accounts durable expenditures is one of the relatively more volatile elements. Our theories and estimated models must confront these important facts.

This chapter focuses on the consumption of nondurables and services. We start with a simple two-period model to build intuition. We then progress to more complex models of consumption behavior by going to the infinite horizon, adding various forms of uncertainty and also considering borrowing restrictions. In keeping with the theme of this book, we pay particular attention to empirical studies that naturally grow out of consideration of these dynamic optimization problems.

6.2   Two-Period Problem

The two-period problem is, as always, a good starting point to build intuition about the consumption and savings decisions. We start with a statement of this problem and its solution, and then discuss some extensions.

6.2.1 Basic Problem

The consumer maximizes the discount present value of consumption over the two-period horizon. Assuming that preferences are separable across periods, we represent lifetime utility as:

$$\sum_{t=0}^{1} \beta^t u(c_t) = u(c_0) + \beta u(c_1), \tag{6.1}$$

where $\beta \in [0,1]$ and is called the discount factor. Recall from the optimal growth model that the taste factor is tied to the marginal product of capital as part of an equilibrium allocation. It is treated here as a fixed parameter. Period 0 is the initial period, so we make use of $\beta^0 = 1$.

The consumer is endowed with some initial wealth at the start of period 0 and earns income y_t in period $t = 0, 1$. For now we treat these income flows as exogenous; we later discuss adding a labor supply decision to the choice problem. We assume that the agent can freely borrow and lend at a fixed interest rate between each of the two periods of life. Thus the consumer faces a pair of constraints, one for each period of life, given by

$$a_1 = r_0(a_0 + y_0 - c_0)$$

and

$$a_2 = r_1(a_1 + y_1 - c_1).$$

Here y_t is period t income and a_t is the agent's wealth at the start of period t. It is important to appreciate the timing and notational assumptions made in these budget constraints. First, r_t represents the gross return on wealth between period t and period $t+1$. Second, the consumer earns this interest on wealth plus income less consumption over the period. It is as if the income and consumption decisions are made at the start of the period and then interest is earned over the period. Nothing critical hinges on these timing decisions, but it is necessary to be consistent about them.

There are some additional constraints to note. First, we restrict consumption to be nonnegative. Second, the stock of assets remaining at the end of the consumer's life (a_2) must be nonnegative. Else, the consumer would set $a_2 = -\infty$ and die (relatively happily) with an enormous outstanding debt. We leave open the possibility of $a_2 > 0$.

This formulation of the consumers' constraints are similar to the ones used throughout this book in our statement of dynamic programming problems. These constraints are often termed flow constraints, since they emphasize the intertemporal evolution of the stock of assets being influenced by consumption. As we will see, it is natural to think of the stock of assets as a state variables and consumption as a control variable.

There is an alternative way to express the consumer's constraints that combines these two flow conditions by substituting the first into the second. After some rearranging, it yields

$$\frac{a_2}{r_1 r_0} + \frac{c_1}{r_0} + c_0 = (a_0 + y_0) + \frac{y_1}{r_0}. \tag{6.2}$$

The left side of this expression represents the expenditures of the consumer on goods in both periods of life and on the stock of assets held at the start of period 2. The right side measures the total amount of resources available to the household for spending over its lifetime. This is a type of sources as opposed to uses formulation of the lifetime budget constraint. The numéraire for this expression of the budget constraint is period 0 consumption goods.

Maximization of (6.1) with respect to (c_0, c_1) subject to (6.2) yields

$$u'(c_0) = \lambda = \beta r_0 u'(c_1) \tag{6.3}$$

as a necessary condition for optimality, where λ is the multiplier on (6.2). This is an intertemporal first-order condition (often termed the consumer's Euler equation) that relates the marginal utility of consumption across two periods.

It is best to think of this condition as a deviation from a proposed solution to the consumer's optimization problem. So, given a candidate solution, suppose that the consumer reduces consumption by a small amount in period 0 and increases savings by the same amount. The cost of the deviation is obtained by $u'(c_0)$ in (6.3). The household will earn r_0 between the two periods and will consume those extra units of consumption in period 1. This leads to a discounted gain in utility given by the right side of (6.3). When this condition holds, lifetime utility cannot be increased through such a perturbation from the optimal path.

As in our discussion of the cake-eating problem in chapter 2, this is just a necessary condition, since (6.3) captures a very special type of deviation from a proposed path: reduce consumption today and increase it tomorrow. For more general problems (more than two periods) there will be other deviations to consider. But, even in the two-period problem, the consumer could have taken the reduced consumption in period 0 and used it to increase a_2.

Of course, there is another first-order condition associated with (6.1): the choice of a_2. The derivative with respect to a_2 is given by

$$\lambda = \phi,$$

where ϕ is the multiplier on the nonnegativity constraint for a_2. Clearly, the nonnegativity constraint binds ($\phi > 0$) if and only if the marginal utility of consumption is positive ($\lambda > 0$). That is, it is suboptimal to leave money in the bank when more consumption is desirable.

This (somewhat obvious but very important) point has two implications to keep in mind. First, in thinking about perturbations from a candidate solution, we are right to ignore the possibility of using the reduction in c_0 to increase a_2 as this is definitely not desirable. Second, and perhaps more important, knowing that $a_2 = 0$ is also critical to solving this problem. Looking at the Euler equation (6.3) alone guarantees that consumption is optimally allocated across periods, but this condition can hold for any value of a_2. So, applying (6.3) is but one necessary condition for optimality; $a_2 = 0$ must be included as well.

With $a_2 = 0$, the consumer's constraint simplifies to

$$\frac{c_1}{r_0} + c_0 = a_0 + y_0 + \frac{y_1}{r_0} \equiv w_0, \tag{6.4}$$

where w_0 is lifetime wealth for the agent in terms of period 0 goods. The optimal consumption choices depend on the measure of lifetime wealth (w_0) and the intertemporal terms of trade (r_0). In the absence of any capital market restrictions, the timing of income across the households lifetime is irrelevant for their consumption decisions. Instead, variations in the timing of income, given w_0, are reflected in the level of savings between the two periods.[1]

---

1. This has a well-understood implication for the timing of taxes. Essentially a government with a fixed level of spending must decide on the timing of its taxes. If we interpret the income flows in our example as net of taxes, then intertemporal variation in taxes (holding fixed their present value) will only change the timing of household income and not its present value. Thus tax policy will influence savings but not consumption decisions.

As an example, suppose utility is quadratic in consumption:

$$u(c) = a + bc - \frac{d}{2}c^2,$$

where we require that $u'(c) = b - dc > 0$. In this case the Euler condition simplifies to

$$b - dc_0 = \beta r_0(b - dc_1).$$

With the further simplification that $\beta r_0 = 1$, we have constant consumption: $c_0 = c_1$. Note that this prediction is independent of the timing of income over periods 0 and 1. This is an example of a more general phenomenon termed consumption smoothing. The smoothing effect will guide our discussion of consumption policy functions.

6.2.2 Stochastic Income

We now add uncertainty to the problem by supposing that income in period 1 (y_1) is not known to the consumer in period 0. Further we use the result of $A_2 = 0$ and rewrite the optimization problem more compactly as

$$\max_{c_0} E_{y_1 | y_0}[u(c_0) + \beta u(R_0(A_0 + y_0 - c_0) + y_1)],$$

where we have substituted for c_1 using the budget constraint. Note that the expectation is taken here with respect to the only unknown variable (y_1) conditional on knowing y_0, period 0 income. In fact we assume that

$$y_1 = \rho y_0 + \varepsilon_1,$$

where $|\rho| \in [0, 1]$. Here ε_1 is a shock to income that is not forecastable using period 0 information. In the optimization problem the consumer is assumed to take the information about future income conveyed by observed current income into account.

The Euler equation for this problem is given by

$$u'(c_0) = E_{y_1 | y_0} \beta R_0 u'(R_0(A_0 + y_0 - c_0) + y_1).$$

Note here that the marginal utility of future consumption is stochastic. Thus the trade-off in the Euler equation reflects the loss of utility today from reducing consumption relative to the expected gain, which depends on the realization of income in period 1.

The special case of quadratic utility and $\beta R_0 = 1$ highlights the dependence of the consumption decision on the persistence of income fluctuations. For this case the Euler equation simplifies to

$$c_0 = E_{y_1 \mid y_0} c_1 = R_0(A_0 + y_0 - c_0) + E_{y_1 \mid y_0} y_1.$$

Solving for c_0 and calculating $E_{y_1 \mid y_0} y_1$ yields

$$c_0 = \frac{R_0(A_0 + y_0)}{(1 + R_0)} + \frac{\rho y_0}{(1 + R_0)} = \frac{R_0 A_0}{(1 + R_0)} + y_0 \frac{(R_0 + \rho)}{(1 + R_0)}. \qquad (6.5)$$

This expression relates period 0 consumption to period 0 income through two separate channels. First, variations in y_0 directly affect the resources currently available to the household. Second, variations in y_0 provide information about future income (unless $\rho = 0$).

From (6.5) we have

$$\frac{\partial c_0}{\partial y_0} = \frac{(R_0 + \rho)}{(1 + R_0)}.$$

In the extreme case of iid income shocks ($\rho = 0$), consumers will save a fraction of an income increase and consume the remainder. In the opposite extreme of permanent shocks ($\rho = 1$), current consumption moves one for one with current income. Then savings does not respond to income at all. The sensitivity of consumption to income variations depends on the permanence of those shocks.[2]

Both extremes reflect a fundamental property of the optimal problem of consumption smoothing. By this property, variations in current income are spread over time periods in order to satisfy the Euler equation condition that marginal utility today is equal to the discounted marginal utility of consumption tomorrow, given the return R_0. In effect, consumption smoothing is the intertemporal expression of the normality of goods property found in static demand theory.

But our example helps highlight an interesting aspect of consumption smoothing: as the persistence of shocks increases, so does the responsiveness of consumption to income variations. This actually makes good sense: if income increases today are likely to persist, there is no need to save any of the current income gain as it will reappear in the next period. These themes of consumption smooth-

---

2. If $\rho > 1$, then $\partial c_0 / \partial y_0$ will exceed 1.

ing and the importance of the persistence of shocks will reappear throughout our discussion of the infinite horizon consumer optimization problem.

6.2.3 Portfolio Choice

A second extension of the two-period problem is the addition of multiple assets. Historically there has been a close link between the optimization problem of a consumer and asset pricing models. We will explain these links as we proceed. We begin here with a savings problem in which there are two assets.

Assume that the household has no initial wealth and can save current income through these two assets. One is nonstochastic and has a one period gross return of R^s. The second asset is risky with a return denoted by $\tilde{R}^r$ and a mean return of $\bar{R}^r$. Let a^r and a^s denote the consumer's holdings of asset type $j = r, s$. Assets' prices are normalized at 1 in period 0.

The consumer's choice problem can then be written as

$$\max_{a^r, a^s} u(y_0 - a^r - a^s) + E_{\tilde{R}^r} \beta u(\tilde{R}^r a^r + R^s a^s + y_1).$$

Here we make the simplifying assumption that y_1 is known with certainty. The first-order conditions are

$$u'(y_0 - a^r - a^s) = \beta R^s E_{\tilde{R}^r} u'(\tilde{R}^r a^r + R^s a^s + y_1)$$

and

$$u'(y_0 - a^r - a^s) = \beta E_{\tilde{R}^r} \tilde{R}^r u'(\tilde{R}^r a^r + R^s a^s + y_1).$$

Note we have not imposed any conditions regarding the holding of these assets. In particular, we have allowed the agent to buy or sell the two assets.

Suppose that $u(c)$ is strictly concave so that the agent is risk averse. Further suppose that we search for conditions such that the household is willing to hold positive amounts of both assets. Then we would expect that the agent would have to be compensated for the risk associated with holding the risky asset. This can be seen by equating these two first-order conditions (which hold with equality) and then using the fact that the expectation of the product of two random variables is the product of the expectations plus the covariance. This manipulation yields

$$R^s = \bar{R}^r + \frac{\text{cov}[\tilde{R}^r, u'(\tilde{R}^r a^r + R^s a^s + y_1)]}{E_{\tilde{R}^r} u'(\tilde{R}^r a^r + R^s a^s + y_1)}. \tag{6.6}$$

The sign of the numerator of the ratio on the right depends on the sign of a^r.

If the agent holds both the riskless and the risky asset ($a^r > 0$ and $a^s > 0$), then the strict concavity of $u(c)$ implies that the covariance must be negative. In this case, $\bar{R}^r$ must exceed R^s: the agent must be compensated for holding the risky asset.

If the average returns are equal, then the agent will not hold the risky asset ($a_r = 0$) and (6.6) will hold. Finally, if $\bar{R}^r$ is less than R^s, the agent will sell the risky asset and buy additional units of the riskless asset.

6.2.4   Borrowing Restrictions

A final extension of the two-period model is to impose a restriction on the borrowing of agents. To illustrate, consider a very extreme constraint where the consumer is able to save but not to borrow: $c_0 \leq y_0$. Thus the optimization problem of the agent is

$$\max_{c_0 \leq y_0} [u(c_0) + \beta u(R_0(A_0 + y_0 - c_0) + y_1)].$$

Denote the multiplier on the borrowing constraint by μ, the first-order condition is given by

$$u'(c_0) = \beta R_0 u'(R_0(A_0 + y_0 - c_0) + y_1) + \mu.$$

If the constraint does not bind, then the consumer has nonnegative savings and the familiar Euler equation for the two-period problem holds. However, if $\mu > 0$, then $c_0 = y_0$ and

$$u'(y_0) > \beta R_0 u'(y_1).$$

The borrowing constraint is less likely to bind if βR_0 is very large and if y_0 is large relative to y_1.

An important implication of the model with borrowing constraints is that consumption will depend on the timing of income receipts and not just W_0. That is, imagine a restructuring of income that increased y_0 and decreased y_1, leaving W_0 unchanged. In the absence of a borrowing restriction, consumption patterns would not change. But, if the borrowing constraint binds, then this restructuring of income will lead to an increase in c_0 and a reduction in c_1 as consumption "follows" income. To the extent that this change in the timing of income flows could reflect government tax policy (y_t is then viewed as after-tax income), the presence of borrowing restrictions implies that the timing of taxes can matter for consumption flows and thus for welfare.

The weakness of this and more general models is that the basis for the borrowing restrictions is not provided. So it is not surprising that researchers have been interested in understanding the source of borrowing restrictions. We return to this point in a later section.

6.3   Infinite Horizon Formulation: Theory and Empirical Evidence

We now consider the infinite horizon version of the optimal consumption problem. We are interested in seeing how the basic intuition of consumption smoothing and other aspects of optimal consumption allocations carry over to the infinite horizon setting. In addition we introduce empirical evidence into our presentation.

6.3.1   Bellman's Equation for the Infinite Horizon Problem

Consider a household with a stock of wealth denoted by A, a current flow of income y, and a return on its investments over the past period given by R_{-1}. The state vector of the consumer's problem is (A, y, R_{-1}), and the associated Bellman equation is

$$v(A, y, R_{-1}) = \max_c \ u(c) + \beta E_{y', R \mid R_{-1}, y} v(A', y', R) \qquad \text{for all } (A, y, R_{-1}),$$

where the transition equation for wealth is given by

$$A' = R(A + y - c).$$

We assume that the problem is stationary so that no time subscripts are necessary.[3] This requires, among other things, that income and returns be stationary random variables and that the joint distribution of (y', R) depend only on (y, R_{-1}).

The transition equation has the same timing as we assumed in the two-period problem: interest is earned on wealth plus income less

---

3. We assume that there exists a solution to this function equation. This requires, as always, that the choice be bounded, perhaps by a constraint on the total debt that a household can accumulate.

consumption over the period. Further the interest rate that applies is not necessarily known at the time of the consumption decision. Thus the expectation in Bellman's equation is over the two unknowns (y', R') where the given state variables provide information on forecasting these variables.[4]

6.3.2 Stochastic Income

To analyze this problem, we first consider the special case where the return on savings is known and the individual faces uncertainty only with respect to income. We then build on this model by adding in a portfolio choice, endogenous labor supply, and borrowing restrictions.

Theory
The case we study is

$$v(A, y) = \max_c u(c) + \beta E_{y'|y} v(A', y'), \tag{6.7}$$

where $A' = R(A + y - c)$ for all (A, y). The solution to this problem is a policy function that relates consumption to the state vector: $c = \phi(A, y)$. The first-order condition is

$$u'(c) = \beta R E_{y'|y} v_A(A', y'), \tag{6.8}$$

which holds for all (A, y), where $v_A(A', y')$ denotes $\partial v(A', y')/\partial A'$.

Using (6.7) to solve for $E_{y'|y} v_A(A', y')$ yields the Euler equation

$$u'(c) = \beta R E_{y'|y} u'(c'). \tag{6.9}$$

The interpretation of this equation is that the marginal loss of reducing consumption is balanced by the discounted expected marginal utility from consuming the proceeds in the following period. As usual, this Euler equation implies that a one-period deviation from a proposed solution that satisfies this relationship will not increase utility. The Euler equation, (6.9), holds when consumption today and tomorrow is evaluated using this policy function. In the special case of $\beta R = 1$, the theory predicts that the marginal utility of consumption follows a random walk.

In general, one cannot generate a closed-form solution of the policy function from these conditions for optimality. Still, some

---

4. If there are other variables known to the decision maker that provide information on (y', R), then these variables would be included in the state vector as well.

properties of the policy functions can be deduced. Given that $u(c)$ is strictly concave, one can show that $v(A, y)$ is strictly concave in A. As argued in chapter 2, the value function will inherit some of the curvature properties of the return function. Using this and (6.8), the policy function, $\phi(A, y)$, must be increasing in A. Else, an increase in A would reduce consumption and thus increase A'. This would contradict (6.8).

As a leading example, consider the specification of utility

$$u(c) = \frac{c^{1-\gamma} - 1}{1 - \gamma},$$

where $\gamma = 1$ is the special case of $u(c) = \ln(c)$. This is called the constant relative risk aversion case (CRRA), since $-cu''(c)/u'(c) = \gamma$.

Using this utility function, we rewrite (6.9) as

$$1 = \beta R E \left(\frac{c'}{c}\right)^{-\gamma},$$

where the expectation is taken with respect to future consumption which, through the policy function, depends on (A', y'). As discussed in some detail below, this equation is then used to estimate the parameters of the utility function, (β, γ).

Evidence
Hall (1978) studies the case where $u(c)$ is quadratic so that the marginal utility of consumption is linear. In this case consumption itself is predicted to follow a random walk. Hall uses this restriction to test the predictions of this model of consumption. In particular, if consumption follows a random walk, then

$$c_{t+1} = c_t + \varepsilon_{t+1}.$$

The theory predicts that the growth in consumption (ε_{t+1}) should be orthogonal to any variables known in period t: $E_t \varepsilon_{t+1} = 0$. Hall uses aggregate quarterly data for nondurable consumption. He shows that lagged stock market prices significantly predict consumption growth, which violates the permanent income hypothesis.[5]

Flavin (1981) extends Hall's analysis, allowing for a general ARMA process for the income. Income is commonly found as a predictor of consumption growth. Flavin points out that this finding is

---

5. Sargent (1978) also provides a test for the permanent income hypothesis and rejects the model.

not necessarily in opposition with the prediction of the model. Current income might be correlated with consumption growth, not because of a failure of the permanent income hypothesis but because current income signals changes in the permanent income. However, she also rejects the model.

The importance of current income to explain consumption growth has been seen as evidence of liquidity constraints (see section 6.3.5). A number of authors have investigated this issue.[6] However, most of the papers use aggregate data to test the model. Blundell et al. (1994) test the model on micro data and find that when one controls for demographics and household characteristics, current income does not appear to predict consumption growth. Meghir and Weber (1996) explicitly test for the presence of liquidity constraints using a U.S. panel data and do not find any evidence.

6.3.3 Stochastic Returns: Portfolio Choice

We have already considered a simple portfolio choice problem for the two-period problem, so this discussion will be intentionally brief. We elucidate the empirical evidence based on this model.

Theory
Assume that there are N assets available. Let R_{-1} denote the N-vector of gross returns between the current and previous period and let A be the current stock of wealth. Let s_i denote the share of asset $i = 1, 2, \ldots, N$ held by the agent. Normalizing the price of each asset to be unity, the current consumption of the agent is then

$$c = A - \sum_i s_i.$$

Substituting this into the Bellman equation, we have

$$v(A, y, R_{-1}) = \max_{s_i} \ u\left(A - \sum_i s_i\right) + \beta E_{R, y' \mid R_{-1}, y} v\left(\sum_i R_i s_i, y', R\right),$$

$$(6.10)$$

where R_i is the stochastic return on asset i. Note that R_{-1} is only in the state vector because of the informational value it provides on the return over the next period, R.

---

6. See, for instance, Zeldes (1989b) and Campbell and Mankiw (1989).

The first-order condition for the optimization problem holds for $i = 1, 2, \ldots, N$, and it is

$$u'(c) = \beta E_{R, y' \mid R_{-1}, y} R_i v_A \left(\sum_i R_i s_i, y', R \right),$$

where again $v_A(\ )$ is defined as $\partial v(\ )/\partial A$. Using (6.10) to solve for the derivative of the value function, we obtain

$$u'(c) = \beta E_{R, y' \mid R_{-1}, y} R_i u'(c') \qquad \text{for } i = 1, 2, \ldots, N,$$

where, of course, the level of future consumption will depend on the vector of returns, R, and the realization of future income, y'.

This system of Euler equations forms the basis for financial models that link asset prices to consumption flows. This system is also the basis for the argument that conventional models are unable to explain the observed differential between the return on equity and relatively safe bonds. Finally, these conditions are also used to estimate the parameters of the utility function, such as the curvature parameter in the traditional CRRA specification.

This approach is best seen through a review of Hansen and Singleton (1982). To understand this approach, recall that Hall uses the orthogonality conditions to test a model of optimal consumption. Note that Hall's exercise does not estimate any parameters as the utility function is assumed to be quadratic and the real interest rate is fixed. Instead, Hall essentially tests a restriction imposed by his model at the assumed parameter values.

The logic pursued by Hansen-Singelton goes a step further. Instead of using the orthogonality constraints to evaluate the predictions of a parameterized model, they use these conditions to estimate a model. Evidently, if one imposes more conditions than there are parameters (i.e., if the exercise is overidentified), the researcher can both estimate the parameters and test the validity of the model.

Empirical Implementation
The starting point for the analysis is the Euler equation for the household's problem with N assets. We rewrite that first-order condition here using time subscripts to show the timing of decisions and realizations of random variables:

$$u'(c_t) = \beta E_t R_{it+1} u'(c_{t+1}) \qquad \text{for } i = 1, 2, \ldots, N, \tag{6.11}$$

where R_{it+1} is defined as the real return on asset i between periods

t and $t + 1$. The expectation here is conditional on all variables observed in period t. Unknown $t + 1$ variables include the return on the assets as well as period $t + 1$ income.

The power of the GMM approach derives from this first-order condition. What the theory tells us is that while ex post this first-order condition need not hold, any deviations from it will be unpredictable given period t information. That is, the period $t + 1$ realization say, of income, may lead the consumer to increase consumption is period $t + 1$, thus implying ex post that (6.11) does not hold. This deviation is consistent with the theory as long as it is not predictable given period t information.

Formally, define $\varepsilon_{t+1}^i(\theta)$ as

$$\varepsilon_{t+1}^i(\theta) \equiv \frac{\beta R_{it+1} u'(c_{t+1})}{u'(c_t)} - 1 \qquad \text{for } i = 1, 2, \ldots, N. \tag{6.12}$$

Thus $\varepsilon_{t+1}^i(\theta)$ is a measure of the deviation for an asset i. We have added θ as an argument in this error to highlight its dependence on the parameters describing the household's preferences. Household optimization implies that

$$E_t(\varepsilon_{t+1}^i(\theta)) = 0 \qquad \text{for } i = 1, 2, \ldots, N.$$

Let z_t be a q-vector of variables that are in the period t information set.[7] This restriction on conditional expectations implies that

$$E(\varepsilon_{t+1}^i(\theta) \otimes z_t) = 0 \qquad \text{for } i = 1, 2, \ldots, N, \tag{6.13}$$

where $\otimes$ is the Kronecker product. So the theory implies the Euler equation errors from any of the N first-order conditions ought to be orthogonal to any of the z_t variables in the information set. There are Nq restrictions created.

The idea of GMM estimation is then to find the vector of structural parameters (θ) such that (6.13) holds. Of course, applied economists only have access to a sample, say of length T. Let $m_T(\theta)$ be an Nq vector where the component relating asset i to one of the variables in z_t, z_t^j, is defined by

$$\frac{1}{T} \sum_{t=1}^{T} (\varepsilon_{t+1}^i(\theta) z_t^j).$$

---

7. The theory does not imply which of the many possible variables should be used when employing these restrictions in an estimation exercise. That is, the question of which moments to match is not answered by the theory.

The GMM estimator is defined as the value of θ that minimizes

$$J_T(\theta) = m_T(\theta)'W_T m_T(\theta).$$

Here W_T is an $Nq \times Nq$ matrix that is used to weight the various moment restrictions.

Hansen and Singleton (1982) use monthly seasonally adjusted aggregate data on U.S. nondurable consumption or nondurables and services between 1959 and 1978. They use as a measure of stock returns, the equally weighted average return on all stocks listed on the New York Stock Exchange. They choose a constant relative risk aversion utility function $u(c) = c^{1-\gamma}/(1-\gamma)$. With this specification there are two parameters to estimate, the curvature of the utility function γ and the discount factor β. Thus $\theta = (\beta, \gamma)$. The authors use as instruments lagged values of (c_t, R_{it+1}) and estimate the model with 1, 2, 4, or 6 lags. Depending on the number of lags and the series used, they find values for γ which vary between 0.67 and 0.97 and values for the discount factor between 0.942 and 0.998. As the model is overidentified, there is scope for an overidentification test. Depending on the number of lags and the series used, the test gives mixed results as the restrictions are sometimes satisfied and sometimes rejected.

Note that the authors do not adjust for possible trends in the estimation. Suppose that log consumption is characterized by a linear trend:

$$c_t = \exp(\alpha t)\tilde{c}_t,$$

where $\tilde{c}_t$ is the detrended consumption. In that case equation (6.12) is rewritten as

$$\varepsilon^i_{t+1}(\theta) \equiv \frac{\beta e^{-\alpha\gamma} R_{it+1} \tilde{c}^{-\gamma}_{t+1}}{\tilde{c}^{-\gamma}_t} - 1 \qquad \text{for } i = 1, 2, \ldots, N.$$

Hence the estimated discount factor is a product between the true discount factor and a trend effect. Ignoring the trend would result in a bias for the discount rate.

6.3.4 Endogenous Labor Supply

Of course, it is natural to add a labor supply decision to this model. We can think of the stochastic income, taken as given above, as coming from a stochastic wage (w) and a labor supply decision (n). In this case consider the following functional equation:

$$v(A, w) = \max_{A', n} U\left(A + wn - \frac{A'}{R}, n\right) + \beta E_{w'|w} v(A', w') \quad \text{for all } (A, w).$$

Here we have substituted in for current consumption so that the agent is choosing labor supply and future wealth.

Note that the labor supply choice, given (A, A'), is purely static. That is, the level of employment and thus labor earnings has no dynamic aspect other than supplementing the resources available to finance current consumption and future wealth. Correspondingly the first-order condition with respect to the level of employment does not directly involve the value function, and it is given by

$$wU_c(c, n) = -U_n(c, n). \tag{6.14}$$

Using $c = A + wn - (A'/R)$, this first-order condition relates n to (A, w, A'). Denote this relationship as $n = \varphi(A, w, A')$. It can then be substituted back into the dynamic programming problem yielding a simpler functional equation:

$$v(A, w) = \max_{A'} Z(A, A', w) + \beta E_{w'|w} v(A', w'),$$

where

$$Z(A, A', w) \equiv U(A + w\varphi(A, w, A') - (A'/R), \varphi(A, w, A')).$$

This simplified Bellman equation can be analyzed by standard methods, thus ignoring the static labor supply decision.[8] Once a solution is found, the level of employment can then be determined from the condition $n = \varphi(A, w, A')$.

By a similar model MaCurdy (1981) studies the labor supply of young men using the Panel Study on Income Dynamics (PSID). The estimation of the model is done in several steps. First, the intraperiod allocation (6.14) is estimated. The coefficients are then used to get at the intertemporal part of the model.

To estimate the parameters of the utility function, one has to observe hours of work and consumption, but in the PSID, total consumption is not reported. To identify the model, MaCurdy uses a

---

8. This is similar to the trick we used in the stochastic growth model with endogenous employment.

utility function that is separable between consumption and labor supply. The utility function is specified as $u(c_t, n_t) = \gamma_{1t} c_t^{\omega_1} - \gamma_{2t} n_t^{\omega_2}$, where γ_{1t} and γ_{2t} are two deterministic functions of observed characteristics that might affect preferences such as age, education, and number of children.

With this specification the marginal utility of leisure, $U_n(c, n)$, is independent of the consumption decision. Using (6.14), hours of work can be expressed as

$$\ln(n_t) = \frac{\ln w_t}{\omega_2 - 1} + \frac{1}{\omega_2 - 1}(\ln U_c(c_t, n_t) - \ln \gamma_{2t} - \ln \omega_2).$$

While the first term in the right-hand-side is observed, the second term contains the unobserved marginal utility of consumption. $U_c(c_t, n_t)$ can be expressed as a function of the Lagrange multiplier associated with the wealth constraint in period 0:

$$U_c(c_t, n_t) = \frac{\lambda_0}{\beta^t(1 + r_1) \dots (1 + r_t)}.$$

The author treats the unobserved multiplier λ_0, as a fixed effect and uses panel data to estimate a subset of the parameters of the utility function from first differences. In a next step the fixed effect is backed out. At this point some additional identification assumptions are needed. A specific functional form is assumed for the Lagrange multiplier, written as a function of wages over the life cycle and initial wealth, all of them being unobserved in the data set. The author uses then fixed characteristics such that education or age to proxy for the Lagrange multiplier. The author finds that a 10 percent increase in the real wage induces a one to 5 percent increase in hours worked.

Eichenbaum et al. (1988) analyze the time series properties of a household model with both a savings and a labor supply decision. They pay particular attention to specifications in which preferences are nonseparable, both across time and between consumption and leisure contemporaneously. They estimate their model using GMM on time series evidence on real consumption (excluding durables) and hours worked. They find support for nontime separability in preferences, though in some cases they found little evidence against the hypothesis that preferences were separable within a period.

6.3.5 Borrowing Constraints

The Model and Policy Function
The extension of the two-period model with borrowing constraints
to the infinite horizon case is discussed by Deaton (1991).[9] One of the
key additional insights from extending the horizon is to note that
even if the borrowing constraint does not bind in a period, this does
not imply that consumption and savings take the same values as
they would in the problem without borrowing constraints. Simply
put, consumers anticipate that borrowing restrictions may bind in
the future (i.e., in other states), and this influences their choices in
the current state.

Following Deaton (1991), let $x = A + y$ represent cash on hand.
Then the transition equation for wealth implies that

$$A' = R(x - c),$$

where c is consumption. In the event that income variations are iid,
we can write the Bellman equation for the household as

$$v(x) = \max_{0 \le c \le x} u(c) + \beta E_{y'} v(R(x - c) + y') \tag{6.15}$$

so that the return R is earned on the available resources less consumption, $x - c$. Note that income is not a state variable here as it is
assumed to be iid. Hence cash on hand completely summarizes the
resources available to the consumer.

The borrowing restriction takes the simple form of $c \le x$ so that the
consumer is unable to borrow. Of course, this is extreme and entirely
ad hoc, but it does allow us to explore the consequences of this
restriction. As argued by Deaton, the Euler equation for this problem
must satisfy

$$u'(c) = \max\{u'(x), \beta R E u'(c')\}. \tag{6.16}$$

Thus, either the borrowing restriction binds so that $c = x$ or it doesn't
so that the more familiar Euler equation holds. Only for low values
of x will $u'(x) > \beta R E u'(c')$, and only in these states, as argued for
the two-period problem, will the constraint bind. To emphasize an
important point: even if the $u'(x) < \beta R E u'(c')$ so that the standard
condition of

---

9. See also Wright and Williams (1984) and Miranda and Helmberger (1988) for an early
contribution on this subject, including numerical solutions and simulations of these models.

$$u'(c) = \beta REu'(c')$$

holds, the actual state dependent levels of consumption may differ from those that are optimal for the problem in which c is not bounded above by x.

Alternatively, one might consider a restriction on wealth of the form: $A \geq A_{\min}(s)$ where s is the state vector describing the household. In this case the household may borrow, but its assets are bounded below. In principle, the limit on wealth may depend on the state variables of the household: all else the same, a household with a high level of income may be able to borrow more. One can look at the implications of this type of constraint and, through estimation, uncover $A_{\min}(s)$. (see Adda and Eaton 1997).

To solve the optimal problem, one can use the value function iteration approach, described in chapters 2 and 3, based on the Bellman equation (6.15). Deaton (1991) uses another approach, working from the Euler equation (6.16). The method is similar to the projection methods presented in chapter 3, but the optimal consumption function is obtained by successive iterations instead of solving a system of nonlinear equations. Although there is no formal proof that iterations on the Euler equation actually converge to the optimal solution, the author note that empirically convergence always occur. Figure 6.1 displays the optimal consumption rule in the case of a serially correlated income. In this case the problem has two state variables—the cash on hand and the current realization of income—that provide information on future income. The policy rule has been computed using a (coarse) grid with three points for the current income and with 60 equally spaced points for the cash on hand. When cash on hand is low, the consumer is constrained and is forced to consume all his cash on hand. The policy rule is then the 45 degree line. For higher values of the cash on hand, the consumer saves part of the cash on hand for future consumption.

Figure 6.2 displays a simulation of consumption and assets over 200 periods. The income follows an AR(1) process with unconditional mean of 100, a persistence of 0.5, and the innovations to income are drawn from $\mathcal{N}(0, 10)$. The path of income is asymmetric as good income shocks are smoothed by savings, whereas the liquidity constraints prevents the smoothing of low income realizations. Consumption is smoother than income, with a standard deviation of 8.9 instead of 11.5.

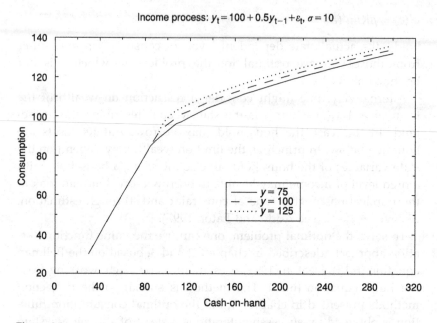

Figure 6.1
Consumption and liquidity constraints: Optimal consumption rule

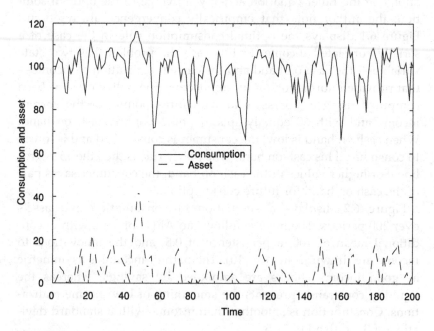

Figure 6.2
Simulations of consumption and assets with serially correlated income

Table 6.1
GMM estimation based on the Euler equation

γ	Liquidity constrained periods	$\hat{\gamma}_{\mathrm{GMM}}$
0.5	80%	2.54
1	50	3.05
2	27	3.92
3	23	4.61
4	11	5.23
5	9	5.78
6	8	6.25

Note: $p = 0$, $\sigma = 10$, $\mu = 100$, $\beta = 0.9$, $r = 0.05$. Estimation done on 3,000 simulated observations.

An Estimation Exercise

In section 6.3.3 we presented a GMM estimation by Hansen and Singleton (1982) based on the Euler equation. Hansen and Singleton (1982) find a value for γ of about 0.8. This is under the null that the model is correctly specified, and in particular, that the Euler equation holds in each period. When liquidity constraints are binding, the standard Euler equation does not hold. An estimation procedure that does not take into account this fact would produce biased estimates.

Suppose that the real world is characterized by potentially binding liquidity constraints. If one ignores them and consider a simpler model without any constraints, how would it affect the estimation of the parameter γ?

To answer this question, we chose different values for γ, solved the model with liquidity constraints, and simulated it. The simulated consumption series are used to get an estimate $\hat{\gamma}_{\mathrm{GMM}}$ such that

$$\hat{\gamma}_{\mathrm{GMM}} = \arg\min_{\gamma} \frac{1}{T} \sum_{t=1}^{T} \varepsilon_t(\gamma) \quad \text{with} \quad \varepsilon_t(\gamma) = \beta(1+r)\frac{c_{t+1}^{-\gamma}}{c_t^{-\gamma}} - 1.$$

The results are displayed in table 6.1. When γ is low, the consumer is less risk averse, consumes more out of the available cash on hand, and saves less. The result is that the liquidity constraints are binding more often. In this case the bias in the GMM estimate is the biggest. The bias is decreasing in the proportion of liquidity-constrained periods, as when liquidity constraints are almost absent, the standard Euler equation holds. From table 6.1 there is no value of γ that would generate a GMM estimate of 0.8 as found by Hansen and Singelton.

6.3.6 Consumption over the Life Cycle

Gourinchas and Parker (2002) investigate the ability of a model of intertemporal choice with realistic income uncertainty to match observed life cycle profiles of consumption. (For a related study see also Attanasio et al. 1999.) They parameterize a model of consumption over the life cycle, which is solved numerically. The parameters of the model are estimated using a simulated method of moments method for data on household consumption over the life cycle. We first present a simplified version of their model. We then discuss the numerical computation and the estimation methods.

Following Zeldes (1989a),[10] the log income process is modeled as a random walk with a moving average error. This specification is similar to the one used in empirical work (see Abowd and Card 1989) and seems to fit the data well. Denote Y_t as the income of the individual:

$$Y_t = P_t U_t,$$

$$P_t = G_t P_{t-1} N_t.$$

Income is the product of two components. U_t is a transitory shock which is independently and identically distributed and takes a value of 0 with a probability p and a positive value with a probability $1 - p$. P_t is a permanent component that grows at a rate G_t, which depends on age. N_t is the innovation to the permanent component. $\ln N_t$ and $\ln U_t$, conditionally on $U_t > 0$, are normally distributed with mean 0 and variance σ_n^2 and σ_u^2 respectively. The consumer faces a budget constraint

$$W_{t+1} = (1 + r)(W_t + Y_t - C_t).$$

The consumer can borrow and save freely. However, under the assumption that there is a probability that income will be zero and that the marginal utility of consumption is infinite at zero, the consumer will choose never to borrow against future income. Hence the outcome of the model is close to the one proposed by Deaton (1991)

---

10. See also Carroll (1992).

and presented in section 6.3.5. Note that in the model the agent can only consume nondurables. The authors ignore the durable decision, or equivalently assume that this decision is exogenous. This might be a strong assumption. Fernández-Villaverde and Krueger (2001) argue that the joint dynamics of durables and nondurables are important to understand the savings and consumption decisions over the life cycle.

Define the cash on hand as the total of assets and income:

$$X_t = W_t + Y_t, \quad X_{t+1} = R(X_t - C_t) + Y_{t+1}.$$

Define $V_t(X_t, P_t)$ as the value function at age $T - t$. The value function is indexed by age as it is assumed that the consumer has a finite life horizon. The value function depends on two state variables: the cash on hand, which indicates the maximal limit that can be consumed, and the realization of the permanent component, which provides information on future values of income. The program of the agent is defined as

$$V_t(X_t, P_t) = \max_{C_t}[u(C_t) + \beta E_t V_{t+1}(X_{t+1}, P_{t+1})].$$

The optimal behavior is given by the Euler equation:

$$u'(C_t) = \beta R E_t u'(C_{t+1}).$$

As income is assumed to be growing over time, cash on hand and consumption are also nonstationary. This problem can be solved by normalizing the variables by the permanent component. Denote $x_t = X_t/P_t$ and $c_t = C_t/P_t$. The normalized cash on hand evolves as

$$x_{t+1} = (x_t - c_t)\frac{R}{G_{t+1}N_{t+1}} + U_{t+1}.$$

Under the assumption that the utility function is $u(c) = c^{(1-\gamma)}/(1-\gamma)$, the Euler equation can be rewritten with only stationary variables:

$$u'(c_t) = \beta R E_t u'(c_{t+1}G_{t+1}N_{t+1}).$$

As the horizon of the agent is finite, one has to postulate some terminal condition for the consumption rule. It is taken to be linear in the normalized cash on hand: $c_{T+1} = \gamma_0 + \gamma_1 x_{T+1}$.

Gourinchas and Parker (2002) use this Euler equation to compute numerically the optimal consumption rule. Normalized consumption is only a function of the normalized cash on hand. By discretizing

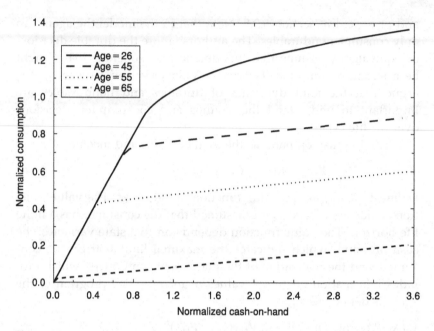

Figure 6.3
Optimal consumption rule

the cash on hand over a grid, the problem is solved recursively by evaluating $c_t(x)$ at each point of the grid using

$$u'(c_t(x))$$

$$= \beta R(1-p) \iint u'\left(c_{t+1}\left((x-c_t)\frac{R}{G_{t+1}N} + U\right)G_{t+1}N\right) dF(N)\, dF(U)$$

$$+ \beta Rp \int u'\left(c_{t+1}\left((x-c_t)\frac{R}{G_{t+1}N}\right)G_{t+1}N\right) dF(N).$$

The first term on the right-hand-side calculates the expected value of the future marginal utility conditional on a zero income, while the second term is the expectation conditional on a strictly positive income. The integrals are solved by a quadrature method (see chapter 3). The optimal consumption rules are obtained by minimizing the distance between the left-hand side and the right-hand side. Figure 6.3 displays the consumption rule at different ages.[11]

11. The figure was computed using the following parameterization: $\beta = 0.96$, $\gamma = 0.5$, $\sigma_u^2 = 0.0212$, $\sigma_n^2 = 0.044$, $p = 0.03$. $\gamma_0 = 0.0196$, and $\gamma_1 = 0.0533$. We are grateful to Gourinchas and Parker for providing us with their codes and data.

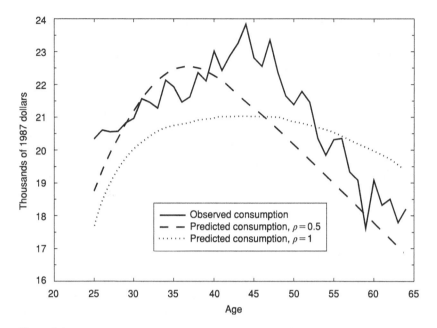

Figure 6.4
Observed and predicted consumption profiles

Once the consumption rules are determined, the model can be simulated to generate average life cycle profiles of consumption. This is done using the approximated consumption rules and by averaging the simulated behavior of a large number of households. The simulated profiles are then compared to actual profiles from U.S. data. Figure 6.4 displays the predicted consumption profile for two values of the intertemporal elasticity of substitution as well as the observed consumption profiles constructed from the U.S. Consumer Expenditure Survey.[12]

More formally, the estimation method is the simulated method of moments (see chapter 4). The authors minimize the distance between observed and predicted consumption at different ages. As neither the cash on hand nor the permanent component of income are directly observed, the authors integrate out the state variables to calculate the unconditional mean of (log) consumption at a given age:

$$\ln C_t(\theta) = \int \ln C_t(x, P, \theta) \, dF_t(x, P, \theta),$$

---

12. See footnote 11 for the parameterization.

where θ is the vector of parameters characterizing the model and where $F_t(\ )$ is the density of the state variables for individuals of age t. Characterizing this density is difficult as it has no closed form solution. Hence the authors use simulations to approximate $\ln C_t(\theta)$. Denote

$$g(\theta) = \frac{1}{I_t}\sum_{i=1}^{I_t} \ln C_{it} - \frac{1}{S}\sum_{s=1}^{S} \ln C_t(X_t^s, P_t^s, \theta).$$

The first part is the average log consumption for households of age t, and I_t is the number of observed household in the data set. The second part is the average predicted consumption over S simulated paths. θ is estimated by minimizing

$$g(\theta)'Wg(\theta),$$

where W is a weighting matrix.

The estimated model is then used to analyze the determinant of savings. There are two reasons to accumulate savings in this model. First, it cushions the agent from uninsurable income shocks, to avoid facing a low marginal utility. Second, savings are used to finance retirement consumption. Gourinchas and Parker (2002) show that the precautionary motive dominates at least until age 40, whereas older agents save mostly for retirement.

6.4   Conclusion

In this chapter we demonstrated how to use the approach of dynamic programming to characterize the solution of the households optimal consumption problem and to link it with observations. The discussion went beyond the savings decision to integrate it with the labor supply and portfolio decisions.

As in other chapters, we gave numerous extensions that are open-ended for the researcher to consider. (In the next chapter we turn to one of these, durable goods.) Further, there are numerous policy exercises that can be evaluated using an estimated model of the household consumption choice, included a variety of policies intended to influence savings decisions.[13]

---

13. Rust and Phelan (1997) provide a good example in exploring the effects of social security policies on labor supply and retirement decisions in a dynamic programming framework.

7   Durable Consumption

7.1   Motivation

So far the consumption goods we looked at are classified as either nondurables or services. This should be clear since consumption expenditures affected utility directly in the period of the purchase and then disappeared.[1] However, durable goods play a prominent role in business cycles as durable expenditures are quite volatile.[2]

In this chapter we study two approaches to understanding durable consumption. The first is an extension of the models studied in the previous chapter in which a representative agent accumulates durables to provide a flow of services. Here we present the results of Mankiw (1982) which effectively rejects the representative agent model.[3]

The second model introduces a nonconvexity into the household's optimization problem. The motivation for doing so is evidence that households do not continuously adjust their stock of durables. We explore this optimization problem through the specification and estimation of a dynamic discrete choice model.

---

1. In a model of habit formation, past consumption can influence current utility even if the consumption is of a nondurable or a service. Then the state vector is supplemented to keep track of that experience. For durable goods we will supplement the state vector to take the stock of durables into account.

2. According to Baxter (1996), the volatility of durable consumption is about five times that of nondurable consumption.

3. To be complete, as we explain, there are also maintained assumptions about preferences, shocks, and the lack of adjustment costs.

7.2 Permanent Income Hypothesis Model of Durable Expenditures

We begin with a model that builds on the permanent income hypothesis structure that we used in the previous chapter to study nondurable expenditures. We first provide the theoretical properties of the model and then discuss its empirical implementation.

7.2.1 Theory

To model expenditures on both durable and nondurable goods, we consider household behavior in which the consumer has a stock of wealth A, a stock of durable goods D, and current income y. The consumer uses wealth plus current income to finance expenditures on current nondurable consumption c and to finance the purchase of durable goods e at a relative price p.

There are two transition equations for this problem. One is the accumulation equation for wealth given by

$$A' = R(A + y - c - pe).$$

The accumulation equation for durables is similar to that used for capital held by the business sector:

$$D' = D(1 - \delta) + e, \tag{7.1}$$

where $\delta \in (0, 1)$ is the depreciation rate for the stock of durables.

Utility depends on the flow of services from the stock of durables and the purchases of nondurables. In terms of timing, assume that durables bought in the current period yield services starting in the next period. So, as with capital, there is a time lag between the order and the use of the durable good.[4]

With these details in mind, the Bellman equation for the household is given by

$$V(A, D, y, p) = \max_{D', A'} u(c, D) + \beta E_{y', p' | y, p} V(A', D', y', p')$$

$$\text{for all } (A, D, y, p) \tag{7.2}$$

with

---

4. Of course, other possible assumptions on timing are implementable in this framework as we show later in the chapter.

$$c = A + y - \frac{A'}{R} - p(D' - (1 - \delta)D) \tag{7.3}$$

and the transition for the stock of durables given by (7.1). The maximization gives rise to two first-order conditions:

$$u_c(c, D) = \beta R E_{y', p' | y, p} V_A(A', D', y') \tag{7.4}$$

and

$$u_c(c, D)p = \beta E_{y', p' | y, p} V_D(A', D', y').$$

In both cases these conditions can be interpreted as equating the marginal costs of reducing either nondurable or durable consumption in the current period with the marginal benefits of increasing the (respective) state variables in the next period.

Using the functional equation (7.2), we can solve for the derivatives of the value function and then update these two first-order conditions. This implies that

$$u_c(c, D) = \beta R E_{y', p' | y, p} u_c(c', D') \tag{7.5}$$

and

$$p u_c(c, D) = \beta E_{y', p' | y, p} [u_D(c', D') + p'(1 - \delta) u_c(c', D')]. \tag{7.6}$$

The first condition should be familiar from the optimal consumption problem without durables. The marginal gain of increasing consumption is offset by the reduction in wealth and thus consumption in the following period. In this specification the marginal utility of nondurable consumption may depend on the level of durables. So, to the extent there is an interaction within the utility function between nondurable and durable goods, empirical work that looks solely at nondurable consumption may be inappropriate.[5]

The second first-order condition compares the benefits of buying durables with the marginal costs. The benefits of a durable expenditure comes from two sources. First, increasing the stock of durables has direct utility benefits in the subsequent period. Second, as the Euler equation characterizes a one-period deviation from a proposed solution, the undepreciated part of the additional stock is sold and consumed. This is reflected by the second term on the right-hand

---

5. That is, movement in the marginal utility of consumption of nondurables may be the consequence of variations in the stock of durables. We return to this point in the discussion of empirical evidence.

side. The marginal cost of the durable purchase is the reduction in expenditures on nondurables that the agent must incur.

A slight variation in the problem assumes that durables purchased in the current period provide services starting in that period. Since this formulation is also found in the literature, we present it here as well. In this case the dynamic programming problem is

$$V(A, D, y, p) = \max_{D', A'} u(c, D') + \beta E_{y', p' | y, p} V(A', D', y', p')$$

$$\text{for all } (A, D, y, p), \tag{7.7}$$

with c defined as in (7.3).

Manipulation of the conditions for optimality implies (7.5) and

$$p u_c(c, D') = [u_D(c, D') + \beta E_{y', p' | y, p} p'(1 - \delta) u_c(c', D'')]. \tag{7.8}$$

For constant prices $(p = p')$, the result is

$$u_D(c, D') = \beta R E_{y' | y} u_D(c', D'').$$

The optimal condition corresponds to a variation where the stock of durables is reduced by ε in the current period, the resources are saved and then used to purchase durables in the next period.[6] As in nondurable consumption, in the special case of $\beta R = 1$, the marginal utility from durables follows a random walk.

Note that regardless of the timing assumption, there are some connections between the two Euler equations, particularly if utility is not separable between durables and nondurables ($u_{cD} \neq 0$). Also shocks to income will influence both durable and nondurable expenditures.

7.2.2 Estimation of a Quadratic Utility Specification

Mankiw (1982) studied the pattern of durable expenditures when $u(c, D')$ is separable and quadratic. In this case Mankiw finds that durable expenditures follows an ARMA$(1, 1)$ process given by

$$e_{t+1} = a_0 + a_1 e_t + \varepsilon_{t+1} - (1 - \delta) \varepsilon_t,$$

where $a_1 = \beta R$. Here the MA piece is parameterized by the rate of depreciation. In estimating the model using U.S. data, Mankiw finds

---

6. This condition does not obtain under the previous timing because of the time to build aspect of durables assumed there.

Table 7.1
ARMA$(1, 1)$ estimates on U.S. and French data

	No trend		Linear trend	
Specification	α_1	δ	α_1	δ
U.S. durable expenditures	1.00 (0.03)	1.5 (0.15)	0.76 (0.12)	1.42 (0.17)
U.S. car registration	0.36 (0.29)	1.34 (0.30)	0.33 (0.30)	1.35 (0.31)
France durable expenditures	0.98 (0.04)	1.20 (0.2)	0.56 (0.24)	1.2 (0.36)
France car expenditures	0.97 (0.06)	1.3 (0.2)	0.49 (0.28)	1.20 (0.32)
France car registrations	0.85 (0.13)	1.00 (0.26)	0.41 (0.4)	1.20 (0.41)

Notes: Annual data. For the United States: FRED database, 1959:1–1997:3. For France: INSEE, 1970:1–1997:2. U.S. registration: 1968–1995.

that empirically, δ is quite close to 1. So durables may not be so durable after all.

Adda and Cooper (2000b) study the robustness of Mankiw's results across different time periods, for different frequencies, and across countries (United States and France). Their results are summarized in table 7.1.

In the table the rows pertain to both aggregated durable expenditures and estimates based on cars (for France, both total expenditures on cars and new car registrations). The model is estimated with and without a linear trend. The rate of depreciation is close to 100 percent each year for most of the specifications. Mankiw's "puzzle" turns out to be robust across categories of durables, countries, time periods, and the method of detrending.

Over the past few years there was considerable effort made in the literature to understand Mankiw's result. One interesting approach was to embellish the basic representation agent model by the addition of adjustment costs and shocks other than variations in income. Another, coming from Bar-Ilan and Blinder (1992) and Bertola and Caballero (1990), was to recognize that at the household level durable expenditures are often discrete. We describe these two lines of research in turn below.

7.2.3 Quadratic Adjustment Costs

Bernanke (1985) goes beyond the quadratic utility formulation by adding price variations and costs of adjustment. As he observes, it is worthwhile to look jointly at the behavior of durable and nondurable expenditures as well.[7] Consider the dynamic optimization problem

$$V(A, D, y, p) = \max_{D', A'} u(c, D, D') + \beta E_{y'|y} V(A', D', y', p')$$

for all (A, D, y, p),   (7.9)

where the functional equation holds for all values of the state vector. Bernanke assumes a quadratic utility function with quadratic adjustment costs of the form

$$u(c, D, D') = -\frac{1}{2}(\bar{c} - c)^2 - \frac{a}{2}(\bar{D} - D)^2 - \frac{d}{2}(D' - D)^2,$$

where c_t is nondurable consumption and D_t is the stock of durables. The adjustment cost is part of the utility function rather than the budget constraints, for tractability reasons. Because of the quadratic structure, the model (7.9) can be solved explicitly as a (nonlinear) function of the parameters. Current nondurable consumption is a function of lagged nondurable consumption, of the current and lagged stock of durables, and of the innovation to the income process. Durables can be expressed as a function of the past stock of durables and of the innovation to income. The two equations with an equation describing the evolution of income are estimated jointly by nonlinear three-stage least squares. Lagged measures of prices, nondurable consumption, durable stocks and disposable income current income, nondurable consumption and the stock of durables, were used as instruments to control for simultaneity and measurement error.

The model is rejected because overall it does not suit the data when testing the overidentifying restrictions. The estimation of the adjustment cost gives conflicting results (as described in some detail by Bernanke 1985). The nonlinear function of this parameter implies a significant adjustment cost, whereas the parameter itself is not statistically different from zero.

Bernanke (1984) tests the permanent hypothesis model at the micro level by looking at car expenditures for a panel of households. Although Bernanke does not reject the model for this type of data, the result is at odds with real-life observations (described below) as

---

7. See also Eichenbaum and Hansen (1990).

it predicts continuous adjustment of the stock whereas car expenditures are typically lumpy at the individual level.

EXERCISE 7.1   Write a program to solve (7.9). Give decision rules by the household. Use these decision rules to create a panel data set, allowing households to have different realizations of income. Consider estimating the Euler equations from the household's optimization problem. If there are nonseparabilities present in $u(c, D, D')$, particularly, $u_{cD} \neq 0$, that were ignored by the researcher, what "incorrect inferences" would be reached?

7.3   Nonconvex Adjustment Costs

The model explored in the previous section is intended to capture the behavior of a representative agent. Despite its theoretical elegance the model does not match two characteristics of the data. First, as noted above, Mankiw's estimate of close to 100 percent depreciation suggests rejection of the model. Second, there is evidence at the household level that adjustment of the stock of durables is not

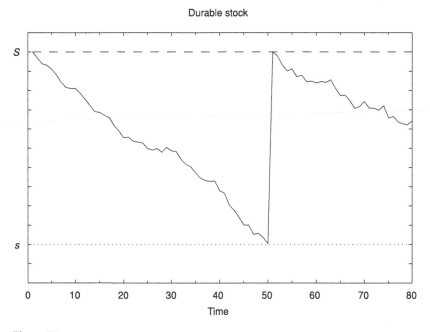

Durable stock

Figure 7.1
$[s, S]$ rule

continuous. Rather, households purchases of some durables, such as cars as studied by Lam (1991), are relatively infrequent. This may reflect irreversibility due to imperfect information about the quality of used durable good, the discrete nature of some durable goods, or the nature of adjustment costs.

Bar-Ilan and Blinder (1992) and Bar-Ilan and Blinder (1988) present a simple setting in which a fixed cost of adjustment implies inaction from the agent when the stock of durable is not too far from the optimal one. They argue that the optimal consumption of durables should follow an (S, s) policy. When the durable stock depreciates to a lower value s, the agent increases the stock to a target value S as depicted in figure 7.1.

7.3.1 General Setting

To gain some insight into the importance of irreversibility, consider the following formalization of a model in which irreversibility is important. By this we mean that because of friction in the market for durables, households receive only a fraction of the true value of a product they wish to sell. This might be thought of as a version of Akerlof's famous lemons' problem.[8]

In particular, suppose that the price of durables is normalized to 1 when they are purchases (e) but that the price of durables when they are sold (s) is given by $p_s < 1$. The Bellman equation for the household's optimization problem is

$$V(A, D, y) = \max(V^b(A, D, y), V^s(A, D, y), V^i(A, D, y)), \qquad (7.10)$$

where

$$V^b(A, D, y) = \max_{e, A'} u\left(A + y - \frac{A'}{R} - e, D\right)$$

$$+ \beta E_{y' \mid y} V(A', D(1 - \delta) + e, y'), \qquad (7.11)$$

$$V^s(A, D, y) = \max_{s, A'} u\left(A + y - \frac{A'}{R} + p_s s, D\right)$$

$$+ \beta E_{y' \mid y} V(A', D(1 - \delta) - s, y'), \qquad (7.12)$$

---

8. See House and Leahy (2000) for a model of durables with an endogenous lemons premium.

$$V^i(A, D, y) = \max_{A'} u\left(A + y - \frac{A'}{R}, D\right)$$

$$+ \beta E_{y'|y} V(A', D(1-\delta), y') \qquad \text{for all } (A, D, y). \qquad (7.13)$$

This is admittedly a complex problem as it includes elements of a discrete choice (to adjust or not) and also an intensive margin (given adjustment, the level of durable purchases (sales) must be determined).

The gap between the buying and selling price of durables will create inaction. Imagine a household with a substantial stock of durables that experiences an income loss due to a layoff. In the absence of irreversibility ($p_s = 1$), the household may optimally sell off some durables. If a job is found and the income flow returns, then the stock of durables can be rebuilt. However, in the presence of irreversibility, the sale and subsequent purchase of durables is costly due to the wedge between the buying and selling price of durables. Thus in response to an income shock the household may be inactive and not adjust its stock.

The functional equation in (7.10) cannot be solved by linearization techniques as there is no simple Euler equation that treats the discrete choice nature of the problem. For that reason value function iteration techniques are needed. As in the dynamic discrete choice problem specified in chapter 3, we would start with initial guesses of the values of the three options and then induce $V(A, D, y)$ through the max operator. From these initial solutions, the iteration procedure begins. As there is also an intensive margin in this problem (given adjustment, the stock of durables one can choose is a continuous variable), a state space for durables as well as assets must be specified. This is a complex setting but one that the value function iteration approach can handle.

So the policy functions can be created using a vector of parameters that describes preferences and the stochastic processes. In principle, in an estimation exercise, these parameters can generate moments that are matched with observations. This method is described in some detail, for a different model, in the subsequent subsections.

7.3.2 Irreversibility and Durable Purchases

Grossman and Laroque (1990) develop a model of durable consumption and also consider an optimal portfolio choice. They assume that

the durable good is illiquid as the agent incurs a proportional transaction cost when selling the good. The authors show that under the
assumption of a constant relative risk aversion utility function, the
state variable is the ratio of wealth A over the stock of durables D.
The optimal behavior of the agent is to follow an $[s, S]$ rule, with a
target $s^* \in [s, S]$. The agent does not change the stock of durable if the
ratio A/D is within the two bands s and S. If the ratio drifts out of
this interval, the agent adjusts it by buying or selling the good such
that $A/D = s^*$.

Eberly (1994) empirically investigates the relevance of some
aspects of the Grossman-Laroque model. She uses data from the
Survey of Consumer Finances which reports information on assets,
income and major purchases. She estimates the bands s and S. These
bands can be computed by observing the ratio A/D for individuals
just before an adjustment is made. The target s^* can be computed as
the average ratio just after adjustment. Eberly (1994) estimates the
band width and investigates its determinants. She finds that the year
to year income variance and the income growth rate are strong pre-
dictors of the width of the band.

Attanasio (2000) develops a more elaborate estimation strategy for
these bands, allowing for unobserved heterogeneity at the individual
level. This heterogeneity is needed as, conditional on household
characteristics and the value of the ratio of wealth to consumption,
some are adjusting their stock and some are not. The estimation is
done by maximum likelihood on data drawn from the Consumer
Expenditure Survey. The width of the bands are functions of household characteristics such as age and race. The estimated model is
then aggregated to study the aggregate demand for durables.

Caballero (1993) uses the Grossman and Laroque (1990) approach
to investigate the aggregate behavior of durable goods. The individual agent is assumed to follow an $[s, S]$ consumption rule because
of transaction costs. In the absence of transaction costs, the agent
would follow a PIH type behavior as described in section 7.2.
Caballero postulates that the optimal behavior of the agent can be
described by the distance between the stock of durables held by the
agent and the "target" defined as the optimal stock in the PIH
model. The agent adjusts the stock when the gap between the realized and the desired stock is big enough. In this setting the state
variables are the stock of durables and the target. The target stock is
assumed to follow a known stochastic process. Hence in this model

it is assumed that the evolution of the target is a sufficient statistic to inform of all the relevant economic variables such as prices or income.

The aggregate demand for durables is the sum of all agents who decide to adjust their stock in a given period. Hence Caballero stresses the importance of the cross sectional distribution of the gap between the target and the realized stock. When there is an aggregate shock on the target, the aggregate response depends not only on the size of the shock but also on the number of individuals close to the adjustment line. The aggregate demand for durables can therefore display complicated dynamic patterns. The model is estimated on aggregate U.S. data.

7.3.3   A Dynamic Discrete Choice Model

Suppose that instead of irreversibility, there is a restriction that households can have either no car or one car.[9] Thus, by assumption, the household solves a dynamic discrete choice problem. We discuss solutions of that problem, estimation of parameters and aggregate implications in this section.[10]

Optimal Behavior

We start with the dynamic programming problem as specified in Adda and Cooper (2000b). At the start of a period the household has a car of a particular age, a level of income and a realization of a taste shock. Formally, the household's state is described by the age of its car, i, a vector $Z = (p, Y, \varepsilon)$ of aggregate variables, and a vector $z = (y)$ of idiosyncratic variables. Here p is the relative price of the (new) durable good. Current income is given by the sum $Y + y$, where Y represents aggregate income and y represents idiosyncratic shocks to nondurable consumption that could reflect variations in household income or required expenditures on car maintenance and other necessities.[11] The final element in the state vector is a taste shock, ε.

---

9. The assumption that one car is the max is just for convenience. What is important is that the car choice set is not continuous.

10. This presentation relies heavily on Adda and Cooper (2000b).

11. Adda and Cooper (2000b) explicitly view this as a household specific income shock, but a broader interpretation is acceptable, particularly in light of the iid assumption associated with this source of variation.

At every point in time the household decides whether to retain a car of age i, trade it, or scrap it. If the household decides to scrap the car, then it receives the scrap value of π and has the option to purchase a new car. If the household retains the car, then it receives the flow of services from that car and cannot, by assumption, purchase another car. Thus the household is constrained to own at most a single car.

Formally, let $V_i(z, Z)$ represent the value of having a car of age i to a household in state (z, Z). Further let $V_i^k(z, Z)$ and $V_i^r(z, Z)$ represent the values from keeping and replacing an age i car in state (z, Z). Then

$$V_i(z, Z) = \max[V_i^k(z, Z), V_i^r(z, Z)],$$

where

$$V_i^k(z, Z) = u(s_i, y + Y, \varepsilon) + \beta(1 - \delta)EV_{i+1}(z', Z')$$
$$+ \beta\delta\{EV_1(z', Z') - u(s_1, y' + Y', \varepsilon')$$
$$+ u(s_1, y' + Y' - p' + \pi, \varepsilon')\} \qquad (7.14)$$

and

$$V_i^r(z, Z) = u(s_1, y + Y - p + \pi, \varepsilon) + \beta(1 - \delta)EV_2(z', Z')$$
$$+ \beta\delta\{EV_1(z', Z') - u(s_1, y' + Y', \varepsilon')$$
$$+ u(s_1, y' + Y' - p' + \pi, \varepsilon')\}.$$

In the definition of $V_i^k(z, Z)$, the car is assumed to be destroyed (from accidents and breakdowns) with probability δ leading the agent to purchase a new car in the next period. The cost of a new car in numéraire terms is $p' - \pi$, which is stochastic since the price of a new car in the next period is random. Further, since it is assumed that there is no borrowing and lending, the utility cost of the new car is given by $u(s_1, y' + Y', \varepsilon') - u(s_1, y' + Y' - p' + \pi, \varepsilon')$ which exceeds $p' - \pi$ as long as $u(\cdot)$ is strictly concave in nondurable consumption. It is precisely at this point that the borrowing restriction appears as an additional transactions cost.

Adding in either borrowing and lending or the purchase and sale of used cars presents no modeling difficulties. But adding in wealth as well as resale prices as state variables certainly increases the dimensionality of the problem. This remains as work in progress.

EXERCISE 7.2   Reformulate (7.14) to allow the household to borrow/ lend and also to resell cars in a used car market. What additional state variables would you have to add when these choices are included? What are the new necessary conditions for optimal behavior of the household?

Further Specification

For the application the utility function is defined to be additively separable between durables and nondurables:

$$u(s_i, c) = \left[i^{-\gamma} + \frac{\varepsilon(c/\lambda)^{1-\xi}}{1-\xi} \right],$$

where c is the consumption of nondurable goods, γ is the curvature for the service flow of car ownership, ξ the curvature for consumption, and λ is a scale factor. In this specification the taste shock (ε) influences the contemporaneous marginal rate of substitution between car services and nondurables.

In order for the agent's optimization problem to be solved, a stochastic process for income, prices, and the aggregate taste shocks must be specified. Aggregate income, prices, and the unobserved preference shock are assumed to follow a VAR(1) process given by[12]

$$Y_t = \mu_Y + \rho_{YY} Y_{t-1} + \rho_{Yp} p_{t-1} + u_{Yt},$$

$$p_t = \mu_p + \rho_{pY} Y_{t-1} + \rho_{pp} p_{t-1} + u_{pt},$$

$$\varepsilon_t = \mu_\varepsilon + \rho_{\varepsilon Y} Y_{t-1} + \rho_{\varepsilon p} p_{t-1} + u_{\varepsilon t}.$$

The covariance matrix of the innovations $u = \{u_{Yt}, u_{pt}, u_{\varepsilon t}\}$ is

$$\Omega = \begin{bmatrix} \omega_Y & \omega_{Yp} & 0 \\ \omega_{pY} & \omega_p & 0 \\ 0 & 0 & \omega_\varepsilon \end{bmatrix}.$$

As the aggregate taste shock is unobserved, we impose a block diagonal structure on the VAR, which enables us to identify all the parameters involving prices and aggregate income in a simple first-step regression. This considerably reduces the number of parameters

---

12. Here only a single lag is assumed to economize on the state space of the agents' problem.

to be estimated in the structural model. We allow prices and income to depend on lagged income and lagged prices.[13]

The aggregate taste shock potentially depends on lagged prices and income. The coefficients of this process along with ω_ε are estimated within the structural model. By allowing a positive correlation between the aggregate taste shock and lagged prices, given that prices are serially correlated, we can reconcile the model with the fact that sales and prices are positively correlated in the data. This allows us to better capture some additional dynamics of sales and prices in the structural estimation. An alternative way would be to model jointly the producer and consumer side of the economy, to get an upward-slopping supply curve. However, solving for the equilibrium is computationally very demanding.

Solving the Model
The model is solved by the value function iteration method. Starting with an initial guess for $V_i(z, Z)$, the value function is updated by backward iterations until convergence.

The policy functions that are generated from this optimization problem are of an optimal stopping variety. That is, given the state of the household, the car is scrapped and replaced if and only if the car is older than a critical age. Letting $h_k(z_t, Z_t; \theta)$ represent the probability that a car of age k is scrapped, the policy functions imply that $h_k(z_t, Z_t; \theta) = \delta$ if $k < J(z_t, Z_t; \theta)$ and $h_k(z_t, Z_t; \theta) = 1$ otherwise. Here $J(z_t, Z_t; \theta)$ is the optimal scrapping age in state (z_t, Z_t) when θ is the vector of parameters describing the economic environment.

In particular, for each value of the idiosyncratic shock z, there is an optimal scrapping age. Integrating over all possible values of this idiosyncratic shock produces an aggregate policy function that indicates the fraction of cars of a given vintage being scrapped when the state of the world is Z_t:

---

13. As in Adda and Cooper (2000b), we assume that the costs of production are independent of the level of production. Combined with an assumption of constant mark-ups, this implies that the product price is independent of the cross-sectional distribution of car vintages.

This assumption of an exogenous price process greatly simplifies the empirical implementation of the model, since we do not have to solve an equilibrium problem. We have even found that adding information on the moments of the cross-sectional distribution of car vintages has no explanatory power in forecasting car prices in the French case. Results are mixed for the U.S. case, as the average age of cars significantly predicts future prices.

$$H_k(Z_t, \theta) = \int h_k(z_t, Z_t, \theta)\phi(z_t)\, dz_t,$$

where $\phi(\cdot)$ is the density function of z_t taken to be the normal distribution. $H_k(\cdot)$ is an increasing function of the vintage and bounded between δ and 1. The aggregated hazard can be used to predict aggregate sales and the cross-sectional distribution of car vintages over time. Letting $f_t(k)$ be the period t cross-sectional distribution of k, aggregate sales are given by

$$S_t(Z_t, \theta) = \sum_k H_k(Z_t, \theta) f_t(k). \tag{7.15}$$

From an initial condition it is possible to generate a time series for the cross-sectional distribution given a particular parameterization of the hazard function. The evolution of $f_t(k)$ is given by

$$f_{t+1}(k, Z_t, \theta) = [1 - H_k(Z_t; \theta)] f_t(k-1) \qquad \text{for } k > 1 \tag{7.16}$$

and

$$f_{t+1}(1, Z_t, \theta) = S_t(Z_t, \theta).$$

Thus, for a given θ and a given draw of T aggregate shocks, one can simulate both sales and the cross-sectional distribution. This can be repeated N times to produce N simulated data sets of length T, which can be used in the estimation. Define $S_{tn}(Z_t, \theta) = S_t(p_t, Y_t, \varepsilon_{nt}, \theta)$ as the predicted aggregate sales given prices, aggregate income and unobserved taste shock ε_{nt}. Define $\bar{S}_t(Z_t, \theta) = 1/N \sum_{n=1}^{N} S_{nt}(Z_t, \theta)$ as the average aggregate sales conditional on prices, aggregate income and period $t-1$ cross-sectional distribution.

Estimation Method and Results
In total there are eight parameters to estimate: $\theta = \{\gamma, \delta, \lambda, \zeta, \sigma_y, \rho_{\varepsilon Y}, \rho_{\varepsilon c}, \omega_\varepsilon\}$. The estimation method follows Adda and Cooper (2000b) and is a mix between simulated non-linear least squares and simulated method of moments. The first part of the criterion matches predicted sales of new cars with the observed ones, conditional on prices and aggregate income. The second part of the criterion matches the predicted shape of the cross-sectional distribution of car vintages to the observed one. The objective function to minimize is written as the sum of the two criteria:

$$\mathscr{L}_N(\theta) = \alpha \mathscr{L}_N^1(\theta) + \mathscr{L}_N^2(\theta),$$

where N is the number of simulated draws for the unobserved aggregate taste shock ε_{nt}. The two criteria are defined by

$$\mathscr{L}_N^1(\theta) = \frac{1}{T} \sum_{t=1}^{T} \left[(S_t - \bar{S}_t(\theta))^2 - \frac{1}{N(N-1)} \sum_{n=1}^{N} (S_{tn}(\theta) - \bar{S}_t(\theta))^2 \right],$$

$$\mathscr{L}_N^2(\theta) = \sum_{i=\{5,10,15,AR,MA\}} \alpha_i (\bar{F}^i - \bar{F}^i(\theta))^2,$$

where $\bar{S}_t(\theta)$ is the average $\bar{F}^i$, $i = 5, 10, 15$ is the average fraction of cars of age i across all periods, and $\bar{F}^i$, $i = AR, MA$ are the autoregressive and moving average coefficients from an ARMA(1, 1) estimated on aggregate sales.

The estimation uses two criteria for identification reasons. Matching aggregate sales at each period extracts information on the effect of prices and income on behavior and helps identify the parameter of the utility function as well as the parameters describing the distribution of the aggregate taste shock. However, the model is able to match aggregate sales under different values for the agent's optimal stopping time. In other words, there can be different cross-sectional distributions that produce aggregated sales close to the observed ones. In particular, the parameter δ is poorly identified by using only the first criterion. The second criterion pins down the shape of the cross-sectional distribution of car vintages.

The data come from France and the United States and include besides the cross-sectional distribution of car vintages over time, the aggregate sales of new cars, prices, and aggregate income. The estimated aggregate hazard functions $H_t(Z)$ over the period 1972 to 1995 for France and 1981 to 1995 for the United States are shown in figures 7.2 and 7.3. Note that the probability of replacement for young cars, which is equal to the δ, is estimated at a low value between 5 to 10 percent. Hence, in contrast with the estimated PIH models described in section 7.2, the model is able to produce a sensible estimate of the rate of depreciation. Moreover, in estimating an ARMA(1, 1), as in section 7.2.2, on the predicted aggregate sales, we find that the MA coefficient is close to zero as in the observed data. Hence, from a PIH perspective, the model appears to support a 100 percent depreciation rate at the aggregate level, but not at the micro level where the depreciation rate is low.

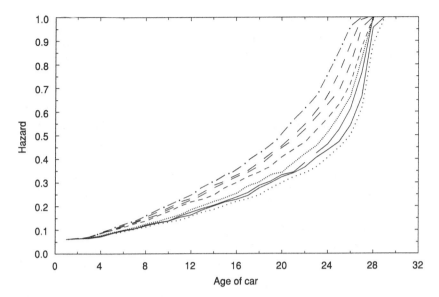

Figure 7.2
Estimated hazard function, France

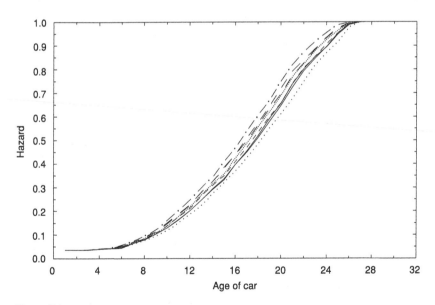

Figure 7.3
Estimated hazard function, United States

Once the model is estimated, Adda and Cooper (2000b) investigate the ability of the model to reproduce a number of other features such as the impulse response of sales to an increase in prices. They also use the estimated model to decompose the source of variation in aggregate sales. Within the model there are two main sources, the endogenous evolution of the cross-sectional distribution and the effect of aggregate variables such as prices or income. Caballero (1993) seems to imply that the evolution of the cross-sectional distribution is an important determinant. However, the empirical decomposition shows that its role is relatively minor, compared with the effect of income and prices.

The Impact of Scrapping Subsidies

Adda and Cooper (2000a) uses the same framework to analyze the impact of scrapping subsidies introduced first in France and later in a number of European countries such as Spain or Italy.

From February 1994 to June 1995 the French government offered individuals 5,000 francs (approximately 5 to 10 percent of the value of a new car) for the scrapping of an old car (ten years or older) and

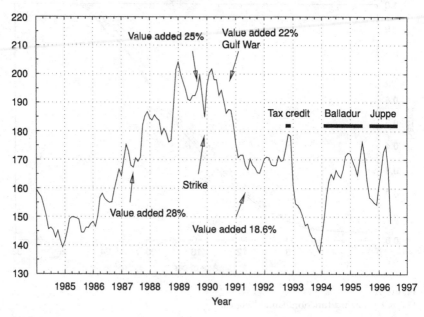

Figure 7.4
Sales of new cars, in thousands, monthly

the purchase of a new car. Sales of new cars which had been low in the preceding period (see figure 7.4) increased markedly during the period the policy was in place. In September 1995 to September 1996, the government re-introduced the policy, with an age limit of eight years. After September 1996, the demand for new cars collapsed at a record low level.

As is evident in figure 7.4, the demand for cars is cyclical and follows the business cycle. The increased demand for new cars during the period 1994 to 1996 could be due either to the policy or to the cyclical nature of demand. If the latter is true, the French government was wasting money on car owners who would have replaced their cars during that period anyway. Even if the increased demand was entirely fueled by the scrapping subsidies, the government was paying out money to car owners who would have replaced their car in the periods ahead anyway. The effect of the policy was then to anticipate new sales and create future, potentially bigger cycles of car demand. As a huge number of new cars were sold in that period, demand for new cars dropped when the policy was ended. However, a peak in demand is expected to appear in about ten years after the cars bought in 1995 and 1996 are scrapped.

Adda and Cooper (2000a) estimate the model in section 7.3.3 for the prepolicy period. The scrapping price π was a constant low value (around 500 French francs) before 1993. With the policy in place, the scrapping price increased and was age specific:

$$\pi(i) = 500 \quad \text{if } i < 10,$$

$$\pi(i) = 5{,}000 \quad \text{if } i \geq 10.$$

In the estimated model the effect of the policy can be simulated as well as the counterfactual without the policy in place. This is done

		State tomorrow			
		1	2	3	4
State today	1	0.01	0.01	0.01	0.97
	2	0.01	0.01	0.01	0.97
	3	0.225	0.225	0.1	0.45
	4	0.01	0.01	0.01	0.97

Figure 7.5
Transition matrix for π

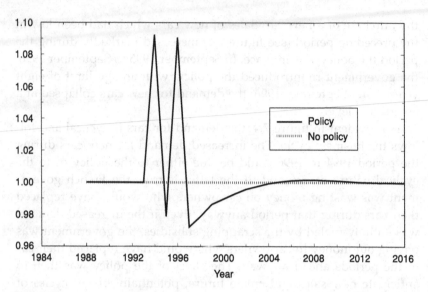

Figure 7.6
Expected aggregate sales, relative to baseline

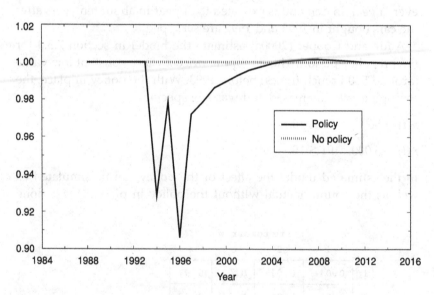

Figure 7.7
Expected government revenue, relative to baseline

conditional on the cross-sectional distribution of cars at the beginning of the period and conditional on the realized income and prices, as the prices of new cars are assumed to be independent of the policy. (This effect is debatable, however, for empirical evidence suggests that prices remained stable throughout the period mainly because the government negotiated a stable price with car producers.)

While the first scrapping subsidy was largely unexpected by consumers, the second was somewhat anticipated, since after the first subsidy, there was discussion on whether to implement another such subsidy. This is taken into account in the model by adding the scrapping price $\pi(i)$ as a stochastic state variable. More precisely, π is assumed to follow a first order Markov process with four states. These four states are shown in figure 7.5. The first state models the 1994 reform and the second one the 1995 reform. State 3 is a state with heightened uncertainty, in which there are no subsidies. State 4 is the baseline state. In state 1, the scrap value is set at 5,500F for cars older than ten years. This state is not assumed to be permanent: there is only a 1 percent chance that the subsidy will be in effect in the next period, conditional on being in force in the current period. In state 2, the scrap value is also 5,500F but for cars older than eight years old.

Figures 7.6 and 7.7 show the predicted sales and government revenue relative to the baseline. The model captures the peak in sales during the two policies, as well as the decline in between due to the uncertainty. The sales are lower for about ten years, with little evidence of a subsequent peak. This result is in line with that discussed in section 7.3.3 where it was found that over time the cross-sectional distribution had little effect on aggregate sales.

Government revenues are lower over the whole period. The government revenue is formed by the value-added taxes from the purchase of new cars minus the paid-out scrapping subsidies. From the perspective of government revenues, the policy is clearly undesirable. The subsidies accounted for about 8 to 10 percent of the increased demand in sales.

8 Investment

8.1 Overview and Motivation

This chapter studies capital accumulation. Investment expenditures are one of the most volatile elements of the aggregate economy. From the perspective of policy intervention, investment is also a key issue. The dependence of investment on real interest rates is critical to many discussions of the impact of monetary policy. Further many fiscal policy instruments, such as investment tax credits and accelerated depreciation allowances, act directly through their influence on capital accumulation.

It should seem then that macroeconomics would have developed and evaluated numerous models to meet this challenge. Yet, relative to the enormous work done on consumption, research on investment lags behind. As noted in Caballero (1999), this has changed dramatically in the last 10 or so years.[1] Partly, we now have the ability to characterize investment behavior in fairly rich settings. Combined with plant-level data sets, researchers are able to confront a rich set of observations with these sophisticated models.

Investment, with its emphasis on uncertainty and nonconvexities is a ripe area for applications of dynamic programming techniques. In this chapter we first analyze a general dynamic optimization problem and then focus on special cases of convex and nonconvex adjustment costs. This sets the stage for the empirical analyzes that follow. We also discuss the use of these estimates for the analysis of policy interventions.

---

1. There are numerous surveys of investment. See Caballero (1999) and Chirinko (1993), and the references therein, for further summaries of existing research.

8.2   General Problem

The unit of analysis will be the plant though for some applications (e.g., consideration of borrowing constraints) focusing on the firm may be more appropriate. The "manager" is assumed to maximize the value of the plant: there are no incentive problems between the manager and the owners. The problem involves the choice of factors of production that are rented for the production period, the hiring of labor and the accumulation of capital. To focus on the investment decision, we assume that demand for the variable inputs (denoted by x) is optimally determined given factor prices (represented by the vector w) and the state variables of the plant's optimization problem, represented by (A, K). Here the vector of flexible factors of production might include labor, materials, and energy inputs into the production process.

The result of this optimization leaves a profit function, denoted by $\Pi(A, K)$, that depends solely on the state of the plant, where

$$\Pi(A, K) = \max_{x} R(\hat{A}, K, x) - wx.$$

Here $R(\hat{A}, K, x)$ denotes revenues given the inputs of capital (K), the variable factors (x), and a shock to revenues and/or productivity, denoted by $\hat{A}$. The reduced form profit function thus depends on the stochastic variable A that encompasses both $\hat{A}$ and w, and the stock of physical capital (K). Thus we often refer to A as a profitability shock since it reflects variations in technology, demand and factor prices.

Taking this profit function as given, we consider variations of the following stationary dynamic programming problem:

$$V(A, K, p) = \max_{K'} \Pi(A, K) - C(K', A, K) - p(K' - (1 - \delta)K)$$

$$+ \beta E_{A', p' | A, p} V(A', K', p') \qquad \text{for all } (A, K, p), \qquad (8.1)$$

where $K' = K(1 - \delta) + I$ is the capital accumulation equation and I is investment. Here unprimed variables are current values and primed variables refer to future values. In this problem the manager chooses the level of the future capital stock denoted K'. The timing assumption is that new investment becomes productive with a one-period lag. The rate of depreciation of the capital stock is denoted by $\delta \in [0, 1]$. The manager discounts the future at a fixed rate of β.[2]

EXERCISE 8.1   Suppose that in contrast to (8.1), investment in period t is productive in that period. Compare these two formulations of the investment problem. Assuming that all functions are differentiable, create Euler equations for each specification. Explain any differences.

EXERCISE 8.2   How would you modify (8.1) to allow the manager's discount factor to be influenced by variations in the real interest rate?

There are no borrowing restrictions in this framework. So the choice of investment and thus future capital is not constrained by current profits or retained earnings. We return to this issue later in the chapter when we discuss the implications of capital market imperfections.

There are two costs of obtaining new capital. The first is the direct purchase price, denoted by p. Notice that this price is part of the state vector as it is a source of variation in this economy.[3]

Second, there are costs of adjustment given by the function $C(K', A, K)$. These costs are assumed to be internal to the plant and might include installation costs, disruption of productive activities in the plant, the need to retrain workers, the need to reconfigure other aspects of the production process, and so on. This function is general enough to have components of both convex and nonconvex costs of adjustment as well as a variety of transactions costs.

8.3   No Adjustment Costs

To make clear the contribution of adjustment costs, it is useful to start with a benchmark case in which these costs are absent: $C(K', A, K) \equiv 0$ for all (K', A, K). Note, though, that there is still a time to build aspect of investment so that capital accumulation remains forward looking. The first-order condition for the optimal investment policy is given by

---

2. This is corresponds to the outcome of a stochastic growth model if there are risk neutral consumers. Otherwise, a formulation with variable real interest rates may be warranted.
3. In many economies it is also influenced by policy variations in the form of investment tax credits.

$$\beta E_{A',p'|A,p} V_k(A', K', p') = p, \tag{8.2}$$

where subscripts on the functions denote partial derivatives. This condition implies that the optimal capital stock depends on the realized value of profitability, A, only through an expectations mechanism: given the time to build, current profitability is not relevant for investment except as a signal of future profitability. Further the optimal capital stock does not depend on the current stock of capital. Using (8.1) to solve for $E_{(A',p'|A,p)} V_k(A', K', p')$ yields

$$\beta E_{(A',p'|A,p)}[\Pi_k(A', K') + (1 - \delta)p'] = p. \tag{8.3}$$

This condition has a natural interpretation. The cost of an additional unit of capital today (p) is equated to the marginal return on capital. This marginal return has two pieces: the marginal profits from the capital, $\Pi_k(A', K')$, and the resale value of undepreciated capital at the future price, $(1 - \delta)p'$.

Substituting for the future price of capital and iterating forward, we find that

$$p_t = \beta \sum_{\tau=0}^{\infty} [\beta(1 - \delta)]^\tau E_{A_{t+\tau}|A_t} \Pi_K(K_{t+\tau+1}, A_{t+\tau+1}),$$

where p_t is the price of capital in period t. So the firm's investment policy equates the purchase price of capital today with the discounted present value of marginal profits in the future. Note that in stating this condition, we are assuming that the firm will be optimally resetting its capital stock in the future so that (8.3) holds in all subsequent periods.

While simple, the model without adjustment costs does not fit the data well. Cooper and Haltiwanger (2000) argue that relative to observations, this model without adjustment costs implies excessive sensitivity of investment to variations in profitability. So one of the empirical motivations for the introduction of adjustment costs is to temper the otherwise excessively volatile movements in investment. Further this model is unable to match the observation of inaction in capital adjustment seen (and discussed below) in plant-level data. For these reasons various models of adjustment costs are considered.[4]

---

4. Moreover the special case of no adjustment costs is generally nested in these other models.

8.4   Convex Adjustment Costs

In this section we assume that $C(K', A, K)$ is a strictly increasing, strictly convex function of future capital, K'.[5] The firm chooses tomorrow's capital (K') using its conditional expectations of future profitability, A'. Of course, to the extent that A' is correlated with A, current profits will be correlated with future profits.

Assuming that $V(K, A, p)$ exists, an optimal policy, obtained by solving the maximization problem in (8.1), must satisfy

$$C_{K'}(K', A, K) + p = \beta E_{(A', p' \mid A, p)} V_{K'}(A', K', p'). \tag{8.4}$$

The left side of this condition is a measure of the marginal cost of capital accumulation and includes the direct cost of new capital as well as the marginal adjustment cost. The right side of this expression measures the expected marginal gains of more capital through the derivative of the value function. This is conventionally termed "marginal Q" and denoted by q. Note the timing: the appropriate measure of marginal Q is the expected discounted value for the following period due to the one-period investment delay.

Using (8.1) to solve for $E_{(A', p' \mid A, p)} V_{K'}(A', K', p')$, we can simplify (8.4) to a Euler equation:

$$
\begin{aligned}
C_{K'}(K', A, K) + p \\
= \beta E_{(A', p' \mid A, p)} \{ \Pi_K(K', A') + p'(1 - \delta) - C_{K'}(K'', A', K') \}. \tag{8.5}
\end{aligned}
$$

To interpret this necessary condition for an optimal solution, consider increasing current investment by a small amount. The cost of this investment is measured on the left side of this expression: there is the direct cost of the capital (p) as well as the marginal adjustment cost. The gain comes in the following period. The additional capital increases profits. Further, as the manager "returns" to the optimal path following this deviation, the undepreciated capital is valued at the future market price p' and adjustment costs are reduced.

EXERCISE 8.3   Suppose that the problem had been written, more conventionally, with the choice of investment rather than the future capital stock. Derive and analyze the resulting Euler equation.

---

5. In some applications the cost of adjustment function depends on investment and is written $C(I, K)$ where $I = K' - (1 - \delta)K$.

8.4.1   Q Theory: Models

One of the difficult aspects of investment theory with adjustment costs is empirical implementation. As the value function and hence its derivative is not observable, (8.4) cannot be directly estimated. Thus the theory is tested either by finding a suitable proxy for the derivative of $V(A, K, p)$ or by estimating the Euler equation, (8.5). We focus here on the development of a theory that facilitates estimation based on using the average value of the firm as a substitute for the marginal value of an additional unit of capital.

This approach, called Q theory, imposes additional structure on (8.1). In particular, following Hayashi (1982), we assume that $\Pi(K, A)$ is proportional to K and that the cost of adjustment function is quadratic.[6] Further we assume that the price of capital is constant. Therefore we have

$$V(A, K) = \max_{K'} AK - \frac{\gamma}{2}\left(\frac{K' - (1 - \delta)K}{K}\right)^2 K$$

$$- p(K' - (1 - \delta)K) + \beta E_{A'|A} V(A', K'). \qquad (8.6)$$

As always, Bellman's equation must be true for all (A, K). Suppose that the shock to profitability, A, follows an autoregressive process given by

$$A' = \rho A + \varepsilon',$$

where $|\rho| < 1$ and ε' is white noise. The first-order condition for the choice of the investment level implies that the investment rate in ($i \equiv I/K$) is given by

$$i = \frac{1}{\gamma}(\beta E_{A'|A} V_K(A', K') - p). \qquad (8.7)$$

Here $E_{A'|A} V_K(A', K')$ is again the expected value of the derivative of the value function, a term we called "marginal Q." To solve this dynamic programming problem, we can guess at a solution and verify that it works. Given the linear-quadratic structure of the problem, it is natural to guess that

$$V(A, K) = \phi(A)K,$$

---

6. Abel and Eberly (1994) contain further discussion of the applicability of Q theory for more general adjustment cost and profit functions.

where $\phi(A)$ is some unknown function. This guess allows us to write the expected marginal Q as a function of A:

$$E_{A'|A}V_K(A', K') = E_{A'|A}\phi(A') \equiv \tilde{\phi}(A).$$

Note that in this case the expected values of marginal and average Q (defined as $V(A, K)/K = \phi(A)$) are the same.[7] Using this value function in the Euler equation, we write

$$i = \frac{1}{\gamma}(\beta\tilde{\phi}(A) - p) \equiv z(A).$$

This expression implies that the investment rate is independent of the current level of the capital stock.

To verify our guess, we substitute this investment policy function into the original functional equation, which implies that

$$\phi(A)K = AK - \frac{\gamma}{2}(z(A))^2 K - pz(A)K + \beta\tilde{\phi}(A)K[(1 - \delta) + z(A)]$$

must hold for all (A, K). Clearly, the guess that the value function is proportional to K is correct: the value of K cancels out. So, from our conjecture that $V(A, K)$ is proportional to K, we find an optimal investment policy that confirms the suggested proportionality. The remaining part of the unknown value function $\phi(A)$ is given implicity by the expression above.[8]

The result that the value function is proportional to the stock of capital is, at this point, a nice property of the linear-quadratic formulation of the capital accumulation problem. In the discussion of empirical evidence it forms the basis for a wide range of applications, since it allows the researcher to substitute the average value of Q (observable from the stock market) for marginal Q (unobservable).

8.4.2   Q Theory: Evidence

Due to its relatively simple structure, the convex adjustment cost model is one of the leading models of investment. In fact, as discussed above, the convex model is often simplified further so that

---

7. Hayashi (1982) was the first to point out that in this case average and marginal Q coincide, though his formulation was nonstochastic.
8. Interestingly the natural conjecture that $\phi(A) = A$ does not satisfy the functional equation.

adjustment costs are quadratic, as in (8.6). Necessary conditions for optimality for this model are expressed in two ways.

First, from the first-order conditions, the investment rate is linearly related to the difference between the future marginal value of new capital and the current price of capital, as in (8.7). Using the arguments from above, this marginal value of capital can under some conditions be replaced by the average value of capital. This sets the basis for the Q theory empirical approach discussed below.

Second, one can base an empirical analysis on the Euler equation that emerges from (8.6). It naturally leads to estimation using GMM as discussed below.

The discussion of estimation based on Q theory draws heavily on two papers. The first by Gilchrist and Himmelberg (1995) provides a clean and clear presentation of the basic approach and evidence on Q theory based estimation of capital adjustment models. A theme in this and related papers is that empirically investment depends on variables other than average Q, particularly measures of cash flow.

The second by Cooper and Ejarque (2001) works from Gilchrist and Himmelberg (1995) to explore the significance of imperfect competition and credit market frictions.[9] This paper illustrates the use of indirect inference.

Tests of Q theory on panel data are frequently conducted using an empirical specification of

$$(I/K)_{it} = a_{i0} + a_1 \beta E \bar{q}_{it+1} + a_2 \frac{X_{it}}{K_{it}} + v_{it}. \tag{8.8}$$

Here the i subscript refers to firm or plant i and the t subscript represents time. From (8.7), a_1 should equal $1/\gamma$. This is an interesting aspect of this specification: under the null hypothesis one can infer the adjustment cost parameter from this regression. There is a constant term in the regression that is plant specific. This comes from a modification of the quadratic cost of adjustment to

$$C(K', K) = \frac{\gamma}{2} \left(\frac{K' - (1 - \delta)K}{K} - a_i \right)^2 K$$

as in Gilchrist and Himmelberg (1995).[10]

---

9. We are grateful to Joao Ejarque for allowing us to use this material.
10. The error term in (8.8) is often ascribed to stochastic elements in the cost of adjustment function; then a_i is modified to become $a_{it} = a_i + \varepsilon_{it}$.

Finally, this regression includes a third term, X_{it}/K_{it}. In fact Q theory does not suggest the inclusion of other variables in (8.8), since all relevant information is incorporated in average Q. Rather, these variables are included as a means of testing the theory, where the theory predicts that these variables from the information set should be insignificant. Hence researchers focus on the statistical and economic significance of a_2. In particular, X_{it} often includes financial variables as a way of evaluating an alternative hypothesis in which the effects of financial constraints are not included in average Q.

The results obtained using this approach have been mixed. Estimates of large adjustment costs are not uncommon. Hayashi (1982) estimates $a_1 = 0.0423$ and thus γ of about 25. Gilchrist and Himmelberg (1995) estimate a_1 at 0.033.

Further many studies estimate a positive value for a_2 when X_{it} is a measure of profits and/or cash flow.[11] This is taken as a rejection of the Q theory, which of course implies that the inference drawn about γ from the estimate of a_1 may not be valid. Moreover the significance of the financial variables has lead researchers to conclude that capital market imperfections must be present.

Cooper and Ejarque (2001) argue that the apparent failure of Q theory stems from misspecification of the firm's optimization problem: market power is ignored. As shown by Hayashi (1982), if firms have market power, then average and marginal Q diverge. Consequently the substitution of marginal for average Q in the standard investment regression induces measurement error that may be positively correlated with profits.[12] Cooper and Ejarque (2001) ask whether one might find positive and significant a_2 in (8.8) in a model without any capital market imperfections.

Their methodology follows the indirect inference procedures described in Gourieroux and Monfort (1996) and Gourieroux et al. (1993). This approach to estimation was discussed in chapter 4. This is a minimum distance estimation routine in which the structural parameters of the optimization problem are chosen to bring the reduced form coefficients from the regression on the simulated data close to those from the actual data. The key is that the same reduced form regression is run on both the actual and simulated data.

---

11. Hubbard (1994) reviews these findings.
12. Cooper and Ejarque (2001) do not attempt to characterize this measurement error analytically but use their simulated environment to understand its implications. See Erickson and Whited (2000) for a detailed and precise discussion of the significance of measurement error in the Q regressions.

Cooper and Ejarque (2001) use the parameter estimates of Gilchrist and Himmelberg (1995) for (8.8) as representative of the Q theory based investment literature. Denote these estimates from their pooled panel sample using the average (Tobin's) Q measure by $(a_1^*, a_2^*) = (0.03, 0.24)$.[13] Cooper and Ejarque (2001) add three other moments reported by Gilchrist and Himmelberg (1995): the serial correlation of investment rates (0.4), the standard deviation of profit rates (0.3), and the average value of average Q (3). Let Ψ^d denote the vector moments from the data. In the Cooper and Ejarque (2001) study,

$$\Psi^d = [0.03\ 0.24\ 0.4\ 0.3\ 3].$$

The estimation focuses on two key parameters: the curvature of the profit function (α) and the level of the adjustment costs (γ). So other parameters are set at levels found in previous studies: $\delta = 0.15$ and $\beta = 0.95$. This leaves (α, γ) and the stochastic process for the firm-specific shocks to profitability as the parameters remaining to be estimated. Cooper and Ejarque (2001) estimate the serial correlation (ρ) and the standard deviation (σ) of the profitability shocks while the aggregate shock process is represented process as a two-state Markov process with a symmetric transition matrix in which the probability of remaining in either of the two aggregate states is 0.8.[14]

As described in chapter 4, the indirect inference procedure proceeds, in this application, as follows:

• Given a vector of parameters, $\Theta \equiv (\alpha, \gamma, \rho, \sigma)$, solve the firm's dynamic programming problem of

$$V(A, K) = \max_{K'} AK^\alpha - \frac{\gamma}{2}\left(\frac{K' - (1-\delta)K}{K}\right)^2 K - p(K' - (1-\delta)K)$$

$$+ \beta E_{A'|A}V(A', K') \qquad \text{for all } (A, K) \tag{8.9}$$

using value function iteration. The method outlined in Tauchen (1986) is used to create a discrete state space representation of the

---

13. Cooper and Ejarque (2001) have no unobserved heterogeneity in the model so that the constant from the regression as well as the fixed effects are ignored. The remaining coefficients are taken to be common across all firms.

14. The estimates are not sensitive to aggregate shocks. The model is essentially estimated from the rich cross-sectional variation as in the panel study of Gilchrist and Himmelberg (1995).

Table 8.1
Estimated structural parameters

	Structural parameters				
	α	γ	ρ	σ	θ
GH95					
CE	0.689 (0.011)	0.149 (0.016)	0.106 (0.008)	0.855 (0.04)	2

Table 8.2
Regression results and moments

	Reduced form coefficient estimates/moments				
	a_1	a_2	$sc \dfrac{I}{K}$	$std \dfrac{\pi}{K}$	$\bar{q}$
GH95	0.03	0.24	0.4	0.25	3
CE	0.041	0.237	0.027	0.251	2.95

shock process given (ρ, σ). Use this in the conditional expectation of the optimization.

• Given the policy functions obtained by solving the dynamic programming problem, create a panel data set by simulation.

• Estimate the Q theory model, as in (8.8), on the simulated model, and calculate relevant moments. Let $\Psi^s(\Theta)$ denote the corresponding moments from the simulated data.

• Compute $J(\Theta)$ defined as

$$J(\Theta) = (\Psi^d - \Psi^s(\Theta))'W(\Psi^d - \Psi^s(\Theta)), \tag{8.10}$$

where W is an estimate of the inverse of the variance-covariance matrix of Ψ^d.

• Find the estimator of Θ, $\hat{\Theta}$, that solves

$$\min_{\Theta} J(\Theta).$$

The second row of table 8.1 presents the estimates of structural parameters and standard errors reported in Cooper and Ejarque (2001).[15] Table 8.2 reports the resulting regression results and

---

15. The computation of standard errors follows the description in chapter 4 of Gourieroux and Monfort (1996).

moments. Here the row labeled GH95 represents the regression results and moments reported by Gilchrist and Himmelberg (1995).

The model, with its four parameters, does a good job of matching four of the five estimates/moments but is unable to reproduce the high level of serial correlation in plant-level investment rates. This appears to be a consequence of the fairly low level of γ which implies that adjustment costs are not very large. Raising the adjustment costs will increase the serial correlation of investment.

The estimated curvature of the profit function of 0.689 implies a markup of about 15 percent.[16] This estimate of α, and hence the markup, is not at variance with results reported in the literature.

The other interesting parameter is the estimate of the level associated with the quadratic cost of adjustment, γ. Relative to other studies, this appears quite low.

However, an interesting point from these results is that the estimate of γ is not identified from the regression coefficient on average Q. From table 8.1, the estimated value of $\gamma = 0.149$ is far from the inverse of the coefficient on average Q (about 4). So clearly the identification of the quadratic cost of adjustment parameter from a_2 is misleading in the presence of market power.

EXERCISE 8.4   Write a progam to solve

$$V(A, K) = \max_{K'} AK^\alpha - \frac{\gamma}{2} \left(\frac{K' - (1 - \delta)K}{K} \right)^2 K$$

$$- p(K' - (1 - \delta)K) + \beta E_{A'|A} V(A', K') \tag{8.11}$$

using a value function iteration routine given a parameterization of the problem. Use the results to explore the relationship of investment to average Q. Is there a nonlinearity in this relationship? How is investment related to profitability in your simulated data set?

8.4.3   Euler Equation Estimation

This approach to estimation shares with the consumption applications presented in chapter 6 a simple but powerful logic. The Euler

---

16. Cooper and Ejarque (2001) show that if $p = y^{-\eta}$ is the demand curve and $y = Ak^\phi l^{(1-\phi)}$ the production function, maximization of profit over the flexible factor l leads to a reduced form profit function where the exponent on capital is $\phi(\eta - 1)/[(1 - \phi)(1 - \eta) - 1]$. Here $\phi = 0.33$ and $\eta = 0.1315$, implying a markup of about 15 percent.

equation given in (8.5) is a necessary condition for optimality. In the quadratic cost of adjustment model case this simplifies to

$$i_t = \frac{1}{\gamma}\left[\beta\left[E_t\left(\pi_K(A_{t+1},K_{t+1}) + p_{t+1}(1-\delta) + \frac{\gamma}{2}i_{t+1}^2 + \gamma(1-\delta)i_{t+1}\right)\right] - p_t\right].$$

Let ε_{t+1} be defined from realized values of these variables:

$$\varepsilon_{t+1} = i_t - \frac{1}{\gamma}\left[\beta\left[\left(\pi_K(A_{t+1},K_{t+1}) + p_{t+1}(1-\delta)\right.\right.\right.$$

$$\left.\left.\left. + \frac{\gamma}{2}i_{t+1}^2 + \gamma(1-\delta)i_{t+1}\right)\right] - p_t\right]. \quad (8.12)$$

Then the restriction imposed by the theory is that $E_t\varepsilon_{t+1} = 0$. It is precisely this orthogonality condition that the GMM procedure exploits in the estimation of underlying structural parameters, $\theta = (\beta,\gamma,\delta,\alpha)$.

To illustrate, we have solved and simulated a model with quadratic adjustment costs ($\gamma = 2$) with constant investment good prices. That data set allows us to estimate the parameters of the firm's problem using GMM.

To make this as transparent as possible, assume that the researcher knows the values of all parameters except for γ. Thus we can rely on a single orthogonality condition to determine γ. Suppose that we use the lagged profitability shock as the instrument. Define

$$\Omega(\gamma) = \frac{1}{T}\sum_t \varepsilon_{t+1}(\gamma)A_t. \quad (8.13)$$

The GMM estimate of γ is obtained from the minimization of $\Omega(\gamma)^2$. This function is shown in figure 8.1. Clearly, this function is minimized near $\gamma = 2$.[17]

Whited (1998) contains a thorough review and analysis of existing evidence on Euler equation estimation of investment models. As Whited notes, the Euler equation approach certainly has a virtue over the Q theory based model: there is no need to try to measure

---

17. The program to estimate this model is very simple. Once $\Omega(\gamma)$ is programmed, it is simply a basic routine to minimize this function. Obtaining $\Omega(\gamma)$ is easy too, using the information on parameters plus observations in the data set on investment rates and the ratio of output to capital (to determine marginal profit rates). The minimization may not occur exactly at $\gamma = 2$ because of a sampling error. The interested reader can extend this analysis to create a distribution of estimates by redrawing shocks, simulating, and then re-estimating γ from the GMM procedure.

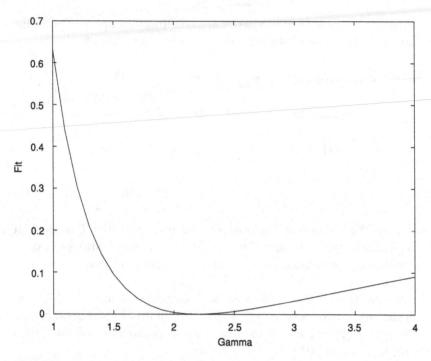

Figure 8.1
Function $\Omega(\gamma)$

marginal Q. Thus some of the restrictions imposed on the estimation, such as the conditions specified by Hayashi, do not have to be
imposed. Estimation based on an investment Euler equation generally leads to rejection of the overidentifying restrictions, and as in
the Q theory based empirical work, the inclusion of financial constraints improves the performance of the model.

The point of Whited (1998) is to dig further into these results.
Importantly, her analysis brings fixed adjustment costs into the
evaluation of the Euler equation estimation. As noted earlier and
discussed at some length below, investment studies have been
broadened to go beyond convex adjustment costs to match the
observations of nonadjustment in the capital stock. Whited (1998)
takes this into account by dividing her sample into the set of firms
that undertakes positive investment. Estimation of the Euler equation for this subset is much more successful. Further Whited (1998)
finds that while financial variables are important overall, they are
also weakly relevant for the firms with ongoing investment.

These results are provocative. They force us to think jointly about the presence of nonconvex adjustment costs and financial variables. We now turn to these important topics.

8.4.4 Borrowing Restrictions

Thus far we have ignored the potential presence of borrowing restrictions. These have a long history in empirical investment analysis. As in our discussion of the empirical Q theory literature, financial frictions are often viewed as the source of the significance of profit rates and/or cash flow in investment regressions.

There is nothing particularly difficult about introducing borrowing restrictions into the capital accumulation problem. Consider

$$V(A, K) = \max_{K' \in \Gamma(A, K)} AK^\alpha - \frac{\gamma}{2} \left(\frac{K' - (1 - \delta)K}{K} \right)^2 K \tag{8.14}$$

$$- p(K' - (1 - \delta)K) + \beta E_{A'|A} V(A', K') \quad \text{for all } (A, K), \tag{8.15}$$

where $\Gamma(A, K)$ constrains the choice set for the future capital stock. For example, if capital purchases had to be financed out of current profits, then the financial restriction is

$$K' - (1 - \delta)K \leq AK^\alpha \tag{8.16}$$

so that

$$\Gamma(A, K) = [0, AK^\alpha + (1 - \delta)K]. \tag{8.17}$$

The dynamic optimization problem with a restriction of (8.17) can certainly be evaluated using value function iteration techniques. The problem of the firm can be broadened to include retained earnings as a state variable and to include other financial variables in the state vector. There are a number of unresolved issues though that have limited research in this area:

• What are the $\Gamma(A, K)$ functions suggested by theory?
• For what $\Gamma(A, K)$ functions is there a wedge between average and marginal Q?

The first point is worthy of note: while we have many models of capital accumulation without borrowing restrictions, the alternative model of investment with borrowing restrictions is not on the table. Thus the rejection of the model without constraints in favor of one with constraints is not as convincing as it could be.

Table 8.3
Descriptive statistics, LRD

Variable	LRD
Average investment rate	12.2%
Inaction rate: Investment	8.1
Fraction of observations with negative investment	10.4
Spike rate: Positive investment	18
Spike rate: Negative investment	1.4

The second point, related to work by Chirinko (1993) and Gomes (2001), returns to the evidence discussed earlier on Q theory based empirical models of investment. The value function $V(A, K)$ that solves (8.15) contains all the information about the constrained optimization problem. As long as this function is differentiable (which restricts the $\Gamma(A, K)$ function), marginal Q will still measure the return to an extra unit of capital. The issue is whether the borrowing friction introduces a wedge between marginal and average Q.[18] Empirically the issue is whether this wedge between marginal and average Q can create the regression results such as those reported in Gilchrist and Himmelberg (1995).

8.5 Nonconvex Adjustment: Theory

Empirically one finds that at the plant level there are frequent periods of investment inactivity and also bursts of investment activity. Table 8.3, taken from Cooper and Haltiwanger (2000), documents the nature of capital adjustment in the Longitudinal Research Database (LRD), a plant-level U.S. manufacturing data set.[19]

Here inaction is defined as a plant-level investment rate less than 0.01 and a spike is an investment rate in excess of 20 percent. Clearly, the data exhibit both inaction as well as large bursts of investment.

As argued by Caballero et al. (1995), Cooper et al. (1999), and Cooper and Haltiwanger (2000), it is difficult to match this type of evidence with a quadratic cost of adjustment model. Thus we turn to alternative models which can produce inaction. In the first type of

---

18. If, in the example above, $\alpha = 1$, then the constraint is proportional to K. In this case it appears that average and marginal Q are equal.
19. Cooper and Haltiwanger provide a full description of the data.

model we relax the convex adjustment cost structure and assume that the costs of adjustment depend only on whether investment has been undertaken, and not its magnitude. We then consider a second type of model in which there is some type of irreversibility. The next section reports on estimation of these models.

8.5.1 Nonconvex Adjustment Costs

For this formulation of adjustment costs, we follow Cooper and Haltiwanger (1993) and Cooper et al. (1999) and consider a dynamic programming problem specified at the plant level as

$$V(A, K, p) = \max\{V^i(A, K, p), V^a(A, K, p)\} \quad \text{for all } (A, K, p), \quad (8.18)$$

where the superscripts refer to active investment a and inactivity i. These options, in turn, are defined by

$$V^i(A, K, p) = \Pi(A, K) + \beta E_{A', p' | A, p} V(A', K(1 - \delta), p')$$

and

$$V^a(A, K, p) = \max_{K'} \ \Pi(A, K)\lambda - FK - p(K' - (1 - \delta)K)$$

$$+ \beta E_{A', p' | A, p} V(A', K', p').$$

Here there are two costs of adjustment that are independent of the level of investment activity. The first is a loss of profit flow equal to $1 - \lambda$. This is intended to capture an opportunity cost of investment in which the plant must be shut down during a period of investment activity. The second nonconvex cost is simply subtracted from the flow of profits as FK. The inclusion of K here is intended to capture the idea that these fixed costs, while independent of the current level of investment activity, may have some scale aspects to them.[20] In this formulation the relative price of capital (p) is allowed to vary as well.

Before proceeding to a discussion of results, it might be useful to recall from chapter 3 how one might obtain a solution to a problem

---

20. See Abel and Eberly (1994) for a model in which fixed costs are proportional to K. If these costs were independent of size, then large plants would face lower adjustment costs (relative to their capital stock) and thus might adjust more frequently. So, as in the quadratic specification, the costs are scaled by size. This is nevertheless an assumption, and the relationship between plant size and investment activity is still an open issue.

such as (8.18).[21] The first step is to specify a profit function, say $\Pi(A, K) = AK^{\alpha}$, for which we set the parameters $(F, \beta, \lambda, \alpha, \delta)$ as well as the stochastic processes for the random variables (A, p). Denote this parameter vector by Θ. The second step is to specify a space for the state variables (A, K, p) and thus for control variable K'. Once these steps are complete, the value function iteration logic (subscripts denote iterations of the mapping) takes over:

• Provide an initial guess for $V_1(A, K, p)$, such as the one-period solution.

• Using this initial guess, compute the values for the two options, $V_1^a(A, K, p)$ and $V_1^i(A, K, p)$.

• Using these values, solve for the next guess of the value function: $V_2(A, K, p) = \max\{V_1^a(A, K, p), V_1^i(A, K, p)\}$.

• Continue this process until convergence.

• After the value function is found, compute the set of state variables such that the action (inaction) is optimal and that the investment level in the event adjustment is optimal.

• From these policy functions, simulate the model and create either a panel or a time series data set.

The policy function for this problem will have two important dimensions. First, there is the determination of whether the plant will adjust its capital stock or not. Second, conditional on adjustment, the plant must determine its level of investment. As usual, the optimal choice of investment depends on the marginal value of capital in the next period. However, in contrast to, say, the quadratic cost of adjustment model, the future value of additional capital depends on future choice with respect to adjustment. Thus there is no simple Euler equation linking the marginal cost of additional capital today with future marginal benefit, as in (8.5), since there is no guarantee that this plant will be adjusting its capital stock in the next period.

Note that the two types of costs have very different implications for the cyclical properties of investment. In particular, when adjustment costs interfere with the flow of profits ($\lambda < 1$), then it is more expensive to invest in periods of high profitability. Yet, if the shocks

---

21. Recall the outline of the basic value function iteration program for the nonstochastic growth model and the modification of that for nonconvex adjustment costs in chapter 3.

are sufficiently correlated, there is a gain to investing in good times. In contrast, if costs are largely lump sum, then given the time-to-build aspect of the accumulation decision, the best time to invest is when it is profitable to do so (A is high) assuming that these shocks are serially correlated. Thus whether investment is procyclical or countercyclical depends on both the nature of the adjustment costs and the persistence of shocks.

We will discuss the policy functions for an estimated version of this model later. For now we look at a simple example to build intuition.

Machine Replacement Example

For an example of a simple model of machine replacement, we turn to a modified version studied by Cooper and Haltiwanger (1993). Here there is no choice of the size of the investment expenditure. Investment means the purchase of a new machine at a net price of p. By assumption, the old machine is scrapped. The size of the new machine is normalized to 1.[22]

To further simplify the argument, we assume that new capital becomes productive immediately. In addition the price of new capital good is assumed to be constant and can be interpreted as including the fixed cost of adjusting the capital stock. In this case we can write the Bellman equation as

$$V(A, K) = \max\{V^i(A, K), V^a(A, K)\} \qquad \text{for all } (A, K),$$

where the superscripts refer to active investment a and inactivity i. These options, in turn, are defined by

$$V^i(A, K) = \Pi(A, K) + \beta E_{A'|A} V(A', K(1 - \delta))$$

and

$$V^a(A, K) = \Pi(A, 1)\lambda - p + \beta E_{A'|A} V(A', (1 - \delta)).$$

Here "action" means that a new machine is bought and is immediately productive. The cost of this is the net price of the new capital and the disruption caused by the adjustment process. Let $\Delta(A, K)$ be the relative gains to action, so

---

22. As discussed by Cooper and Haltiwanger (1993) and Cooper et al. (1999), this assumption that a new machine has fixed size can be derived from a model with embodied technological progress that is rendered stationary by dividing through by the productivity of the new machine. In this case the rate of depreciation measures both physical deterioration and obsolescence.

$$\Delta(A, K) \equiv V^a(A, K) - V^i(A, K) = \Pi(A, 1)\lambda - \Pi(A, K) - p$$

$$+ \beta(E_{A'|A}V(A', (1 - \delta)) - E_{A'|A}V(A', K(1 - \delta))).$$

The problem posed in this fashion is clearly one of the optimal stopping variety. Given the state of profitability (A), there is a critical size of the capital stock $(K^*(A))$ such that machine replacement occurs if and only if $K < K^*(A)$. To see why this policy is optimal, note that by our timing assumption, $V^a(A, K)$ is in fact independent of K. Clearly, $V^i(A, K)$ is increasing in K. Thus there is a unique crossing of these two functions at $K^*(A)$. In other words, $\Delta(A, K)$ is decreasing in K, given A with $\Delta(A, K^*(A)) = 0$.

Is K^* between 0 and 1? With $\Pi(A, 0)$ sufficiently small, $V^i(A, K) < V^a(A, K)$ for K near 0. Hence $K^* > 0$. Further, with the costs of acquiring new capital $(p > 0, \lambda < 1)$ large enough and the rate of depreciation low enough, capital will not be replaced each period: $K^* < 1$. Thus there will be a "replacement cycle" in which there is a burst of investment activity followed by inactivity until the capital ages enough to warrant replacement.[23]

The policy function is then given by $z(A, K) \in \{0, 1\}$, where $z(A, K) = 0$ means inaction and $z(A, K) = 1$ means replacement. From the argument above, for each A there exists $K^*(A)$ such that $z(A, K) = 1$ if and only if $K \leq K^*(A)$.

With the assumption that capital becomes productively immediately, the response of $K^*(A)$ to variations in A can be analyzed.[24] Suppose, for example, that $\lambda = 1$ and A is iid. In this case the dependence of $\Delta(A, K)$ on A is solely through current profits. Thus $\Delta(A, K)$ is increasing in A as long as the marginal productivity of capital is increasing in A, $\Pi_{AK}(A, K) > 0$. So $K^*(A)$ will be increasing in A and replacement will be more likely in good times.

Alternatively, suppose that $\lambda < 1$. In this case, during periods of high productivity, it is desirable to have new capital, but it is also costly to install it. If A is positively serially correlated, then the effect of A on $\Delta(A, K)$ will reflect both the direct effect on current profits and the effects on the future values. If the opportunity cost is large (a small λ) and shocks are not persistent enough, then machine replacement will be delayed until capital is less productive.

---

23. Cooper and Haltiwanger (2000) and Cooper et al. (1999) argue that these features also hold when there is a one-period lag in the installation process.
24. Cooper et al. (1999) analyze the more complicated case of a one-period lag in the installation of new capital.

Aggregate Implications of Machine Replacement

This model of capital adjustment at the plant level can be used to generate aggregate implications. Let $f_t(K)$ be the current distribution of capital across a fixed population of plants. Suppose that the shock in period t, A_t, has two components, $A_t = a_t \varepsilon_t$. The first is aggregate and the second is plant specific. Following Cooper et al. (1999), assume that the aggregate shock takes on two values and the plant specific shock takes on twenty values. Further assume that the idiosyncratic shocks are iid. With this decomposition, write the policy function as $z(a_t, \varepsilon_t, K_t)$, where $z(a_t, \varepsilon_t, K_t) = 1$ signifies action and $z(a_t, \varepsilon_t, K_t) = 0$ indicates inaction. Clearly, the decision on replacement will generally depend differentially on the two types of shocks, since they may be drawn from different stochastic properties. For example, if the aggregate shock is more persistent than the plant-specific one, the response to a variation in a_t will be larger than the response to an innovation in ε_t.

Define

$$H(a_t, K) = \int_\varepsilon z(a_t, \varepsilon_t, K) \, dG_t(\varepsilon),$$

where $G_t(\varepsilon)$ is the period t cumulative distribution function of the plant-specific shocks. Here $H(a_t, K)$ is a hazard function representing the probability of adjustment for all plants with capital K in aggregate state a_t. To the extent that the researcher may be able to observe aggregate but not plant-specific shocks, $H(a_t, K)$ represents a hazard that averages over the $\{0, 1\}$ choices of the individual plants so that $H(a_t, K) \in [0, 1]$.

Using this formulation, let $I(a_t; f_t(K))$ be the rate of investment in state a_t given the distribution of capital holdings $f_t(K)$ across plants. Aggregate investment is defined as

$$I(a_t; f_t(K)) = \sum_K H(a_t, K) f_t(K). \tag{8.19}$$

Thus total investment reflects the interaction between the average adjustment hazard and the cross-sectional distribution of capital holdings.

The evolution of the cross-sectional distribution of capital is given by

$$g_{t+1}((1 - \delta)K) = (1 - H(a_t, K)) g_t(K). \tag{8.20}$$

Expressions such as these are common in aggregate models of discrete adjustment; see, for example, Rust (1985) and Caballero et al. (1995). Given an initial cross-sectional distribution and a hazard function, a sequence of shocks will thus generate a sequence of aggregate investment levels from (8.19) and a sequence of cross-sectional distributions from (8.20).

Thus the machine replacement problem can generate a panel data set and, through aggregation, time series as well. In principle, estimation from aggregate data supplements the perhaps more direct route of estimating a model such as this from a panel.

EXERCISE 8.5 Use a value function iteration routine to solve the dynamic optimization problem with a firm when there are nonconvex adjustment costs. Suppose that there is a panel of such firms. Use the resulting policy functions to simulate the time series of aggregate investment. Then use a value function iteration routine to solve the dynamic optimization problem with a firm when there are quadratic adjustment costs. Create a time series from the simulated panel. How well can a quadratic adjustment cost model approximate the aggregate investment time series created by the model with nonconvex adjustment costs?

8.5.2 Irreversibility

The specifications considered thus far do not distinguish between the buying and selling prices of capital. However, there are good reasons to think that investment is at least partially irreversible so that the selling price of a unit of used capital is less than the cost of a unit of new capital. This reflects frictions in the market for used capital as well as specific aspects of capital equipment that may make them imperfectly suitable for uses at other production sites. To allow for this, we alter our optimization problem to distinguish the buying and selling prices of capital.

The value function for this specification is given by

$$V(A, K) = \max\{V^b(A, K), V^s(A, K), V^i(A, K)\} \qquad \text{for all } (A, K),$$

where the superscripts refer to the act of buying capital b, selling capital s and inaction i. These options, in turn, are defined by

$$V^b(A, K) = \max_I \Pi(A, K) - I + \beta E_{A'|A} V(A', K(1 - \delta) + I),$$

$$V^s(A, K) = \max_R \; \Pi(A, K) + p_s R + \beta E_{A'|A} V(A', K(1 - \delta) - R),$$

and

$$V^i(A, K) = \Pi(A, K) + \beta E_{A'|A} V(A', K(1 - \delta)).$$

Under the buy option, the plant obtains capital at a cost normalized to one. Under the sell option, the plant retires R units of capital at a price p_s. The third option is inaction, so the capital stock depreciates at a rate of δ. Intuitively the gap between the buying and selling price of capital will produce inaction. Suppose that there is an adverse shock to the profitability of the plant. If this shock was known to be temporary, then selling capital and repurchasing it in the near future would not be profitable for the plant as long as $p_s < 1$. Thus inaction may be optimal. Clearly, though, the amount of inaction that this model can produce will depend on both the size of p_s relative to 1 and the serial correlation of the shocks.[25]

8.6 Estimation of a Rich Model of Adjustment Costs

Using this dynamic programming structure to understand the optimal capital decision at the plant (firm) level, we confront the data on investment decisions allowing for a rich structure of adjustment costs.[26] To do so, we follow Cooper and Haltiwanger (2000) and consider a model with quadratic adjustment costs, nonconvex adjustment costs and irreversibility. We describe the optimization problem and then the estimation results obtained by Cooper and Haltiwanger.

8.6.1 General Model

The dynamic programming problem for a plant is given by

$$V(A, K) = \max\{V^b(A, K), V^s(A, K), V^i(A, K)\} \qquad \text{for all } (A, K), \quad (8.21)$$

where, as above, the superscripts refer to the act of buying capital b, selling capital s and inaction i. These options, in turn, are defined by

---

25. An interesting extension of the model would make this gap endogenous.
26. The data set is described by Cooper and Haltiwanger (2000) and is for a balanced panel of U.S. manufacturing plants. Comparable data sets are available in other countries. Similar estimation exercises using these data sets would be of considerable interest.

$$V^b(A, K) = \max_I \ \Pi(A, K) - FK - I - \frac{\gamma}{2}[I/K]^2 K$$

$$+ \beta E_{A'|A} V(A', K(1 - \delta) + I),$$

$$V^s(A, K) = \max_R \ \Pi(A, K) + p_s R - FK - \frac{\gamma}{2}[R/K]^2 K$$

$$+ \beta E_{A'|A} V(A', K(1 - \delta) - R),$$

and

$$V^i(A, K) = \Pi(A, K) + \beta E_{A'|A} V(A', K(1 - \delta)).$$

Cooper and Haltiwanger (2000) estimate three parameters, $\Theta \equiv (F, \gamma, p_s)$ and assume that $\beta = 0.95$, $\delta = 0.069$. Further they specify a profit function of $\Pi(A, K) = AK^\theta$ with $\theta = 0.50$ estimated from a panel data set of manufacturing plants.[27] Note that the adjustment costs in (8.21) exclude any disruptions to the production process so that the $\Pi(A, K)$ can be estimated and the shock process inferred independently of the estimation of adjustment costs. If these additional adjustment costs were added, then the profit function and the shocks would have to be estimated along with the parameters of the adjustment cost function.

These parameters are estimated using an indirect inference routine. The reduced form regression used in the analysis is

$$i_{it} = \alpha_i + \psi_0 + \psi_1 a_{it} + \psi_2 (a_{it})^2 + u_{it}, \tag{8.22}$$

where i_{it} is the investment rate at plant i in period t, a_{it} is the log of a profitability shock at plant i in period t, and α_i is a fixed effect.[28] This specification was chosen as it captures in a parsimonious way the nonlinear relationship between investment rates and fundamentals. The profitability shocks are inferred from the plant-level data using the estimated profit function.[29] Cooper and Haltiwanger document the extent of the nonlinear response of investment to shocks.

---

27. See the discussion by Cooper and Haltiwanger (2000) of the estimation of this profit function.

28. More recent versions of the Cooper-Haltiwanger paper explore adding lagged investment rates to this reduced form to pick up some of the dynamics of the adjustment process.

29. This is an important step in the analysis. Determining the nature of adjustment costs will depend on the characterization of the underlying profitability shocks. For example, if a researcher is trying to identify nonconvex adjustment costs from bursts of investment, then getting the distribution of shocks right is critical.

Table 8.4
Parameter estimates

Specifi-cation	Structural parameter estimates (s.e.)			Parameter estimate for (8.22)		
	γ	F	p_s	ψ_0	ψ_1	ψ_2
LRD				−0.013	0.265	0.20
All	0.043	0.00039	0.967	−0.013	0.255	0.171
	(0.00224)	(0.0000549)	(0.00112)			
F only	0	0.0333	1	−0.02	0.317	0.268
		(0.0000155)				
γ only	0.125	0	1	−0.007	0.241	0.103
	(0.000105)					
p_s only	0	0	0.93	−0.016	0.266	0.223
			(0.000312)			

Table 8.4 reports Cooper and Haltiwanger's results for four different models along with standard errors. The first row shows the estimated parameters for the most general model. The parameter vector $\Theta = [0.043, 0.00039, 0.967]$ implies the presence of statistically significant convex and nonconvex adjustment costs (but nonzero) and a relatively substantial transaction cost. Restricted versions of the model are also reported for purposes of comparison. Clearly, the mixed model does better than any of the restricted models.

Cooper and Haltiwanger argue that these results are reasonable.[30] First, as noted above a low level for the convex cost of adjustment parameter is consistent with the estimates obtained from the Q theory based models due to the presence of imperfect competition. Further the estimation implies that the fixed cost of adjustment is about 0.04 percent of average plant-level profits. Cooper and Haltiwanger find that this cost is significant relative to the difference between adjusting and not adjusting the capital stock. So in fact the estimated fixed cost of adjustment, along with the irreversibility, produces a large amount of inaction. Finally the estimated selling price of capital is much higher than the estimate report in Ramey and Shapiro (2001) for some plants in the aerospace industry.

Cooper and Haltiwanger (2000) also explore the aggregate implications of their model. They contrast the time series behavior of the

---

30. The results are robust to allowing the discount factor to vary with the aggregate shock in order to mimic the relationship between real interest rates and consumption growth from a household's Euler equation.

estimated model with both convex and nonconvex adjustment costs against one in which there are only convex adjustment costs. Even though the model with only convex adjustment costs does relatively poorly on the plant-level data, it does reasonably well in terms of matching time series. In particular, Cooper and Haltiwanger (2000) find that over 90 percent of the time series variation in investment created by a simulation of the estimated model can be accounted for by a quadratic adjustment model. Of course, this also implies that the quadratic model misses 10 percent of the variation.

Note too that this framework for aggregation captures the smoothing by aggregating over heterogeneous plants but misses smoothing created by variations in relative prices. From Thomas (2002) and Kahn and Thomas (2001) we know that this additional source of smoothing can be quite powerful as well.

8.6.2 Maximum Likelihood Estimation

A final approach to estimation follows the approach in Rust (1987). Consider again, for example, the stochastic machine replacement problem given by

$$V(A, K, F) = \max\{V^i(A, K, F), V^a(A, K, F)\} \qquad \text{for all } (A, K, F), \quad (8.23)$$

where

$$V^i(A, K, F) = \Pi(A, K) + \beta E_{A'|A} V(A', K(1 - \delta), F')$$

and

$$V^a(A, K, F) = \max_{K'} \Pi(A, K)\lambda - FK - p(K' - (1 - \delta)K)$$

$$+ \beta E_{A'|A} V(A', K', F').$$

Here we have added the fixed cost of adjustment into the state vector as we assume that the adjustment costs are random at the plant level. Let $G(F)$ represent the cumulative distribution function for these adjustment costs. Assume that these are iid shocks. Then, given a guess for the functions $\{V(A, K, F), V^i(A, K, F), V^a(A, K, F)\}$, the likelihood of inaction can be computed directly from the cumulative distribution function $G(\cdot)$. Thus a likelihood function can be constructed that depends on the parameters of the distribution of adjustment costs and those underlying the dynamic optimization problem. From there, a maximum likelihood estimate can be obtained.[31]

8.7 Conclusion

The theme of this chapter has been the dynamics of capital accumulation. From the plant-level perspective, the investment process is quite rich and entails periods of intense activity followed by times of inaction. This has been documented at the plant level. Using the techniques of the estimation of dynamic programming models, this chapter has presented evidence on the nature of adjustment costs.

Many open issues remain. First, the time series implications of nonconvexities is still not clear. How much does the lumpiness at the plant-level matter for aggregate behavior? Put differently, how much smoothing obtains from the aggregate across heterogeneous plants as well as through variations in relative prices?

Second, there are a host of policy experiments to be considered. What, for example, are the implications of investment tax credits given the estimates of adjustment cost parameters?

EXERCISE 8.6   Add in variations in the price of new capital into the optimization problem given in (8.21). How would you use this to study the impact of, say, an investment tax credit?

---

31. The interested reader should read closely the discussion of Rust (1987) and the papers that followed this line of work. Note that often assumptions are made on $G(\cdot)$ to ease the computation of the likelihood function.

9   Dynamics of Employment Adjustment

9.1   Motivation

This chapter studies labor demand. The usual textbook model of labor demand depicts a firm as choosing the number of workers and their hours given a wage rate. But the determination of wages, employment, and hours is much more complex than this. The key is to recognize that the adjustment of many factors of production, including labor, is not costless. We study the dynamics of capital accumulation elsewhere in this book and in this chapter focus attention on labor demand.

Understanding the nature of adjustment costs and thus the factors determining labor demand is important for a number of reasons. First, many competing models of the business cycle depend crucially on the operation of labor markets. As emphasized in Sargent (1978), a critical point in distinguishing competing theories of the business cycle is whether labor market observations could plausibly be the outcome of a dynamic market-clearing model. Second, attempts to forecast macroeconomic conditions often resort to consideration of observed movements in hours and employment to infer the state of economic activity. Finally, policy interventions in the labor market are numerous and widespread. These include restrictions on wages, restrictions on hours, costs of firing workers, and so forth. Policy evaluate requires a model of labor demand.

We begin the chapter with the simplest models of dynamic labor demand where adjustment costs are assumed to be convex and continuously differentiable. These models are analytically tractable as we can often estimate their parameters directly from first-order conditions. However, they have implications of constant adjustment that are not consistent with microeconomic observations. Nickell (1978) argues:

One point worth noting is that there seems little reason to suppose costs per worker associated with either hiring or firing increase with the rate at which employees flow in or out. Indeed, given the large fixed costs associated with personnel and legal departments, it may even be more reasonable to suppose that the average cost of adjusting the workforce diminishes rather than increases with the speed of adjustment.

This quote is supported by recent evidence in Hamermesh (1989) and Caballero et al. (1997) that labor adjustment is rather erratic at the plant level with periods of inactivity punctuated by large adjustments. Thus this chapter goes beyond the convex case and considers models of adjustment which can mimic these microeconomic facts.

9.2 General Model of Dynamic Labor Demand

In this chapter we consider variants of the following dynamic programming problem:

$$V(A, e_{-1}) = \max_{h,e} R(A, e, h) - \omega(e, h, A) - C(e, e_{-1})$$

$$+ \beta E_{A'|A} V(A', e) \qquad \text{for all } (A, e_{-1}). \qquad (9.1)$$

Here A represents a shock to the profitability of the plant and/or firm. As in our discussion of the investment problem, this shock could reflect variations in product demands or variations in the productivity of inputs. Generally, A will have a component that is common across plants, denoted a, and one that is plant specific, denoted ε.[1] The function $R(A, e, h)$ represents the revenues that depend on the hours worked (h) and the number of workers (e) as well as the profitability shock. Other factors of production, such as capital, are assumed to be rented and optimization over these inputs are incorporated into $R(A, e, h)$.[2]

The function $\omega(e, h, A)$ is the total cost of hiring e workers when each supplies h units of labor time. This general specification

---

1. Here we are also assuming that the discount factor is fixed. In general, the discount would depend on a and a'.
2. In contrast to the chapter on capital adjustment, here we assume that there are no costs to adjusting the stock of capital. This is for convenience only, and a complete model would incorporate both forms of adjustment costs.

allows for overtime pay and other provisions. Assume that this compensation function is increasing in both of its arguments and is convex with respect to hours. Further we allow this compensation function to be state dependent. This may reflect a covariance with the idiosyncratic profitability shocks (due, perhaps, to profit-sharing arrangements) or an exogenous stochastic component in aggregate wages.

The function $C(e, e_{-1})$ is the cost of adjusting the number of workers. Hamermesh (1993) and Hamermesh and Pfann (1996) provide a lengthy discussion of various interpretations and motivations for adjustment costs. This function is meant to cover costs associated with the following:

- Search and recruiting
- Training
- Explicit firing costs
- Variations in complementary activities (capital accumulation, reorganization of production activities, etc.)

It is important to note the timing implicit in the statement of the optimization problem. The state vector includes the stock of workers in the previous period, e_{-1}. In contrast to the capital accumulation problem, the number of workers in the current period is not predetermined. Instead, workers hired in the current period are immediately utilized in the production process: there is no "time to build."

The next section of the chapter is devoted to the study of adjustment cost functions such that the marginal cost of adjustment is positive and increasing in e given e_{-1}. We then turn to more general adjustment cost functions that allow for more nonlinear and discontinuous behavior.

9.3 Quadratic Adjustment Costs

Without putting additional structure on the problem, particularly the nature of adjustment costs, it is difficult to say much about dynamic labor demand. As a starting point, suppose that the cost of adjustment is given by

$$C(e, e_{-1}) = \frac{\eta}{2}(e - (1 - q)e_{-1})^2, \tag{9.2}$$

so $C(e, e_{-1})$ is convex in e and continuously differentiable. Here, q is an exogenous quit rate.

In this specification of adjustment costs, the plant/firm incurs a cost of changing the level of employment relative to the stock of workers $((1 - q)e_{-1})$ that remain on the job from the previous period. Of course, this is a modeling choice: one can also consider the case where the adjustment cost is based on net rather than gross hires.[3]

The first-order conditions for (9.1) using (9.2) are

$$R_h(A, e, h) = \omega_h(e, h, A), \tag{9.3}$$

$$R_e(A, e, h) - \omega_e(e, h, A) - \eta(e - (1 - q)e_{-1}) + \beta EV_e(A', e) = 0. \tag{9.4}$$

Here the choice of hours, given in (9.3), is static: the firm weighs the gains to the increasing labor input against the marginal cost (assumed to be increasing in hours) of increasing hours.

In contrast, (9.4) is a dynamic relationship since the number of employees is a state variable. Assuming that the value function is differentiable, $EV_e(A', e')$ can be evaluated using (9.1), leading to

$$R_e(A, e, h) - \omega_e(e, h, A) - \eta(e - (1 - q)e_{-1})$$

$$+ \beta E[\eta(e' - (1 - q)e)(1 - q)] = 0. \tag{9.5}$$

The solution to this problem will yield policy functions for hours and employment given the state vector. Let $e = \phi(A, e_{-1})$ denote the employment policy function and $h = H(A, e_{-1})$ denote the hours policy function. These functions jointly satisfy (9.3) and (9.5).

As a benchmark, suppose there were no adjustment costs, $\eta \equiv 0$, and the compensation function is given by

$$\omega(e, h, A) = e\tilde{\omega}(h).$$

Here compensation per worker depends only on hours worked. Further, suppose that revenues depend on the product eh so that only total hours matters for the production process. Specifically,

$$R(A, e, h) = A\tilde{R}(eh) \tag{9.6}$$

with $\tilde{R}(eh)$ strictly increasing and strictly concave.

In this special case, the two first-order conditions can be manipulated to imply that

---

3. We can study the implications of that specification by setting $q = 0$ in (9.2) to study the alternative.

$$1 = h\frac{\tilde{\omega}'(h)}{\tilde{\omega}(h)}.$$

So, in the absence of adjustment costs and with the functional forms given above, hours are independent of both e and A. Consequently all variations in the labor input arise from variations in the number of workers rather than hours. This is efficient given that the marginal cost of hours is increasing in the number of hours worked while there are no adjustment costs associated with varying the number of workers.

At another extreme, suppose there are adjustment costs ($\eta \neq 0$). Further, suppose that compensation is simply

$$\omega(e, h, A) = eh,$$

so there are no costs to hours variation. In this case (9.3) implies $A\tilde{R}'(eh) = 1$. Using this, we see that (9.5) is clearly satisfied at a constant level of e. Hence the variation in the labor input would be only in terms of hours, and we would never observe employment variations.

Of course, in the presence of adjustment costs and a strictly convex (in h) compensation function, the plant/firm will optimally balance the costs of adjusting hours against those of adjusting the labor force. This is empirically relevant since in the data both employment and hours variation are observed. Note, though, that it is only adjustment in the number of workers that contains a dynamic element. The dynamics in hours is derived from the dynamic adjustment of employees.[4] It is this trade-off between hours and worker adjustment that lies at the heart of the optimization problem.

Given functional forms, these first-order conditions can be used in an estimation routine that exploits the implied orthogonality conditions. Alternatively, a value function iteration routine can be used to approximate the solution to (9.1) using (9.2). We consider below some specifications.

A Simulated Example

Here we follow Cooper and Willis (2001) and study the policy functions generated by a quadratic adjustment cost model with some particular functional form assumptions.[5] Suppose that output is

---

4. Add to this the dynamic adjustment of other factors, such as capital.
5. As discussed later in this chapter, this model is used by Cooper and Willis (2001) for their quantitative analysis of the gap approach.

a Cobb-Douglas function of total labor input (eh) and capital, and assume the firm has market power as a seller. In this case consider

$$R(A, e, h) = A(eh)^{\alpha}, \tag{9.7}$$

where α reflects labor's share in the production function as well as the elasticity of the demand curve faced by the firm. Further, impose a compensation schedule that follows Bils (1987):

$$\omega(e, h) = w * e * [w_0 + h + w_1(h - 40) + w_2(h - 40)^2], \tag{9.8}$$

where w is the straight-time wage.

Instead of working with (9.5), Cooper and Willis (2001) solve the dynamic programming problem (9.1) with the functional forms above, using value function iteration. The functional equation for the problem is

$$V(A, e_{-1}) = \max_{h, e} A(eh)^{\alpha} - \omega(e, h) - \frac{\eta}{2} \frac{(e - e_{-1})^2}{e_{-1}}$$

$$+ \beta E_{A'|A} V(A', e) \qquad \text{for all } (A, e_{-1}). \tag{9.9}$$

In this analysis, decisions are assumed to be made at the plant level. Accordingly we assume that the profitability shocks have two components: a piece that is common across plants (an aggregate shock) and a piece that is plant specific. Both types of shocks are assumed to follow first-order Markov processes. These are embedded in the conditional expectation in (9.9).

In this formulation the adjustment costs are paid on net changes in employment. Further the adjustment costs depend on the rate of adjustment rather than the absolute change alone.[6]

The policy function that solves (9.9) is given by $e = \phi(A, e_{-1})$. This policy function can be characterized given a parameterization of (9.9).

Cooper and Willis (2001) assume the following:

• Labor's share is 0.65 and the markup is 25 percent so that α in (9.7) is 0.72.

• The compensation function uses the estimates of Bils (1987) and Shapiro (1986): $\{w_0, w_1, w_2\} = \{1.5, 0.19, 0.03\}$; the straight-time wage

---

6. The literature on labor adjustment costs contains both specifications. Cooper and Willis (2001) find that their results are not sensitive to this part of the specification.

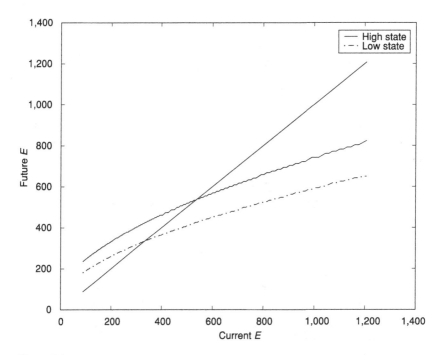

Figure 9.1
Employment policy functions: Quadratic costs

w is normalized to 0.05 for convenience. The elasticity of the wage with respect to hours is close to 1, on average.

• The profitability shocks are represented by a first-order Markov process and are decomposed into aggregate (A) and idiosyncratic components (ε). $A \in \{0.9, 1.1\}$ and ε takes on 15 possible values. The serial correlation for the plant-level shocks is 0.83 and is 0.8 for the aggregate shocks.[7]

This specification leaves open the parameterization of η in the cost of adjustment function. In the literature this is a key parameter to estimate.

The policy functions computed for two values of A at these parameter choices are depicted in figure 9.1. Here we have set $\eta = 1$ which is at the low end of estimates in the literature. These policy functions have two important characteristics:

---

7. Alternatively, the parameters of these processes could be part of an estimation exercise.

- $\phi(A, e_{-1})$ is increasing in (e_{-1}).
- $\phi(A, e_{-1})$ is increasing in A. As profitability increases, so does the marginal gain to adjustment, and thus e is higher.

The quadratic adjustment cost model can be estimated either from plant (firm) data or aggregate data. To illustrate this, we next discuss the approach of Sargent (1978). We then discuss a more general approach to estimation in a model with a richer specification of adjustment costs.

EXERCISE 9.1   Write down the necessary conditions for the optimal choices of hours and employment in (9.9). Provide an interpretation of these conditions.

Sargent: Linear Quadratic Specification

A leading example of bringing the quadratic adjustment cost model directly to the data is Sargent (1978). In that application, Sargent assumes there are two types of labor input: straight-time and over-time workers. The production function is linear-quadratic in each of the two inputs, and the costs of adjustment are quadratic and sepa-rable across the types of labor. As the two types of labor inputs do not interact in either the production function or the adjustment cost function, we will focus on the model of straight-time employment in isolation. Following Sargent, assume that revenue from straight-time employment is given by

$$R(A, e) = (R_0 + A)e - \frac{R_1}{2}e^2. \tag{9.10}$$

Here A is a productivity shock and follows an AR(1) process. Sar-gent does not include hours variation in his model except through the use of overtime labor. Accordingly there is no direct dependence of the wage bill on hours. Instead, he assumes that the wage rate follows an exogenous process (with respect to employment) given by

$$w_t = v_0 + \sum_{i=1}^{i=n} v_i w_{t-i} + \zeta_t. \tag{9.11}$$

In principle, the innovation to wages can be correlated with the shocks to revenues.[8]

---

8. The factors that help the firm forecast future wages are then included in the state space of the problem; that is, they are in the aggregate component of A.

With this structure the firm's first-order condition with respect to employment is given by

$$\beta E_t e_{t+1} - e_t \left(\frac{R_1}{\eta} + (1 + \beta) \right) + e_{t-1} = \frac{1}{\eta} (w_t - R_0 - A_t). \qquad (9.12)$$

From this Euler equation, current employment will depend on the lagged level of employment (through the cost of adjustment) and on (expected) future values of the stochastic variables, productivity, and wages, as these variables influence the future level of employment. As described by Sargent, the solution to this Euler equation can be obtained so that employment in a given period depends on lagged employment, current and (conditional expectations of) future wages, and current and (conditional expectations of) future productivity shocks. Given the driving process for wages and productivity shocks, this conditional expectation can be evaluated so that employment in period t is solely a function of lagged employment, current and past wages. The past wages are relevant for predicting future wages.

Sargent estimates the resulting VAR model of wages employment using maximum likelihood techniques.[9] The parameters he estimated included (R_1, η, ρ), where ρ is the serial correlation of the productivity shocks. In addition Sargent estimated the parameters of the wage process.

The model is estimated using quarterly data on total U.S. civilian employment. Interestingly he also decided to use seasonally unadjusted data for some of the estimation, arguing in effect that there is no reason to separate the responses to seasonal and nonseasonal variations. The data are detrended to correspond to the stationarity of the model.

He finds evidence of adjustment costs insofar as η is significantly different from zero.[10] Sargent argues that these results "... are moderately comforting to the view that the employment-real-wage observations lie along a demand schedule for employment" (p. 1041).

---

9. Sargent (1978) estimates a model with both regular and overtime employment. For simplicity we presented the model of regular employment alone.

10. He also discusses at length the issue of identification and finds multiple peaks in the likelihood function. Informally the issue is distinguishing between the serial correlation in employment induced by lagged employment from that induced by the serial correlation of the productivity shocks.

EXERCISE 9.2   There are a number of exercises to consider working from this simple model.

1. Write a program to solve (9.9) for the employment and hours policy functions using value function iteration. What are the properties of these policy functions? How do these functions change as you vary the elasticity of the compensation function and the cost of adjustment parameter?

2. Solve (9.9) using a log-linearization technique. Compare your results with those obtained by the value function iteration approach.

3. Consider some moments such as the relative variability of hours and employment and the serial correlations of these two variables. Calculate these moments from a simulated panel and also from a time series constructed from the panel. Look for studies that characterize these moments at the micro and/or aggregate levels. Or, better yet, calculate them yourself. Construct an estimation exercise using these moments.

4. Suppose that you wanted to estimate the parameters of (9.9) using GMM. How would you proceed?

9.4   Richer Models of Adjustment

In part, the popularity of the quadratic adjustment cost structure reflects it's tractability. But the implications of this specification of adjustment costs conflict with evidence of inactivity and bursts at the plant level. Thus researchers have been motivated to consider a richer set of models. Those are studied here and then are used for estimation purposes below. For these models of adjustment we discuss the dynamic optimization problem and present policy functions.

9.4.1   Piecewise Linear Adjustment Costs

One of the criticisms of the quadratic adjustment cost specification is the implications of continuous adjustment. At the plant level, as mentioned earlier, there is evidence that adjustment is much more erratic than the pattern implied by the quadratic model. Piecewise linear adjustment costs can produce inaction.

For this case the cost of adjustment function is

$$C(e, e_{-1}) = \begin{cases} \gamma^+ \Delta e & \text{if } \Delta e > 0, \\ \gamma^- \Delta e & \text{if } \Delta e < 0. \end{cases} \tag{9.13}$$

The optimal policy rules are then determined by solving (9.1) using this specification of the adjustment cost function.

The optimal policy rule will look quite different from the one produced with quadratic adjustment costs. This difference is a consequence of the lack of differentiability in the neighborhood of zero adjustment. Consequently small adjustments will not occur since the marginal cost of adjustment does not go to zero as the size of the adjustment goes to zero. Further this specificiation of adjustment costs implies there is no partial adjustment. Since the marginal cost of adjustment is constant, there is no basis for smoothing adjustment.

The optimal policy is characterized by two boundaries: $e^-(A)$ and $e^+(A)$. If $e_{-1} \in [e^-(A), e^+(A)]$, then there is no adjustment. In the event of adjustment, the optimal adjustment is to $e^-(A)$ if $e_{-1} < e^-(A)$ and is to $e^+(A)$ if $e_{-1} > e^+(A)$.

Following Cooper and Willis (2001) and using the same basic parameters as described above, we can study the optimal policy function for this type of adjustment cost. Assume that $\gamma^+ = \gamma^- = 0.05$, which produces inaction at the plant level in 23 percent of the observations.[11] Then (9.1) along with (9.13) can be solved using value function iteration and the resulting policy functions evaluated.

These are shown in figure 9.2. Note that there is no adjustment for values of e_{-1} in an interval: the employment policy function coincides with the 45-degree line. Outside of that internal there are two targets: $e^-(A)$ and $e^+(A)$. Again, this policy function is indexed by the values of γ^+ and γ^-. So these parameters can be estimated by matching the implications of the model against observations of employment adjustment at the plant and/or aggregate levels. We will return to this point below.

EXERCISE 9.3 Specify the dynamic programming problem for labor adjustment using a piecewise linear adjustment cost structure. What determines the region of inaction? Study this model numerically by solving the dynamic programming problem and obtaining policy functions.

---

11. This inaction rate is too high relative to observation: the parameterization is for illustration only.

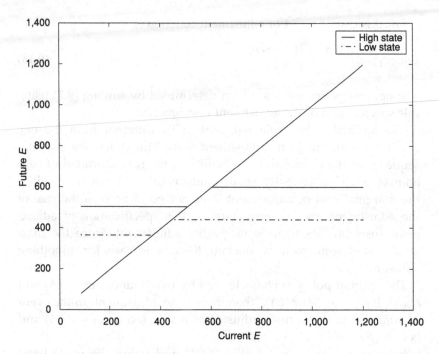

Figure 9.2
Employment policy functions: Piecewise linear adjustment costs

9.4.2 *Nonconvex Adjustment Costs*

The observations of inactivity at the plant level that motivate the piecewise linear specification are also used to motivate consideration of fixed costs in the adjustment process. As noted by Hamermesh and Pfann (1996), the annual recruiting activities of economics departments provide a familiar example of the role of fixed costs. In the United States, hiring requires posting of an advertisement of vacancies, extensive review of material provided by candidates, travel of a recruiting team to a convention site, interviews of leading candidates, university visits, and finally a vote to select among the candidates. Clearly, there are fixed cost components to many of these activities that comprise the hiring of new employees.[12]

---

12. This depiction motivates consideration of a search model as the primitive that underlies a model of adjustment costs. See the discussion of Yashiv (2000) in chapter 10.

As a formal model of this, consider

$$V(A, e_{-1}) = \max[V^a(A, e_{-1}), V^n(A, e_{-1})] \quad \text{for all } (A, e_{-1}), \quad (9.14)$$

where $V^a(A, e_{-1})$ represents the value of adjusting employment and $V^n(A, e_{-1})$ represents the value of not adjusting employment. These are given by

$$V^a(A, e_{-1}) = \max_{h, e} \ R(A, e, h) - \omega(e, h) - F + \beta E_{A'|A} V(A', e), \quad (9.15)$$

$$V^n(A, e_{-1}) = \max_{h} \ R(A, e_{-1}, h) - \omega(e_{-1}, h) + \beta E_{A'|A} V(A', e_{-1}). \quad (9.16)$$

In this specification the firm can either adjust the number of employees or not. These two options are labeled action ($V^a(A, e_{-1})$) and inaction ($V^n(A, e_{-1})$). In either case, hours are assumed to be freely adjusted and thus will respond to variations in profitability even if there is no adjustment in the number of workers. Note too that this specification assumes adjustment costs depend on gross changes in the number of workers. In this way the model can potentially match the inaction in employment adjustment at the plant level defined by zero changes in the number of workers.

The optimal policy has three dimensions. First, there is the choice of whether to adjust or not. Let $z(A, e_{-1}) \in \{0, 1\}$ indicate this choice where $z(A, e_{-1}) = 1$ if and only if there is adjustment. Second, there is the choice of employment in the event of adjustment. Let $\phi(A, e_{-1})$ denote that choice where $\phi(A, e_{-1}) = e_{-1}$ if $z(A, e_{-1}) = 0$. Finally, there is the choice of hours, $h(A, e_{-1})$, which will reflect the decision of the firm whether or not to adjust employment. As these employment adjustments depend on (A, e_{-1}) through $e = \phi(A, e_{-1})$, one can always consider hours to be a function of the state vector alone.

There are some rich trade-offs between hours and employment variations embedded in this model. Suppose that there is a positive shock to profitability: A rises. If this variation is large and permanent, then the optimal response of the firm will be to adjust employment. Hours will vary only slightly. If the shock to profitability is not large or permanent enough to trigger adjustment, then by definition, employment will remain fixed. In that case the main variation will be in worker hours.

These variations in hours and employment are shown in figure 9.3. The policy functions underlying this figure were created using a

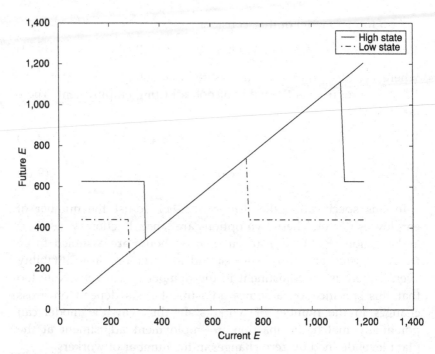

Figure 9.3
Employment policy functions: Nonconvex adjustment costs

baseline parameters with fixed costs at 0.1 of the steady state profits.[13]

EXERCISE 9.4   Specify the dynamic programming problem for labor adjustment using a nonconvex adjustment cost structure. What determines the frequency of inaction? What comovement of hours and employment is predicted by the model? What features of the policy functions distinguish this model from the one with piecewise linear adjustment costs? Study this model numerically by solving the dynamic programming problem and obtaining policy functions.

9.4.3   Asymmetries

As discussed in Hamermesh and Pfann (1996), there is certainly evidence in favor of asymmetries in the adjustment costs. For example,

---

13. At this level of fixed costs, there is about 50 percent employment inaction. Again, the parameterization is just for illustration.

there may be a cost of advertising and evaluation that is proportional to the number of workers hired but no costs of firing workers. Alternatively, it may be of interest to evaluate the effects of firing costs on hiring policies as discussed in the context of some European economies.

It is relatively straightforward to introduce asymmetries into the model. Given the approach to obtaining policy functions by solving (9.1) through a value function iteration routine, asymmetries do not present any additional difficulties. As with the other parameterizations of adjustment costs, these model can be estimated using a variety of techniques. Pfann and Palm (1993) provide a nice example of this approach. They specify an adjustment cost function of

$$C(e, e_{-1}) = -1 + e^{\gamma \Delta e} - \gamma \Delta e + \frac{1}{2}\eta(\Delta e)^2, \tag{9.17}$$

where $\Delta e \equiv (e - e_{-1})$. If $\gamma \equiv 0$, then this reduces to (9.2) with $q = 0$.

As Pfann and Palm (1993) illustrate, the asymmetry in adjustment costs is controlled by γ. For example, if $\gamma < 0$, then firing costs exceed hiring costs.

Using this model of adjustment costs, Pfann and Palm (1993) estimate parameters using a GMM approach on data for manufacturing in the Netherlands (quarterly, seasonally unadjusted data, 1971.I–1984.IV) and annual data for U.K. manufacturing. They have data on both production and nonproduction workers, and the employment choices are interdependent, given the production function.

For both countries they find evidence of the standard quadratic adjustment cost model: η is positive and significantly different from zero for both types of workers. Moreover there is evidence of asymmetry. They report that the costs of firing production workers are lower than the hiring costs. But, the opposite is true for nonproduction workers.

9.5 The Gap Approach

The work in Caballero and Engel (1993b) and Caballero et al. (1997) pursues an alternative approach to studying dynamic labor adjustment. Instead of solving an explicit dynamic optimization problem, they postulate that labor adjustment will respond to a gap between the actual and desired employment level at a plant. They then test for nonlinearities in this relationship.

The theme of creating an employment target to define an employment gap as a proxy for the current state is quite intuitive and powerful. As noted in our discussion of nonconvex adjustment costs, when a firm is hit by a profitability shock, a gap naturally emerges between the current level of employment and the level of employment the firm would choose if there were no costs of adjustment. This gap should then be a good proxy for the gains to adjustment. These gains, of course, are then compared to the costs of adjustment, which depend on the specification of the adjustment cost function. This section studies some attempts to characterize the nature of adjustment costs using this approach.[14]

The power of the gap approach is the simplification of the dynamic optimization problem as the target level of employment summarizes the current state. However, as we will see, these gains may be difficult to realize. The problem arises from the fact that the target level of employment, and thus the gap, is not observable to the researcher.

To understand this approach, it is useful to begin with a discussion of the partial adjustment model. We then return to evidence on adjustment costs from this approach.

9.5.1 Partial Adjustment Model

Researchers often specify a partial adjustment model in which the firm is assumed to adjust the level of employment to a target.[15] The assumed model of labor adjustment would be

$$e_t - e_{t-1} = \lambda(e^* - e_{t-1}). \tag{9.18}$$

So here the change in employment $e_t - e_{t-1}$ is proportional to the difference between the previous level of employment and a target, e^*, where λ parameterizes how quickly the gap is closed.

Where does this partial adjustment structure come from? What does the target represent? Cooper and Willis (2001) consider a dynamic programming problem given by

$$\mathscr{L}(e^*, e_{-1}) = \min_e \frac{(e - e^*)^2}{2} + \frac{\kappa}{2}(e - e_{-1})^2 + \beta E_{e^{*\prime}\,|\,e^*}\mathscr{L}(e^{*\prime}, e), \tag{9.19}$$

---

14. This presentation draws heavily on Cooper and Willis (2001). We are grateful to John Haltiwanger and Jon Willis for helpful discussions on this topic.
15. The structure is used to study adjustment of capital as well.

where the loss depends on the gap between the current stock of workers (e) and the target (e^*). The target is taken as an exogenous process, though in general it reflects the underlying shocks to profitability that are explicit in the optimizing model. In particular, suppose that e^* follows an AR(1) process with serial correlation of ρ. Further assume that there are quadratic adjustment costs, parameterized by κ.

The first-order condition to the optimization problem is

$$(e - e^*) + \kappa(e - e_{-1}) - \beta\kappa E(e' - e) = 0, \tag{9.20}$$

where the last term was obtained from using (9.19) to solve for $\partial\mathscr{L}/\partial e$. Given that the problem is quadratic, it is natural to conjecture a policy function in which the control variable (e) is linearly related to the two elements of the state vector (e^*, e_{-1}):

$$e = \lambda_1 e^* + \lambda_2 e_{-1}. \tag{9.21}$$

Using this conjecture in (9.20) and taking expectations of the future value of e^* yields

$$(e - e^*) + \kappa(e - e_{-1}) - \beta\kappa(\lambda_1 \rho e^* + (\lambda_2 - 1)e) = 0. \tag{9.22}$$

This can be used to solve for e as a linear function of (e^*, e_{-1}) with coefficients given by

$$\lambda_1 = \frac{1 + \beta\kappa\lambda_1\rho}{1 + \kappa - \beta\kappa(\lambda_2 - 1)} \tag{9.23}$$

and

$$\lambda_2 = \frac{\kappa}{(1 + \kappa - \beta\kappa(\lambda_2 - 1))}. \tag{9.24}$$

Clearly, if the shocks follow a random walk ($\rho = 1$), then partial adjustment is optimal ($\lambda_1 + \lambda_2 = 1$). Otherwise, the optimal policy created by minimization of the quadratic loss is linear but does not dictate partial adjustment.

9.5.2   Measuring the Target and the Gap

Taking this type of model directly to the data is problematic as the target e^* is not observable. In the literature (e.g., see the discussion in Caballero and Engel 1993b) the target is intended to represent the destination of the adjustment process. There are two representations of the target.

One, termed a *static* target, treats e^* as the solution of a static optimization problem, as if adjustment costs did not exist. Thus e^* solves (9.5) with $\eta \equiv 0$ and hours set optimally.

A second approach treats e^* as the level of employment that the firm would choose if there were no adjustment costs for a single period. This is termed the *frictionless* target. This level of employment solves $e = \phi(A, e)$, where $\phi(A, e_{-1})$ is the policy function for employment for the quadratic adjustment cost model. Thus the target is the level of employment where the policy function, contingent on the profitability shock, crosses the 45-degree line as in figure 9.1.

Following Caballero et al. (1997), define the gap as the difference between desired $(e^*_{i,t})$ and actual employment levels (in logs):

$$\tilde{z}_{i,t} \equiv e^*_{i,t} - e_{i,t-1}. \tag{9.25}$$

Here $e_{i,t-1}$ is number of workers inherited from the previous period. So $\tilde{z}_{i,t}$ measures the gap between the desired and actual levels of employment in period t, prior to any adjustments, but after any relevant period t random variables are realized as these shocks are embedded in the target and thus the gap.

The policy function for the firm is assumed to be[16]

$$\Delta e_{i,t} = \phi(\tilde{z}_{i,t}). \tag{9.26}$$

The key of the empirical work is to estimate the function $\phi(\cdot)$.

Unfortunately, estimation of (9.26) is not feasible as the target, and thus the gap are not observable. So the basic theory must be augmented with a technique to measure the gap. There are two approaches in the literature corresponding to the two notions of a target level of employment, described earlier.

Caballero et al. (1997) pursue the theme of a frictionless target. To implement this, they postulate a second relationship between another (closely related) measure of the gap, $(\tilde{z}^1_{i,t})$ and plant-specific deviations in hours:

$$\tilde{z}^1_{i,t} = \theta(h_{i,t} - \bar{h}). \tag{9.27}$$

Here $\tilde{z}^1_{i,t}$ is the gap in period t after adjustments in the level of e have been made: $\tilde{z}^1_{i,t} = \tilde{z}_{i,t} - \Delta e_{i,t}$.

---

16. Based on discussions above, the policy function of the firm should depend jointly on (A, e_{-1}) and not on the gap alone.

The argument in favor of this approach again returns to our discussion of the choice between employment and hours variation in the presence of adjustment costs. In that case we saw that the firm chose between these two forms of increasing output when profitability rose. Thus, if hours are measured to be above average, this will reflect a gap between actual and desired workers. If there was no cost of adjustment, the firm would choose to hire more workers. But in the presence of these costs the firm maintains a positive gap, and hours worked are above average.

The key to (9.27) is θ. Since the left-hand side of (9.27) is also not observable, the analysis is further amended to generate an estimate of θ. Caballero et al. (1997) estimate θ from

$$\Delta e_{i,t} = \alpha - \theta \Delta h_{i,t} + \varepsilon_{i,t}, \tag{9.28}$$

where the error term includes unobserved changes in the target level of employment $(\Delta e_{i,t}^*)$ as well as measurement error. Caballero et al. (1997) note that the equation may have omitted variable bias as the change in the target may be correlated with changes in hours. From the discussion in Cooper and Willis (2001), this omitted variable bias can be quite important.

Once θ is estimated, Caballero et al. (1997) can construct plant specific gap measures using observed hours variations. In principle, the model of employment adjustment using these gap measures can be estimated from plant-level data. Instead, Caballero et al. (1997) focus on the aggregate time series implications of their model. In particular, the growth rate of aggregate employment is given by

$$\Delta E_t = \int_z z \Phi(z) f_t(z), \tag{9.29}$$

where $\Phi(z)$ is the adjustment rate or hazard function characterizing the fraction of the gap that is closed by employment adjustment. From aggregate data this expression can be used to estimate $\Phi(z)$. As discussed in Caballero et al. (1997), if $\Phi(z)$ is, say, a quadratic, then (9.29) can be expanded implying that employment growth will depend on the first and third moments of the cross-sectional distribution of gaps.

The findings of Caballero et al. (1997) can be summarized as follows:

• Using (9.28), θ is estimated at 1.26.

• The relationship between the average adjustment rate and the gap is nonlinear.

• There is some evidence of inaction in employment adjustment.

• Aggregate employment growth depends on the second moment of the distribution of employment gaps.

In contrast, Caballero and Engel (1993b) do not estimate θ. Instead, they calibrate it from a structural model of static optimization by a firm with market power. In doing so, they are adopting a target that ignores the dynamics of adjustment. From their perspective, the gap is defined using (9.25) where $e_{i,t}^*$ corresponds to the solution of a static optimization problem over both hours and employment without any adjustment costs. They argue that this static target will approximate the frictionless target quite well if shocks are random walks. As with Caballero et al. (1997), once the target is determined, a measure of the gap can be created.

This approach to approximating the dynamic optimization problem is applied extensively because it is so easy to characterize. Further it is a natural extension of the partial adjustment model. But, as argued in Cooper and Willis (2001), the approach may place excessive emphasis on static optimization.[17]

Caballero and Engel (1993b) estimate their model using aggregate observations on net and gross flows for U.S. manufacturing employment. They find that a quadratic hazard specification fits the aggregate data better than the flat hazard specification.

The key point in both of these papers is the rejection of the flat hazard model. Both Caballero et al. (1997) and Caballero and Engel (1993b) argue that the estimates of the hazard function from aggregate data imply that the cross-sectional distribution "matters" for aggregate dynamics. Put differently, both studies reject a flat hazard specification in which a constant fraction of the gap is closed each period.

Given that this evidence is obtained from time series, this implies that the nonconvexities at the plant-level have aggregate implications. This is an important finding in terms of the way macroeconomists build models of labor adjustment.

---

17. This point was made some years ago. Nickell (1978) says: "... the majority of existing models of factor demand simply analyze the optimal adjustment of the firm towards a static equilibrium and it is very difficult to deduce from this anything whatever about optimal behavior when there is no 'equilibrium' to aim at."

To the extent that the flat hazard model is the outcome of a quadratic adjustment cost model, both papers reject that specification in favor of a model that generates some nonlinearities in the adjustment process. But, as these papers do not consider explicit models of adjustment, one cannot infer from these results anything about the underlying adjustment cost structure.

Further, as argued by Cooper and Willis (2001), the methodology of these studies may itself induce the nonlinear relationship between employment adjustment and the gap. Cooper and Willis (2001) construct a model economy with quadratic adjustment costs. They assume that shocks follow a first-order Markov process, with serial correlation less than unity.[18] They find that in using either the Caballero et al. (1997) or Caballero and Engel (1993b) measurements of the gap, the cross-sectional distribution of employment gaps may be significant in a time series regression of employment growth.

9.6 Estimation of a Rich Model of Adjustment Costs

Thus far we have discussed some evidence associated with the quadratic adjustment cost models and provided some insights into the optimal policy functions from more complex adjustment cost models. In this section we go a step further and discuss attempts to evaluate models that may have both convex and nonconvex adjustment costs.

As with other dynamic optimization problems studied in this book, there is, of course, a direct way to estimate the parameters of labor adjustment costs. This requires the specification of a model of adjustment that nests the variety of special cases described above along with a technique to estimate the parameters. In this subsection we outline this approach.[19]

Letting A represent the profitability of a production unit (e.g., a plant), we consider the following dynamic programming problem:

$$V(A, e_{-1}) = \max_{h,e} R(A, e, h) - \omega(e, h, A) - C(A, e_{-1}, e) + \beta E_{A' | A} V(A', e).$$

$$(9.30)$$

---

18. The process is taken from the Cooper and Haltiwanger (2000) study of capital adjustment. As these shocks were measured using static labor first-order condition, Cooper and Willis (2001) study the robustness of their results to variations in these Markov processes.

19. This discussion parallels the approach in Cooper and Haltiwanger (2000).

As above, let

$$R(A,e,h) = A(eh)^{\alpha}, \tag{9.31}$$

where the parameter α is again determined by the shares of capital and labor in the production function as well as the elasticity of demand.

The function $\omega(e,h,A)$ represents total compensation to workers as a function of the number of workers and their average hours. As before, this compensation function could be taken from other studies or perhaps a constant elasticity formulation might be adequate: $w = w_0 + w_1 h^{\varsigma}$.

The costs of adjustment function nests quadratic and nonconvex adjustment costs of changing employment

$$C(A,e_{-1},e) = \begin{cases} F^H + \dfrac{v}{2}\left(\dfrac{e - e_{-1}}{e_{-1}}\right)^2 e_{-1} & \text{if } e > e_{-1}, \\[2mm] F^F + \dfrac{v}{2}\left(\dfrac{e - e_{-1}}{e_{-1}}\right)^2 e_{-1} & \text{if } e < e_{-1}, \end{cases} \tag{9.32}$$

where F^H and F^F represent the respective fixed costs of hiring and firing workers. Note that quadratic adjustment costs are based upon net *not* gross hires. In (9.32), v parameterizes the level of the adjustment cost function. This adjustment cost function yields the following dynamic optimization problem:

$$V(A,e_{-1}) = \max\{V^H(A,e_{-1}), V^F(A,e_{-1}), V^N(A,e_{-1})\} \quad \text{for all } (A,e_{-1}), \tag{9.33}$$

where N refers to the choice of no adjustment of employment. These options are defined by

$$V^H(A,e_{-1}) = \max_{h,e} R(A,e,h) - \omega(e,h,A) - F^H$$

$$- \frac{v}{2}\left(\frac{e - e_{-1}}{e_{-1}}\right)^2 e_{-1} + \beta E_{A'|A} V(A',e) \quad \text{if } e > e_{-1},$$

$$V^F(A,e_{-1}) = \max_{h,e} R(A,e,h) - \omega(e,h,A) - F^F$$

$$- \frac{v}{2}\left(\frac{e - e_{-1}}{e_{-1}}\right)^2 e_{-1} + \beta E_{A'|A} V(A',e) \quad \text{if } e < e_{-1},$$

$$V^N(A,e_{-1}) = \max_{h} R(A,e_{-1},h) - \omega(e_{-1},h,A) + \beta E_{A'|A} V(A',e_{-1}).$$

Problem (9.33) looks formidable. It contains both an extensive (adjustment or no adjustment) as well an an intensive (the choice of e, given adjustment) margin. Further there is no simple Euler equation to study given the nonconvex adjustment costs.[20]

But, given the methodology of this book, attacking a problem like this is feasible. In fact one could build additional features into this model, such as allowing for a piecewise linear adjustment cost a structure.[21]

From our previous discussion, we know that "solving" a model with this complexity is relatively straightforward. Let Θ represent the vector of parameters necessary to solve the model.[22] Then, for a given value of this vector, a value function iteration procedure will generate a solution to (9.30).

Once a solution to the functional equation is obtained, then policy functions can be easily created. Figure 9.4 produces a policy function for the case of $\eta = 1$ and $F^F = F^H = 0.01$.

One can obtain correlations from a simulated panel. For this parameterization, some moments of interest are: $\text{corr}(e, A) = 0.856$; $\text{corr}(h, A) = 0.839$, and $\text{corr}(e, h) = 0.461$. Clearly, employment and hours adjustments are both positively related to the shock. Further we find that the correlation of hours and employment is positive indicating that the adjustment toward a target, in which the correlation is negative, is offset by the joint response of these variables to a shock.

Computation of these moments for a given Θ opens the door to estimation. If these moments can be computed for a given Θ, then:

• It is easy to compute other moments (including regression coefficients).

• It is easy to find a value of Θ to bring the actual and simulated moments close together.

The techniques of this book are then easily applied to a study of labor market dynamics using either panel or time series data.[23] Of course, this exercise may be even more interesting using data from

---

20. However, see the discussion of Aguirregabiria (1997) for progress in this direction.
21. Of course, it then becomes a question of identification: Can one distinguish between the nonconvex and piecewise linear models.
22. Note that Θ would include the parameters of the stochastic processes.
23. This is the goal of an ongoing project.

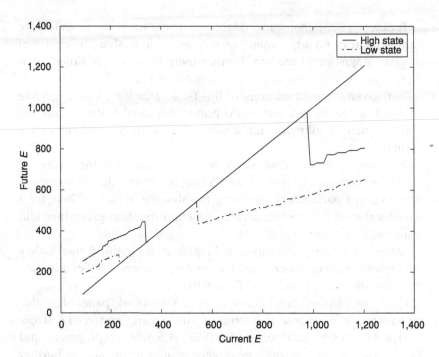

Figure 9.4
Employment policy functions: Mixed adjustment costs

countries other than the US who, through institutional constraints, have richer adjustment costs.

9.7 Conclusion

This point of this chapter has been to explore the dynamics of labor adjustment. In the presence of adjustment costs, the conventional model of static labor demand is replaced by a possibly complex dynamic optimization problem. Solving these problems and estimating parameters using either plant-level or aggregate observations is certainly feasible using the techniques developed in this book.

In terms of policy implications, governments often impose restrictions on employment and hours. The dynamic optimization framework facilitates the analysis of those interventions.[24] Further

---

24. In some cases a more general equilibrium approach is needed to assess the complete implications of the policy.

these policies (such as restrictions on hours and/or the introduction of firing costs) may provide an opportunity to infer key structural parameters characterizing labor adjustment costs.[25]

25. This suggestion is along the lines of the so-called natural experimental approach to estimation where the researcher searches for "exogenous" events that may allow for the identification of key parameters. Evaluating this approach in the context of structural model is an exercise of some interest.

10   Future Developments

10.1   Overview and Motivation

This final section of this book covers an assortment of additional topics. These represent active areas of research which utilize the approach of this book. In some cases the research is not yet that far along. Examples of this would include ongoing work on the integration of pricing and inventory problems or the joint evolution of capital and labor. In a second category are search models of the labor market that illustrate the usefulness of empirical work on dynamic programming, though generally these models are not part of standard courses in applied macroeconomics.

Consequently the presentation is different than other chapters. Here we focus mainly on the statement of coherent dynamic optimization problems and properties of policy functions. To the extent that there are empirical studies, we summarize them.

10.2   Price Setting

We begin with a very important problem in macroeconomics, the determination of prices. For this discussion we do not rely on the Walrasian auctioneer to miraculously set prices. Instead, we allow firms to set prices and study this interaction in a monopolistic competition setting.[1]

The natural specification includes a fixed cost of adjusting prices so that the firm optimally chooses between adjusting or not. Hence

---

1. Early formulations of the framework we discuss include Benassy (1982), Blanchard and Kiyotaki (1987), Caballero and Engel (1993a), Caplin and Leahy (1991) and Caplin and Leahy (1997).

we term this the state-dependent pricing model. These have been most recently termed *menu cost* models in the literature to highlight the fact that a leading parable of the model is one where a seller finds it costly to literally change the posted price. In fact this terminology is somewhat unfortunate as it tends to trivialize the problem. Instead, it is best to view these costs as representing a wide range of sources of frictions in the pricing of goods.

Besides presenting a basic optimization problem, this section summarizes two empirical exercises. The first reports on an attempt to use indirect inference to estimate the cost of price adjustment for magazine prices. The second is a study of the aggregate implications of state dependent pricing.

10.2.1 Optimization Problem

Consider a dynamic optimization problem at the firm level where, by assumption, prices are costly to adjust. The firm has some market power, represented by a downward-sloping demand curve. This demand curve may shift around so that the price the firm would set in the absence of adjustment costs is stochastic. The question is: How, in the presence of adjustment costs, do firms behave?

Suppose, to be concrete, that product demand comes from the CES (constant elasticity of substitution) specification of utility so that the demand for product i is given by

$$q_i^d(p, D, P) = \left(\frac{p}{P}\right)^{-\gamma} \frac{D}{P}.$$

(10.1)

Here all variables are nominal. The price of product i is p while the general price level is P. Finally, nominal spending, taken to be exogenous and stochastic, is denoted D.

Given this specification of demand and the realized state, (p, D, P), the firm's real profits are

$$\pi(p, D, P) = q_i^d(p, D, P) \frac{p}{P} - c(q_i^d(p, D, P)),$$

(10.2)

where $c(\cdot)$ is assumed to be a strictly increasing and strictly convex function of output.

The dynamic optimization problem of the firm, taking the current values and evolution of (D, P) as given, is

$$V(p,D,P,F) = \max\{V^a(p,D,P,F), V^n(p,D,P,F)\} \quad \text{for all } (p,D,P,F),$$

$$(10.3)$$

where

$$V^a(p,D,P,F) = \max_{\tilde{p}} \; \pi(\tilde{p},D,P) - F + \beta E_{(D',P',F'\,|\,D,P,F)} V(\tilde{p},D',P',F'),$$

$$(10.4)$$

$$V^n(p,D,P,F) = \pi(p,D,P) + \beta E_{(D',P',F'\,|\,D,P,F)} V(p,D',P',F').$$

$$(10.5)$$

Here the state vector is (p,D,P,F). The cost of changing a price is F. It enters the state vector, since in this specification we allow this adjustment cost to be stochastic.[2]

The firm has two options. If the firm does not change its price, it enjoys a profit flow, avoids adjustment costs, and then, in the next period, has the same nominal price. Of course, if the aggregate price level changes ($P \neq P'$), then the firm's relative price will change over time. Note that the cost here is associated with adjustment of the nominal price.

Alternatively, the firm can pay the menu cost F and adjust its price to $\tilde{p}$. This price change becomes effective immediately so that the profit flow given adjustment is $\pi(\tilde{p},D,P)$. This price then becomes part of the state vector for the next period.

The policy function for this problem will have two components. First, there is a discrete component indicating whether or not price adjustment will take place. Second, conditional on adjustment, there is the policy function characterizing the dependence of $\tilde{p}$ on the state vector (D,P,F). Interestingly the choice of $\tilde{p}$ is independent of p once the decision to adjust has been made.

There is a very important difference between this optimization problem and most of the others studied in this book. From (10.3) we know that the choice at the individual firm level depends on the choices of other firms, summarized by P. Thus, given the specification of demand, the behavior of a single firm must depend on the behavior of other firms.[3] This feature opens up a number of alternative ways of solving the model.

As a starting point, one might characterize the exogenous evolution of P, perhaps through a regression model, and impose this in the

2. This is similar to the stochastic adjustment cost structure used by Rust (1987).
3. As discussed, for example, in Blanchard and Kiyotaki (1987), there is a complementarity that naturally arises in the pricing decisions in this environment.

optimization problem of the firm.[4] In this case the individual optimizer is simply using an empirical model of the evolution of P.

By this approach, there is no guarantee that the aggregate evolution of P assumed by the individual agent actually accords with the aggregated behavior of these agents. This suggests a second approach in which this consistency between the beliefs of agents and their aggregate actions is imposed on the model. Essentially this amounts to the following steps:

1. Solve (10.3) given a transition equation for P.

2. Use the resulting policy functions to solve for the predicted evolution of P.

3. Stop if these functions are essentially the same.

4. Iterate if they are not.

There is a point of caution here. For the dynamic programming problem we can rely on the contraction mapping property to guarantee that the value function iteration process will find the unique solution to the functional equation. We have no such theorem to guide us in the iterative procedure described above. Consequently finding an equilibrium may be difficult, and further there is no reason to suspect that the equilibrium is unique.[5]

10.2.2 Evidence on Magazine Prices

Willis (2000a) studies the determination of magazine price adjustment using a data set initially used by Cecchetti (1986). The idea is to use data on the frequency and magnitude of magazine price adjustment to estimate a dynamic menu cost model.[6]

Willis postulates a theory model similar to that given above. For the empirical analysis, he specifies an auxiliary equation in which the probability of price adjustment is assumed to depend on the following:

---

4. This may entail adding additional elements to the state space; see Adda and Cooper (2000a) and Willis (2000a) for discussions of this point.

5. Ball and Romer (1990) provide an example. John and Wolman (1999) study these issues in a dynamic setting of price adjustment.

6. The contribution here is bringing the dynamic menu cost model to the data. Bils and Klenow (2002) provide further evidence on price-setting behavior based on BLS price data.

• Number of years since the last price adjustment.
• Cumulative inflation since the last price adjustment.
• Cumulative growth in industry demand since the last price adjustment.
• Current inflation.
• Current industry demand.

This specification is partly chosen as it mimics some of the key elements of the specification in Cecchetti (1986). Further the cumulative inflation and demand since the last price change are, from the dynamic programming problem, key elements in the incentive to adjust prices. Interestingly there seems to be little support for any time dependence, given the presence of the proxies for the state variables.

Willis estimates this auxiliary model and then uses it, through an indirect inference procedure, to estimate the structural parameters of his model. These parameters include the following:

• The curvature of the profit function.
• The curvature of the cost function.
• The distribution of menu costs.

Willis (2000a) finds that magazine sellers have a significant amount of market power but that production is essentially constant returns to scale. Finally, Willis is able the distinguish the average adjustment cost in the distribution from the average that is actually paid. He finds that the former is about 35 percent of revenues, while the latter is only about 4 percent of revenues.[7]

10.2.3   Aggregate Implications

A large part of the motivation for studying models with some form of price rigidity reflects the arguments, advanced by macroeconomists, that inflexible prices are a source of aggregate inefficiency. Further rigidity of prices and/or wages provides a basis for the nonneutrality of money, thus generating a link between the stock

---

7. For this specification there is assumed to be no serial correlation in the adjustment costs. See Willis (2000a) for further discussion of this point and for estimates that relax this restriction.

of nominal money and real economic activity. But these arguments rest on the presence of quantitatively relevant rigidities at the level of individual sellers. Can these costs of adjusting prices "explain" observations at both the microeconomic and aggregate levels?

One approach to studying these issues is to model the pricing behavior of sellers in a particular industry. This estimated model can then be aggregated to study the effects of, say, money on output. An alternative, more aggregate approach is to specify and estimate a macroeconomic model with price rigidities.

At this point, while the estimation of such a model is not complete, there is some progress. A recent paper by Dotsey et al. (1999) studies the quantitative implications of state-dependent pricing for aggregate variables. We summarize those results here.

The economy studied by Dotsey et al. (1999) has a number of key elements:

• As in Blanchard and Kiyotaki (1987), the model is based on monopolistic competition between producers of final goods.
• Sellers face a (stochastic) iid fixed cost of adjusting their price (expressed in terms of labor time).
• Sellers meet all demand forthcoming at their current price.
• There is an exogenously specified demand for money.

At the individual level, firms solve a version of (10.3) where the cost of adjustment F is assumed to be iid. Further heterogeneity across firms is restricted to two dimensions, (F, p). That is, firms may be in different states because they began the period with a different price or because their price adjustment cost for that period is different from that of other firms. There is a very important consequence of this restricted form of heterogeneity: if two firms choose to adjust, they select the same price.

Interestingly Dotsey et al. (1999) solve the dynamic optimization problem of a firm by using a first-order condition. This is somewhat surprising as we have not used first-order conditions to characterize the solutions to dynamic discrete choice problems. Consider the choice of a price by a firm conditional on adjustment, as in (10.4). The firm optimally sets the price taking into account the effects on current profits and on the future value.

In the price-setting model the price only effects the future value if the firm elects not to adjust in the next period. If the firm adjusts its price in the next period, as in (10.4), then the value of the price at the start of the period is irrelevant.

So there is a first-order condition that weighs the effects of the price on current profits and on future values along the no-adjustment branch of the value function. As long as the value function of the firm along this branch is differentiable in $\tilde{p}$, there will be a first-order condition characterizing this optimal choice given by

$$\frac{\partial \pi(\tilde{p}, D, P)}{\partial p} + \frac{\beta G(F^*) E_{(D', P', F' \mid D, P, F)} \partial V^n(\tilde{p}, D', P', F')}{\partial p} = 0, \qquad (10.6)$$

where $G(F^*)$ is the state contingent probability of not adjusting in the next period.

This is not quite an Euler equation as the derivative of the future value remains in this expression. Dotsey et al. iterate this condition forward, and using a restriction that the firm eventually adjusts, they find that derivatives of the primitive profit function can substitute for $\partial V^n(\tilde{p}, D', P', F') / \partial p$.[8]

The solution of the optimization problem and the equilibrium analysis relies on a discrete representation of the possible states of the firms. Given a value of p, there will exist a critical adjustment cost such that sellers adjust if and only if the realized value of F is less than this critical level. So, given the state of the system, there is an endogenously determined probability of adjustment for each seller. Dotsey et al. (1999) use this discrete representation, these endogenous probabilities of adjustment, and the (common) price charged by sellers who adjust to characterize the equilibrium evolution of their model economy.

Details on computing an equilibrium are provided in Dotsey et al. (1999). They find the effects of money on output as follows:

• If the inflation rate is constant at 10 percent, then prices are adjusted at least once every five quarters.

• Comparing different constant inflation rate regimes, the higher the inflation rate, the shorter is the average time to adjustment, and the markup only increases slightly.

---

8. In principle, one could use this condition for estimation of some parameters of the model taking orthogonality conditions as moments. See the discussion of this point by Pakes (1994) and Aguirregabiria (1997), where the latter paper includes a labor example.

• An unanticipated, permanent monetary expansion leads to higher prices and higher output at impact, and there is some persistence in the output effects.

• As the money shocks become less persistent, the price response dampens and consequently the output effect is larger.

This discussion of the aggregate implications of monetary shocks in an environment with state-dependent prices nicely complements our earlier discussion of the estimation of a state-dependent pricing model using micro data. Clearly, there is an open issue here concerning the estimation of a state-dependent pricing model using aggregate data.[9]

10.3 Optimal Inventory Policy

The models we have studied thus far miss an important element of firm behavior, the holding of inventories. This is somewhat ironic as the optimal inventory problem was one of the earlier dynamic optimization problems studied in economics.[10]

We begin with a traditional model of inventories in which a seller with a convex cost function uses inventories to smooth production when demand is stochastic. We then turn to models which include nonconvexities. The section ends with a brief discussion of a model with dynamic choices over prices and inventories.

10.3.1 Inventories and the Production-Smoothing Model

The basic production smoothing argument for the holding of inventories rests on the assumption that the marginal cost of production is increasing. In the face of fluctuating demand, the firm would then profit by smoothing production relative to sales. This requires the firm to build inventories in periods of low demand and to liquidate them in periods of high demand.

Formally, consider

$$V(s, I) = \max_y r(s) - c(y) + \beta E_{s'|s} V(s', I') \qquad \text{for all } (s, I). \qquad (10.7)$$

---

9. The findings of Dotsey et al. (1999) are based on a parameterization of the adjustment cost distribution and the other assumptions noted above. Whether these properties obtain in an estimated model is an open issue. See Willis (2000b) for progress on this issue.

10. See the discussion in Arrow et al. (1951) and the references therein.

Here the state vector is the level of sales s and the stock of inventories at the start of the period, I. The level of sales is assumed to be random and outside of the firm's control. From sales, the firm earns revenues of $r(s)$. The firm chooses its level of production (y) where $c(y)$ is a strictly increasing, strictly convex cost function. Inventories at the start of the next period are given by a transition equation

$$I' = R(I + y - s), \tag{10.8}$$

where R is the return on a marginal unit of inventory (which may be less than unity).[11] From this problem, a necessary condition for optimality is

$$c'(y) = \beta R E_{s'|s} c'(y'), \tag{10.9}$$

where future output is stochastic and will generally depend on the sales realization in the next period.

To make clear the idea of production smoothing, suppose that sales follow an iid process: $E_{s'|s} s$ is independent of s. In this case the right-hand side of (10.9) is independent of the current realization of sales. Hence, since (10.9) must hold for all s, the left-hand side must be constant too. Since production costs are assumed to be strictly convex, this implies that y must be independent of s.

EXERCISE 10.1   Solve (10.7) using a value function iteration routine (or another for comparison purposes). Under what conditions will the variance of production be less than the variance of sales?

Despite its appeal, the implications of the production smoothing model contrast sharply with observation. In particular, the model's prediction that production will be smoother than sales, but the data do not exhibit such production smoothing.[12]

One response to this difference between the model's predictions and observation is to introduce other shocks into the problem to increase the variability of production. A natural candidate would be variations in productivity or the costs of production. Letting A denote a productivity shock, consider

11. Taken literally R in excess of unity means that inventories accumulate on their own, which may seem odd. The literature is much more explicit about various marginal gains to holding inventories. If R is less than unity, than output will be independent of the state but will be rising over time. This policy may require negative inventories, an issue we address below.

12. See Blinder (1986), Blinder and Maccini (1991), and the references therein, for the extensive literature on these points.

$$V(s,I,A) = \max_y r(s) - c(y,A) + \beta E_{A',s'|A,s} V(s',I',A') \tag{10.10}$$

so that the cost of producing y units is stochastic. In this case, (10.9) becomes

$$c_y(y,A) = \beta RE_{A',s'|A,s} c_y(y',A'). \tag{10.11}$$

In this case inventories are used so that goods can be produced during periods of relatively low cost and, in the absence of demand variations, sold smoothly over time.[13]

Kahn (1987) studies a model of stock-out avoidance. Note that in (10.7), the seller was allowed to hold negative inventories. As discussed in Kahn (1987), some researchers add a nonnegativity constraint to the inventory problem, while others are more explicit about a cost of being away from a target level of inventories (e.g., a fraction of sales). Kahn (1987) finds that even without a strictly convex cost function, the nonnegativity constraint alone can increase the volatility of output relative to sales.

EXERCISE 10.2   Solve (10.10) using a value function iteration routine (or another for comparison purposes). Under what conditions on the variance of the two types of shocks and on the cost function will the variance of production be less than the variance of sales? Supplement the model with a nonnegativity constraint on inventories and/ or an explicit target level of investment. Explore the relationship between the variance of sales and the variance of output.

Alternatively, researchers have introduced nonconvexities into this problem. One approach, as in Cooper and Haltiwanger (1992), is to introduce production bunching due to the fixed costs of a production run. For that model consider a version of (10.7) where the cost of production is given by

$$c(y) = \begin{cases} 0 & \text{for } y = 0, \\ K + ay & \text{for } y \in (0, Y], \\ \infty & \text{otherwise.} \end{cases} \tag{10.12}$$

Here Y represents the total output produced if there is a production run. It represents a capacity constraint on the existing capital. Production is naturally more volatile than sales as the firm has an

---

13. See, for example, the discussion in Blinder (1986), Eichenbaum (1989), and Christiano (1988).

incentive to have a large production run and then to sell from inventories until the next burst of production.[14]

Further, the original inventory models that gave rise to the development of the (S, s) literature were based on a fixed cost of ordering.[15] One dynamic stochastic formalization of the models discussed in Arrow et al. (1951) might be

$$v(x, y) = \max\{v^o(x, y), v^n(x, y)\}, \tag{10.13}$$

where x measures the state of demand and y the inventories on hand at the sales site. The optimizer has two options: to order new goods for inventory (v^o) or not (v^n). These options are defined as

$$v^o(x, y) = \max_q r(s) - c(q) - K + \beta E_{x'|x} v(x', (y - s + q)(1 - \delta)) \tag{10.14}$$

and

$$v^n(x, y) = r(s) + \beta E_{x'|x} v(x', (y - s)(1 - \delta)). \tag{10.15}$$

Here s is a measure of sales and is given as the maximum of (x, y): demand can only be met from inventories on hand. The function $r(s)$ is simply the revenues earned from selling s units.

If the firm orders new inventories, it incurs a fixed cost of K and pays $c(q)$, an increasing and convex function, to obtain q units. In the case of ordering new goods, the inventories in the next period reflect the sales and the new orders. The rate of inventory depreciation is given by δ.

If the firm does not order inventories, then its inventories in the following period are the depreciated level of initial inventories less sales. This is zero as the firm stocks out.

This problem, which is similar to the stochastic investment problem with nonconvex adjustment costs, can be easily solved numerically. It combines a discrete choice along with a continuous decision given that the firm decides to order new goods.[16]

---

14. Hall (2000) studies a model of production scheduling using data on automobile assembly plants and finds some support for hypothesis that nonconvexities in the production process lie behind the observations on the relative volatility of production and sales.

15. See Scarf (1959) for developments of this argument.

16. Hall and Rust (2000) examine a model of optimal inventory behavior in an environment where there is a fixed ordering cost with a stochastic product price. They argue that a calibrated version of their model fits important aspects of their data from a U.S. steel wholesaler.

10.3.2   Prices and Inventory Adjustment

Thus far we have treated pricing problems and inventory problems separately. So, in the model of costly price adjustment, sellers had no inventories. In the inventory models, sales are usually taken as given. Yet there is good reason to think jointly about pricing decisions and inventories.[17]

First, one of the motivations for the holding of inventories is to smooth production relative to sales. But there is another mechanism for smoothing sales: as its demand fluctuates, the firm (assuming it has some market power) could adjust its price. Yet, if prices are costly to adjust, this may be an expensive mechanism. So the choices of pricing and inventory policies reflect the efficient response of a profit maximizing firm to variations in demand and/or technology.

At one extreme, suppose that the firm can hold inventories and faces a cost of changing its price. In this case the functional equation for the firm is given by

$$V(p, I; S, P) = \max\{V^a(p, I; S, P), V^n(p, I; S, P)\}, \tag{10.16}$$

where

$$V^a(p, I; S, P) = \max_{\tilde{p}} \pi(\tilde{p}, I; S, P) - F + \beta E_{(S', P'|S, P)} V(\tilde{p}, I'; S', P'), \tag{10.17}$$

$$V^n(p, I; S, P) = \pi(p, I; S, P) + \beta E_{(S', P'|S, P)} V(p, I'; S', P'), \tag{10.18}$$

where the transition equation for inventories is again $I' = R(I + y - s)$. In this optimization problem, p is again the price of the seller and I is the stock of inventories. These are both controlled by the firm. The other elements in the state vector, S and P, represent a shock to profits and the general price level respectively. The function $\pi(p, I; S, P)$ represent the flow of profit when the firm charges a price p, holding inventories I when the demand shock is S and the general price level is P.

Here, in contrast to the inventory problems described above, sales are not exogenous. Instead, sales come a stochastic demand function that depends on the firm's price (p) and the price index (P). From this we see that the firm can influence sales by its price adjustment. But, of course, this adjustment is costly so that the firm must balance

---

17. Kahn (1987) includes a period of price predetermination.

meeting fluctuating demand through variations in inventories, variations in production or through price changes. The optimal pattern of adjustment will presumably depend on the driving process of the shocks, the cost of price adjustment and the curvature of the production cost function (underlying $\pi(p, I; S, P)$).

EXERCISE 10.3   A recent literature asserts that technology shocks are negatively correlated with employment in the presence of sticky prices. Use (10.19) to study this issue by interpreting S as a technology shock.

At the other extreme, suppose that new goods are delivered infrequently due to the presence of a fixed ordering cost. In that case the firm will seek other ways to meet fluctuations in demand, such as changing its price. Formally, consider the optimization problem of the seller if there is a fixed cost to ordering and, in contrast to (10.13), prices are endogenous:

$$V(p, I; S, P) = \max\{V^o(p, I; S, P), V^n(p, I; S, P)\}, \tag{10.19}$$

where

$$V^o(p, I; S, P) = \max_{\tilde{p}, q} \pi(\tilde{p}, I; S, P) - K - c(q) + \beta E_{(S', P' \mid S, P)} V(\tilde{p}, I'; S', P'), \tag{10.20}$$

$$V^n(p, I; S, P) = \max_{\tilde{p}} \pi(\tilde{p}, I; S, P) + \beta E_{(S', P' \mid S, P)} V(\tilde{p}, I'; S', P'). \tag{10.21}$$

The transition equation for inventories is again $I' = R(I + q - s)$.

Aguirregabiria (1999) studies a model with menu costs and lump-sum costs of adjusting inventories. This research is partly motivated by the presence of long periods of time in which prices are not adjusted and by observations of sales promotions.

Interestingly the model has predictions for the joint behavior of markups and inventories even if the costs of adjustment are independent. Aguirregabiria (1999) argues that markups will be high when inventories are low. This reflects the effects of stock-outs on the elasticity of sales. Specifically, Aguirregabiria assumes that

$$s = \min(D(p), q + I), \tag{10.22}$$

where, as above, s is sales, q is orders of new goods for inventory, and I is the stock of inventories. Here $D(p)$ represents demand that depends, among other things, on the current price set by the seller.

So, when demand is less than output and the stock of inventories, then sales equal demand and the price elasticity of sales is equal to that of demand. But, when demand exceeds $q + I$, then the elasticity of sales with respect to price is zero: when the stock-out constraint binds, realized "demand" is very inelastic. In the model of Aguirregabiria (1999) the firm chooses its price and the level of inventories prior to the realizations of a demand shock so that stock-outs may occur.

Aguirregabiria (1999) estimates the model using monthly data on a supermarket chain. His initial estimation is of a reduced form model for the choice to adjust prices and/or inventories. In this discrete choice framework he finds an interesting interaction between the adjustments of inventories and prices. The level of inventories are significant in the likelihood of price adjustment: large inventories increases the probability of price adjustment.

Aguirregabiria (1999) estimates a structural model based upon a dynamic programming model.[18] He finds support for the presence of both types of lump-sum adjustment costs. Moreover he argues that the costs of increasing a price appear to exceed the cost of price reductions.

10.4   Capital and Labor

The grand problem we consider here allows for adjustment costs for both labor and capital.[19] Intuitively many of the stories of adjustment costs for one factor have implications for the adjustment of the other. For example, if part of the adjustment cost for capital requires the shutting down of a plant to install new equipment, then this may also be a good time to train new workers. Moreover we observe inaction in the adjustment of both labor and capital and bursts as well. So it seems reasonable to entertain the possibility that both factors are costly to adjust and that the adjustment processes are interdependent.

For this more general dynamic factor demand problem, we assume that the dynamic programming problem for a plant is given by

---

18. The estimation methodology is complex and the reader is urged to study Aguirregabiria (1999).

19. Estimation of this more general structure using plant level data is part of ongoing research of R. Cooper and J. Haltiwanger. See Sakellaris (2001) for some interesting facts concerning the interaction of capital and labor adjustment.

$$V(A, K, L) = \max_{K', L', h} \Pi(A, K, L', h) - \omega(L', h, K, A) - C(A, K, L, K', L')$$

$$+ \beta E_{A'|A} V(A', K', L') \qquad \text{for all } (A, K, L). \qquad (10.23)$$

Here the flow of profits, $\Pi(A, K, L', h)$, depends on the profitability shock A, the predetermined capital stock K, the number of workers L', and the hours workers h. The function $\omega(L', h, K, A)$ represents the total state-dependent compensation paid to workers. Finally, the general adjustment cost function is given by $C(A, K, L, K', L')$.

To allow the model to capture inaction, the adjustment cost function in (10.23) contains convex and nonconvex adjustment costs for both labor and capital. Further one or both of these components might be interactive. So, for example, there may be a fixed cost of adjusting capital that may "cover" any adjustments in labor as well. Or, within the convex piece of the adjustment cost function, there may be some interaction between the factors.

Writing down and analyzing this dynamic optimization problem is by itself not difficult. There are some computational challenges posed by the larger state space. The key is the estimation of the richer set of parameters.

One approach would be to continue in the indirect inference spirit and consider a VAR estimated from plant-level data in, say, hours, employment, and capital. As with the single factor models, we might also include some nonlinearities in the specification. We could use the reduced form parameters as the basis for indirect inference of the structural parameters.

One of the interesting applications of the estimated model will be policy experiments. In particular, the model with both factors will be useful in evaluating the implications of policy that directly influences one factor on the other. So, for example, we can study how restrictions on worker hours might influence the demand for equipment. Or, how do investment tax credits impact on labor demand?

10.5   Technological Complementarities: Equilibrium Analysis

Here we continue discussion of a topic broached in chapter 5 where we studied the stochastic growth model. There we noted that researchers, starting with Bryant (1983) and Baxter and King (1991), introduced interactions across agents through the production function. The model captures, in a tractable way, the theme that high levels of activity by other agents increases the productivity of each agent.[20]

Let y represent the output at a given firm, Y be aggregate output, k and n the firm's input of capital and labor respectively. Consider a production function of

$$y = Ak^{\alpha}n^{\phi}Y^{\gamma}Y_{-1}^{\varepsilon}, \tag{10.24}$$

where A is a productivity shock that is common across producers. Here γ parameterizes the contemporaneous interaction between producers. If γ is positive, then there is a complementarity at work: as other agents produce more, the productivity of the individual agent increases as well. In addition this specification allows for a dynamic interaction as well parameterized by ε, where Y_{-1} is the lagged level of aggregate output. As discussed in Cooper and Johri (1997), this may be interpreted as a dynamic technological complementarity or even as a learning-by-doing effect. This production function can be embedded into a stochastic growth model.

Consider the problem of a representative household with access to a production technology given by (10.24). This is essentially a version of the stochastic growth model with labor but with a different technology.

There are two ways to solve this problem. The first is to write the dynamic programming problem, carefully distinguishing between individual and aggregate variables. As in our discussion of the recursive equilibrium concept, a law of motion must be specified for the evolution of the aggregate variables. Given this law of motion, the individual household's problem is solved and the resulting policy function compared to the one that governs the economywide variables. If these policy functions match, then there is an equilibrium. Else, another law of motion for the aggregate variables is specified and the search continues. This is similar to the approach described above for finding the equilibrium in the state-dependent pricing model.[21]

---

20. This is the underlying theme of the macroeconomic complementarities literature, as in Cooper (1999).

21. In contrast to the contraction mapping theorem, there is no guarantee that this process will converge. In some cases the household's response to an aggregate law of motion can be used as the next guess on the aggregate law of motion. Iteration of this may lead to a recursive equilibrium.

Alternatively, one can use the first-order conditions for the individual's optimization problem. As all agents are identical and all shocks are common, the representative household will accumulate its own capital, supply its own labor, and interact with other agents only due to the technological complementarity. In a symmetric equilibrium, $y_t = Y_t$. As in Baxter and King (1991), this equilibrium condition is neatly imposed through the first-order conditions when the marginal products of labor and capital are calculated. From the set of first-order conditions, the symmetric equilibrium can be analyzed through by approximation around a steady state.

The distinguishing feature of this economy from the traditional real business cycle model is the presence of the technological complementarity parameters, γ and ε. It is possible to estimate these parameters directly from the production function or to infer them from the equilibrium relationships.[22]

10.6   Search Models

This is a very large and active area of research in which the structural approach to individual decision making has found fertile ground. This partly reflects the elegance of the search problem at the individual level, the important policy question surrounding the provision of unemployment insurance and the existence of rich data sets on firms and workers. This subsection will only introduce the problem and briefly touch on empirical methodology and results.

10.6.1   A Simple Labor Search Model

Our starting point is a model in the spirit of McCall (1970).[23] A prospective worker has a job offer, denoted by ω. If this job is accepted, then the worker stays in this job for life and receives a return of $u(\omega)/(1 - \beta)$. Alternatively, the offer can be rejected. In this case the worker can receive unemployment benefits of b for a period and then may draw again from the distribution. Assume that the draws from the wage distribution are iid.[24]

---

22. See Cooper (1999) and the references therein.
23. Interestingly McCall mentions that his paper draws on Stanford notes from a class taught by K. Arrow on the reservation wage property.
24. This model is frequently used for expositional purposes in other presentations of the search process. It can be enriched in many ways by adding fires, quits, and costly search, for example.

The Bellman equation for a worker with a wage offer of ω in hand is

$$v(\omega) = \max\left\{\frac{u(\omega)}{1-\beta}, u(b) + \beta E v(\omega')\right\} \qquad \text{for all } \omega. \tag{10.25}$$

The worker either accepts the job, the first option, or rejects it in favor of taking a draw in the next period.

Given the assumption of iid draws, the return to another draw, $Ev(\omega')$, is just a constant, denoted κ. It is intuitive to think of this functional equation from the perspective of value function iteration. For a given value of κ, (10.25) implies a function $v(\omega)$. Use this to create a new expected value of search and thus a new value for κ. Continue to iterate in this fashion until the process converges.[25]

Clearly, the gain to accepting the job is increasing in ω, while the return associated with rejecting the job and drawing again is independent of ω. Assuming that the lower (upper) support of the wage offer distribution is sufficiently low (high) relative to b, there will exist a critical wage, termed the *reservation wage*, such that the worker is indifferent between accepting and rejecting the job. The reservation wage, w^* is determined from

$$\frac{u(w^*)}{1-\beta} = u(b) + \beta\kappa, \tag{10.26}$$

where

$$\kappa = Ev(w) = \int_{-\infty}^{+\infty} v(w)\, dF(w)$$

$$= F(w^*)(u(b) + \beta\kappa) + \int_{w^*}^{\infty} \frac{u(w)}{1-\beta}\, dF(w). \tag{10.27}$$

For wages below the reservation wage, the value $v(\cdot)$ is constant and independent of w as the individual chooses to stay in unemployment. For wages above w^*, the individual accept the offer and gets the utility of the wage forever.

EXERCISE 10.4   Write a program to solve (10.25) using the approach suggested above.

---

25. Writing a small program to do this would be a useful exercise. Note that this dynamic programming model is close to the discrete cake-eating problem presented in chapters 2 to 4.

10.6.2   Estimation of the Labor Search Model

There is now a large literature on the estimation of these models. Here we focus on estimating the simple model given above and then discuss other parts of the literature.

The theory implies that there exists a reservation wage that depends on the underlying parameters of the search problem: $w^*(\Theta)$.[26] Suppose that the researcher has data on a set of I individuals over T periods. In particular, suppose that an observation for agent i in period t is $z_{it} \in \{0, 1\}$, where $z_{it} = 0$ means that the agent is searching and $z_{it} = 1$ means that the agent has a job. For the purpose of discussion we assume that the model is correct: once an agent has a job, he keeps it forever.

Consider then the record for agent i who, say, accepted a job in period $k + 1$. According to the model, the likelihood of this is

$$F(w^*)^k (1 - F(w^*)). \tag{10.28}$$

The likelihood function for this problem is equivalent to the coin-flipping example that we introduced in chapter 4. There we saw that the likelihood function would provide a way to estimate the probability of "heads" but would not allow the researcher to identify the parameters that jointly determine this probability.

The same point is true for the search problem. Using (10.28) for all agents in the sample, we can represent the likelihood of observing the various durations of search. But, in the end, the likelihood will only depend on the vector Θ through w^*.

Wolpin (1987) estimates a version of this search model with a finite horizon and costly search. This implies, among other things, that the reservation wage is not constant as the problem is no longer stationary. Instead, he argues that the reservation wage falls over time.[27] This time variation in the reservation wage is useful for identification since it creates time variation in the acceptance probability for given Θ.

Wolpin (1987) also assumes that agents receive an offer each period with a probability less than one. In order to estimate the model, he specifies a function for the likelihood an agent receives an

---

26. Here Θ would include the parameters for the individual agent (e.g., those characterizing $u(w)$ as well as β) and the parameters of the wage distribution.
27. Sometimes unobserved heterogeneity is added to create the same effect.

offer in a given period. This probability is allowed to depend on the duration of unemployment.

Wolpin uses data on both duration to employment and accepted wages. The addition of wage data is interesting for a couple of reasons. First, the lowest accepted wage yields an upper bound on the reservation wage. Second, the researcher generally observes the accepted wage but not the offered wage. Thus there is an interesting problem of deducing the wage distribution from data on accepted wages.

Wolpin (1987) estimates the model using a panel from the 1979 NLS youth cohort. In doing so, he allows for measurement error in the wage and also specifies a distribution for wage offers. Among other things, he finds that a log-normal distribution of wages fits better than a normal distribution. Further the estimated hazard function (giving the likelihood of accepting a job after j periods of search) mimics the negative slope of that found in the data.

10.6.3   Extensions

Of course, much has been accomplished in the search literature over the recent years. This includes introducing equilibrium aspects to the problem so that the wage distribution is not completely exogenous. Other contributions introduce bargaining and search intensity, such as in Eckstein and Wolpin (1995). Postel-Vinay and Robin (2002) develop an equilibrium model where the distribution of wage offers is endogenous to the model and results from heterogenous workers and firms and from frictions in the matching process. The model is then estimated on French data by maximum likelihood techniques.

The simple model of labour search (10.25) can be extended to include transitions into unemployment, learning by doing and experience effects, as well as the effect of unobserved heterogeneity. The model of labor search can also be extended to education choices. The education choices can be a function of an immediate cost of education and the future rewards in terms of increased wages. Eckstein and Wolpin (1999) develop such a model.

Wages and Experience
The model in (10.25) can also be extended to understand why wages are increasing in age. An important part of the labor literature has tried to understand this phenomenon. This increase can come from

two sources, either through an increase in productivity, through general experience or possibly seniority within the firm, or through labor market mobility and on-the-job search. Altonji and Shakotko (1987), Topel (1991), Altonji and Williams (1997), and Dustmann and Meghir (2001) explore these issues, although in a nonstructural framework.

Distinguishing the effect of experience from seniority is mainly done by comparing individuals with similar experience but with different seniority. However, seniority depends on the job-to-job mobility which is a choice for the agent, possibly influenced by heterogeneity in the return to experience. Hence seniority (and experience) has to be considered as an endogenous variable. It is difficult to find good instruments that can deal with the endogeneity. Altonji and Shakotko (1987) instrument the seniority variable with deviations from job means, while Dustmann and Meghir (2001) use workers who are fired when whole plants close down as an exogenous event.

We present a structural model below that can potentially be used to distinguish between the two sources of wage determinants. The wage is a function of labor market experience X, of seniority in the firm S, of an unobserved fixed component ε, which is possibly individual specific, and a stochastic individual component η which is specific to the match between the agent and the firm and is potentially serially correlated. An employed individual earns a wage $w(X, S, \varepsilon, \eta)$. At the end of the period the agent has a probability δ of being fired. If not, in the next period the individual receives a job offer represented by a wage $w(X', 0, \varepsilon, \tilde{\eta}')$. This is compared to a wage within the firm of $w(X', S', \varepsilon, \eta')$. The value of work and of unemployment are defined as[28]

$$V^W(X, S, \varepsilon, \eta) = w(X, S, \varepsilon, \eta) + \beta \delta V^U(X', \varepsilon)$$

$$+ \beta(1 - \delta) E_{\eta' \mid \eta, \tilde{\eta}'} \max[V^W(X', S', \varepsilon, \eta'), V^W(X', 0, \varepsilon, \tilde{\eta}')],$$
(10.29)

$$V^U(X, \varepsilon) = b(X) + \beta E_{\eta'} \max[V^U(X, \varepsilon), V^W(X, 0, \varepsilon, \eta')].$$

When employed, the labor market experience evolves as $X' = X + 1$, and seniority, S, evolves in a similar way. When unemployed, the individual earns an unemployment benefit $b(X)$ and receive at the

---

28. Adda et al. (2002) estimate a related model using panel data of German workers.

end of the period a job offer characterized by a wage $w(X, 0, \varepsilon, \eta')$. The individual then chooses whether to accept the job or to remain for at least an additional period in unemployment.

An important issue is the unobserved heterogeneity in the return to experience. The model capture this with the term ε. Here the identification of the different sources of wage growth comes from the structural framework and no instruments are needed. This model could be solved numerically using a value function iteration approach and then estimated by maximum likelihood, integrating out the unobserved heterogeneity. This can be done as in Heckman and Singer (1984) allowing for mass point heterogeneity (e.g., see Eckstein and Wolpin 1999 for an implementation in the context of a structural dynamic programming problem).

Equilibrium Search
Yashiv (2000) specifies and estimates a model of search and matching. The important feature of this exercise is that it accounts for the behavior of both firms and workers. In this model unemployed workers search for jobs and firms with vacancies search for workers.

Firms have stochastic profit functions and face costs of attracting workers through the posting of vacancies. Workers have an objective of maximizing the discounted expected earnings. Workers too face a cost of search and choose their search intensity. These choices yield Euler equations which are used in the GMM estimation.

The key piece of the model is a matching function that brings the search of the workers and the vacancies of the firms together. The matching function has inputs of the vacancies opened by firms and the search intensity by the unemployed workers. Though all agents (firms and workers) take the matching probability as given, this probability is determined by their joint efforts in equilibrium. Empirically an important component of the analysis is the estimation of the matching function. Yashiv (2000) finds that the matching function exhibits increasing returns, contrary to the assumption made in much of the empirical literature on matching.

There is a very interesting link between this research and the discussion of dynamic labor demand. While researchers have specified labor adjustment costs, the exact source of these costs is less clear. The analysis in Yashiv (2000) is a step toward bridging this gap: he provides an interpretation of labor adjustment costs in the estimated search model.

10.7 Conclusion

The intention of this book was to describe a research methodology for bringing dynamic optimization problems to panel and time series data. In this chapter we have described some ongoing research programs that utilize this methodology.

Still, there are many avenues for further contributions. In particular, the applications described here have generally been associated with the dynamic optimization problem of a single agent. Of course, this agent may be influenced by relative prices, but these prices have been exogenous to the agent.

This does not present a problem as long as we are content to study individual optimization. But, as noted in the motivation of the book, one of the potential gains associated with the estimation of structural parameters is the confidence gained in the examination of alternative policies. In that case we need to include policy-induced variations in equilibrium variables. That is, we need to go beyond the single-agent problem to study equilibrium behavior. While some progress has been made on these issues, estimation of a dynamic equilibrium model with heterogeneous agents and allowing for nonconvex adjustment of factors of production and/or prices still lies ahead.[29]

Related to this point, the models we have studied do not allow any strategic interaction between agents. One might consider the estimation of a structure in which a small set of agents interact in a dynamic game. The natural approach is to compute a Markov-perfect equilibrium and use it as a basis for estimating observed behavior by the agents. Pakes (2000) provides a thorough review of these issues in the context of applications in industrial organization. Again, extensions to applied problems in macroeconomics lie ahead.

---

29. As noted earlier, Willis (2000b) makes some progress on this in a pricing problem, and Thomas (2000) studies some of these issues in the context of an investment problem.

Bibliography

Abel, A., and J. Eberly. 1994. A unified model of investment under uncertainty. *American Economic Review* 94: 1369–84.

Abowd, J., and D. Card. 1989. On the covariance structure of earnings and hours changes. *Econometrica* 57: 411–45.

Adda, J., and R. Cooper. 2000a. Balladurette and Juppette: A discrete analysis of scrapping subsidies. *Journal of Political Economy* 108(4): 778–806.

Adda, J., and R. Cooper. 2000b. The dynamics of car sales: A discrete choice approach. NBER Working Paper 7785.

Adda, J., C. Dustmann, C. Meghir, and J.-M. Robin. 2002. Human capital investment and job transitions. Mimeo. University College London.

Adda, J., and J. Eaton. 1997. Borrowing with unobserved liquidity constraints: Structural estimation with an application to sovereign debt. Mimeo. Boston University.

Aguirregabiria, V. 1997. Estimation of dynamic programming models with censored dependent variables. *Investigaciones Economicas* 21: 167–208.

Aguirregabiria, V. 1999. The dynamics of markups and inventories in retailing firms. *Review of Economic Studies* 66: 275–308.

Altonji, J., and R. Shakotko. 1987. Do wages rise with job seniority? *Review of Economic Studies* 54(3): 437–59.

Altonji, J., and N. Williams. 1997. Do wages rise with job security? *Review of Economic Studies* 54(179): 437–60.

Altug, S. 1989. Time to build and aggregate fluctuations: Some new evidence. *International Economic Review* 30: 889–920.

Amman, H. M., D. A. Kendrick, and J. Rust. 1996. *Handbook of Computational Economics*, vol. 1. Amsterdam: Elsevier Science, North-Holland.

Arrow, K. J., T. Harris, and J. Marschak. 1951. Optimal inventory policy. *Econometrica* 19(3): 250–72.

Attanasio, O. 2000. Consumer durables and inertial behaviour: Estimation and aggregation of (S,s) rules for automobile purchases. *Review of Economic Studies* 67(4): 667–96.

Attanasio, O., J. Banks, C. Meghir, and G. Weber. 1999. Humps and bumps in lifetime consumption. *Journal of Business and Economic Statistics* 17(1): 22–35.

Ball, L., and D. Romer. 1990. Real rigidities and the non-neutrality of money. *Review of Economic Studies* 57(2): 183–204.

Bar-Ilan, A., and A. Blinder. 1988. The life-cycle permanent-income model and consumer durables. *Annales d'Economie et de Statistique* (9): 71–91.

Bar-Ilan, A., and A. S. Blinder. 1992. Consumer durables: Evidence on the optimality of usually doing nothing. *Journal of Money, Credit and Banking* 24: 258–72.

Baxter, M. 1996. Are consumer durables important for business cycles? *Review of Economics and Statistics* 77: 147–55.

Baxter, M., and R. King. 1991. Production externalities and business cycles. Discussion Paper 53. Federal Reserve Bank of Minneapolis.

Bellman, R. 1957. *Dynamic Programming*. Princeton: Princeton University Press.

Benassy, J. 1982. *The Economics of Market Disequilibrium*. New York: Academic Press.

Beneveniste, L., and J. Scheinkman. 1979. On the differentiability of the value function in dynamic models of economics. *Econometrica* 47(3): 727–32.

Benhabib, J., and R. Farmer. 1994. Indeterminacy and increasing returns. *Journal of Economic Theory* 63: 19–41.

Bernanke, B. 1984. Permanent income, liquidity and expenditures on automobiles: Evidence from panel data. *Quarterly Journal of Economics* 99: 587–614.

Bernanke, B. 1985. Adjustment costs, durables and aggregate consumption. *Journal of Monetary Economics* 15: 41–68.

Bertola, G., and R. J. Caballero. 1990. Kinked adjustment cost and aggregate dynamics. *NBER Macroeconomics Annual* 5: 237–95.

Bertsekas, D. 1976. *Dynamic Programming and Stochastic Control*. New York: Academic Press.

Bils, M. 1987. The cyclical behavior of marginal cost and price. *American Economic Review* 77: 838–55.

Bils, M., and P. Klenow. 2002. Some evidence on the importance of sticky prices. NBER Working Paper 9069.

Blackwell, D. 1965. Discounted dynamic programming. *Annals of Mathematical Statistics* 36: 226–35.

Blanchard, O., and N. Kiyotaki. 1987. Monopolistic competition and the effects of aggregate demand. *American Economic Review* 77: 647–66.

Blinder, A. 1986. Can the production smoothing model of inventory behavior be saved? *Quarterly Journal of Economics* 101: 431–53.

Blinder, A., and L. Maccini. 1991. Taking stock: A critical assessment of recent research on inventories. *Journal of Economic Perspectives* 5(1): 73–96.

Blundell, R., M. Browning, and C. Meghir. 1994. Consumer demand and the life-cycle allocation of household expenditures. *Review of Economic Studies* 61: 57–80.

Braun, R. 1994. Tax disturbances and real economic activity in post-war United States. *Journal of Monetary Economics* 33(3): 441–62.

Bryant, J. 1983. A simple rational expectations Keynes-type model. *Quarterly Journal of Economics* 97: 525–29.

Caballero, R. 1999. Aggregate investment. In *Handbook of Macroeconomics*, ed. by J. Taylor and M. Woodford. Amsterdam: North-Holland.

Caballero, R., and E. Engel. 1993a. Heterogeneity and output fluctuation in a dynamic menu-cost economy. *Review of Economic Studies* 60: 95–119.

Caballero, R., and E. Engel. 1993b. Heterogeneity and output fluctuations in a dynamic menu-cost economy. *Review of Economic Studies* 60: 95–119.

Caballero, R., E. Engel, and J. Haltiwanger. 1995. Plant level adjustment and aggregate investment dynamics. *Brookings Papers on Economic Activity* 1995(2): 1–39.

Caballero, R., E. Engel, and J. Haltiwanger. 1997. Aggregate employment dynamics: Building from microeconomic evidence. *American Economic Review* 87: 115–37.

Caballero, R. J. 1993. Durable goods: An explanation for their slow adjustment. *Journal of Political Economy* 101: 351–84.

Campbell, J., and G. Mankiw. 1989. Consumption, income and interest rates: Reinterpreting the time series evidence. *NBER Macroeconomic Annual* 4: 1–50.

Caplin, A., and J. Leahy. 1991. State dependent pricing and the dynamics of money and output. *Quarterly Journal of Economics* 106: 683–708.

Caplin, A., and J. Leahy. 1997. Durable goods cycles. Mimeo. Boston University.

Carroll, C. D. 1992. The buffer-stock theory of saving: Some macroeconomic evidence. *Brookings Papers on Economic Activity* 2: 61–156.

Cecchetti, S. 1986. The frequency of price adjustment: A study of newstand prices of magazines. *Journal of Econometrics* 31: 255–74.

Chirinko, R. 1993. Business fixed investment spending. *Journal of Economic Literature* 31: 1875–1911.

Christiano, L. 1988. Why does inventory investment fluctuate so much? *Journal of Monetary Economics* 21(2): 247–80.

Christiano, L., and M. Eichenbaum. 1992. Current real-business-cycle theories and aggregate labor market fluctuations. *American Economic Review* 82: 430–50.

Cooper, R. 1999. *Coordination Games: Complementarities and Macroeconomics*. Cambridge: Cambridge University Press.

Cooper, R. 2002. Estimation and identification of structural parameters in the presence of multiple equilibria. NBER Working Paper 8941.

Cooper, R., and J. Ejarque. 2000. Financial intermediation and aggregate fluctuations: A quantitative analysis. *Macroeconomic Dynamics* 4: 423–47.

Cooper, R., and J. Ejarque. 2001. Exhuming Q: Market power vs. capital market imperfections. NBER Working Paper 8182.

Cooper, R., and J. Haltiwanger. 1993. On the aggregate implications of machine replacement: Theory and evidence. *American Economic Review* 83: 360–82.

Cooper, R., and J. Haltiwanger. 2000. On the nature of the capital adjustment process. NBER Working Paper 7925.

Cooper, R., J. Haltiwanger, and L. Power. 1999. Machine replacement and the business cycle: Lumps and bumps. *American Economic Review* 89: 921–46.

Cooper, R., and A. Johri. 1997. Dynamic complementarities: A quantitative analysis. *Journal of Monetary Economics* 40: 97–119.

Cooper, R., and J. Willis. 2001. The economics of labor adjustment: Mind the gap. NBER Working Paper 8527.

Cooper, R. W., and J. C. Haltiwanger. 1992. Macroeconomic implications of production bunching. *Journal of Monetary Economics* 30(1): 107–27.

De Boor, C. 1978. *A Practical Guide to Splines*. New York: Springer-Verlag.

Deaton, A. 1991. Savings and liquidity constraints. *Econometrica* 59: 1221–48.

Dotsey, M., R. King, and A. Wolman. 1999. State-dependent pricing and the general equilibrium dynamics of prices and output. *Quarterly Journal of Economics* 114: 655–90.

Duffie, D., and K. Singleton. 1993. Simulated moment estimation of Markov models of asset prices. *Econometrica* 61(4): 929–52.

Dustmann, C., and C. Meghir. 2001. Wages, experience and seniority. IFS Working Paper W01/01.

Eberly, J. C. 1994. Adjustment of consumers' durables stocks: Evidence from automobile purchases. *Journal of Political Economy* 102: 403–36.

Eckstein, Z., and K. Wolpin. 1989. The specification and estimation of dynamic stochastic discrete choice models. *Journal of Human Resources* 24: 562–98.

Eckstein, Z., and K. Wolpin. 1995. Duration to first job and the return to schooling: Estimates from a search-matching model. *Review of Economic Studies* 62: 263–86.

Eckstein, Z., and K. I. Wolpin. 1999. Why youths drop out of high school: The impact of preferences, opportunities and abilities. *Econometrica* 67(6): 1295–1339.

Eichenbaum, M. 1989. Some empirical evidence on the production level and production cost smoothing models of inventory investment. *American Economic Review* 79(4): 853–64.

Eichenbaum, M., L. Hansen, and K. Singleton. 1988. A time series analysis of representative agent models of consumption and leisure choice under uncertainty. *Quarterly Journal of Economics* 103: 51–78.

Eichenbaum, M., and L. P. Hansen. 1990. Estimating models with intertemporal substitution using aggregate time series data. *Journal of Business and Economic Statistics* 8: 53–69.

Erickson, T., and T. Whited. 2000. Measurement error and the relationship between investment and Q. *Journal of Policy Economy* 108: 1027–57.

Farmer, R., and J. T. Guo. 1994. Real business cycles and the animal spirits hypothesis. *Journal of Economic Theory* 63: 42–72.

Fermanian, J.-D., and B. Salanié. 2001. A nonparametric simulated maximum likelihood estimation method. Mimeo. CREST-INSEE.

Fernández-Villaverde, J., and D. Krueger. 2001. Consumption and saving over the life cycle: How important are consumer durables? Mimeo. Stanford University.

Flavin, M. 1981. The adjustment of consumption to changing expectations about future income. *Journal of Political Economy* 89: 974–1009.

Gallant, R. A., and G. Tauchen. 1996. Which moments to match? *Econometric Theory* 12(4): 657–81.

Gilchrist, S., and C. Himmelberg. 1995. Evidence on the role of cash flow for investment. *Journal of Monetary Economics* 36: 541–72.

Gomes, J. 2001. Financing investment. *American Economic Review* 91(5): 1263–85.

Gourieroux, C., and A. Monfort. 1996. *Simulation-Based Econometric Methods*. Oxford: Oxford University Press.

Gourieroux, C., A. Monfort, and E. Renault. 1993. Indirect inference. *Journal of Applied Econometrics* 8: S85–118.

Gourinchas, P.-O., and J. Parker. 2002. Consumption over the life cycle. *Econometrica* 70(1): 47–89.

Greenwood, J., Z. Hercowitz, and G. Huffman. 1988. Investment, capacity utilization and the real business cycle. *American Economic Review* 78: 402–17.

Grossman, S. J., and G. Laroque. 1990. Asset pricing and optimal portfolio choice in the presence of illiquid durable consumption goods. *Econometrica* 58: 25–51.

Hajivassiliou, V. A., and P. A. Ruud. 1994. Classical estimation methods for LDV models using simulation. In *Handbook of Econometrics*, ed. by D. McFadden and R. Engle, vol. 4. Amsterdam: North-Holland, pp. 2383–441.

Hall, G. 1996. Overtime, effort and the propagation of business cycle shocks. *Journal of Monetary Economics* 38: 139–60.

Hall, G. 2000. Non-convex costs and capital utilization: A study of production scheduling at automobile assembly plants. *Journal of Monetary Economics* 45: 681–716.

Hall, G., and J. Rust. 2000. An empirical model of inventory investment by durable commodity intermediaries. *Carnegie-Rochester Conference Series on Public Policy* 52: 171–214.

Hall, R. E. 1978. Stochastic implications of the life cycle–permanent income hypothesis: Theory and evidence. *Journal of Political Economy* 86: 971–87.

Hamermesh, D. 1989. Labor demand and the structure of adjustment costs. *American Economic Review* 79: 674–89.

Hamermesh, D. 1993. *Labor Demand*. Princeton: Princeton University Press.

Hamermesh, D., and G. Pfann. 1996. Adjustment costs in factor demand. *Journal of Economic Literature* 34: 1264–92.

Hansen, G. 1985. Indivisible labor and the business cycle. *Journal of Monetary Economics* 16: 309–27.

Hansen, G., and T. Sargent. 1988. Straight time and overtime in equilibrium. *Journal of Monetary Economics* 21: 281–308.

Hansen, L. P., E. McGrattan, and T. Sargent. 1994. Mechanics of forming and estimating dynamic linear economies. Federal Reserve Bank of Minneapolis, Staff Report 182.

Hansen, L. P., and K. J. Singleton. 1982. Generalized instrumental variables estimation of nonlinear rational expectations models. *Econometrica* 50: 1269–86.

Hayashi, F. 1982. Tobin's marginal Q and average Q: A neoclassical interpretation. *Econometrica* 50: 215–24.

Heckman, J., and B. Singer. 1984. A method for minimizing the impact of distributional assumptions in econometric models for duration data. *Econometrica* 52(2): 271–320.

House, C., and J. Leahy. 2000. An s, S model with adverse selection. NBER Working Paper 8030.

Hubbard, G. 1994. Investment under uncertainty: Keeping one's options open. *Journal of Economic Literature* 32(4): 1816–31.

John, A., and A. Wolman. 1999. Does state-dependent pricing imply coordination failure? Mimeo. Federal Reserve Bank of Richmond.

Judd, K. 1992. Projection methods for solving aggregate growth models. *Journal of Economic Theory* 58: 410–52.

Judd, K. 1996. Approximation, perturbation and projection methods in economic analysis. In *Handbook of Computational Economics*, ed. by H. M. Amman, D. A. Kendrick, and J. Rust. Amsterdam: Elsevier Science, North-Holland.

Judd, K. 1998. *Numerical Methods in Economics*. Cambridge: MIT Press.

Kahn, A., and J. Thomas. 2001. Nonconvex factor adjustments in equilibrium business cycle models: Do nonlinearities matter? Mimeo. University of Minnesota.

Kahn, J. 1987. Inventories and the volatility of production. *American Economic Review* 77(4): 667–79.

Keane, M. P., and K. I. Wolpin. 1994. The solution and estimation of discrete choice dynamic programming models by simulation and interpolation: Monte Carlo evidence. *Review of Economics and Statistics* 76(4): 648–72.

King, R., C. Plosser, and S. Rebelo. 1988. Production, growth and business cycles I. The basic neoclassical model. *Journal of Monetary Economics* 21: 195–232.

Kocherlakota, N., B. F. Ingram, and N. E. Savin. 1994. Explaining business cycles: A multiple shock approach. *Journal of Monetary Economics* 34: 415–28.

Kydland, F., and E. Prescott. 1982. Time to build and aggregate fluctuations. *Econometrica* 50: 1345–70.

Laffont, J.-J., H. Ossard, and Q. Vuong. 1995. Econometrics of first-price auctions. *Econometrica* 63: 953–80.

Lam, P. 1991. Permanent income, liquidity and adjustments of automobile stocks: Evidence form panel data. *Quarterly Journal of Economics* 106: 203–30.

Laroque, G., and B. Salanié. 1989. Estimation of multi-market fix-price models: An application of pseudo maximum likelihood methods. *Eca* 57(4): 831–60.

Laroque, G., and B. Salanié. 1993. Simulation based estimation models with lagged latent variables. *Journal of Applied Econometrics* 8: S119–33.

Lee, B.-S., and B. F. Ingram. 1991. Simulation estimation of time-series models. *Journal of Econometrics* 47: 197–205.

Lerman, S., and C. Manski. 1981. On the use of simulated frequencies to approximate choice probabilities. In *Structural Analysis of Discrete Data with Econometric Applications*, ed. by C. Manski and D. McFadden. Cambridge: MIT Press, pp. 305–19.

Ljungqvist, L., and T. Sargent. 2000. *Recursive Macroeconomic Theory*. Cambridge: MIT Press.

MaCurdy, T. E. 1981. An empirical model of labor supply in a life-cycle setting. *Journal of Political Economy* 89(6): 1059–85.

Mankiw, G. N. 1982. Hall's consumption hypothesis and durable goods. *Journal of Monetary Economics* 10: 417–25.

Manski, C. 1993. Identification of endogenous social effects: The reflection problem. *Review of Economic Studies* 60(3): 531–42.

McCall, J. 1970. Economics of information and job search. *Quarterly Journal of Economics* 84(1): 113–26.

McFadden, D. 1989. A method of simulated moments for estimation of discrete response models without numerical integration. *Econometrica* 57: 995–1026.

McFadden, D., and P. A. Ruud. 1994. Estimation by simulation. *Review of Economics and Statistics* 76(4): 591–608.

McGrattan, E. 1994. The macroeconomic effects of distortionary taxes. *Journal of Monetary Economics* 33: 573–601.

McGrattan, E. R. 1996. Solving the stochastic growth model with a finite element method. *Journal of Economic Dynamics and Control* 20: 19–42.

Meghir, C., and G. Weber. 1996. Intertemporal non-separability or borrowing restrictions? A disaggregate analysis using US CEX panel. *Econometrica* 64(5): 1151–81.

Miranda, M. J., and P. G. Helmberger. 1988. The effects of commodity price stabilization programs. *American Economic Review* 78(1): 46–58.

Newey, W. K., and K. D. West. 1987. A simple, positive, semi-definite, heteroskedasticity and autocorrelation consistent covariance matrix. *Econometrica* 55: 703–8.

Nickell, S. 1978. Fixed costs, employment and labour demand over the cycle. *Economica* 45(180): 329–45.

Pakes, A. 1994. Dynamic structural models, problems and prospects: Mixed continuous discrete controls and market interactions. In *Advances in Econometrics, Sixth World Congress*, ed. by C. Sims. Cambridge: Cambridge University Press, pp. 171–259.

Pakes, A. 2000. A framework for applied dynamic analysis in I.O. NBER Working Paper 8024.

Pakes, A., and D. Pollard. 1989. Simulation and the asymptotics of optimization estimators. *Econometrica* 57: 1027–57.

Pfann, G., and F. Palm. 1993. Asymmetric adjustment costs in non-linear labour models for the Netherlands and U.K. manufacturing sectors. *Review of Economic Studies* 60: 397–412.

Postel-Vinay, F., and J.-M. Robin. 2002. Equilibrium wage dispersion with worker and employer heterogeneity. *Econometrica*, forthcoming.

Press, W., B. Flannery, S. Teukolsky, and W. Vetterling. 1986. *Numerical Recipes: The Art of Scientific Computing*. Cambridge: Cambridge University Press.

Ramey, V., and M. Shapiro. 2001. Displaced capital. *Journal of Political Economy* 109: 958–92.

Reddy, J. 1993. *An Introduction to the Finite Element Method*. New York: McGraw-Hill.

Rogerson, R. 1988. Indivisible labor, lotteries and equilibrium. *Journal of Monetary Economics* 21: 3–16.

Rust, J. 1985. Stationary equilibrium in a market for durable assets. *Econometrica* 53(4): 783–805.

Rust, J. 1987. Optimal replacement of GMC bus engines: An empirical model of Harold Zurcher. *Econometrica* 55(5): 999–1033.

Rust, J., and C. Phelan. 1997. How social security and medicare affect retirement behavior in a world of incomplete markets. *Econometrica* 65(4): 781–832.

Sakellaris, P. 2001. Patterns of plant adjustment. Working Paper 2001-05. Finance and Economics Discussion Series, Division of Research and Statistics and Monetary Affairs, Federal Reserve Board, Washington, DC.

Sargent, T. 1978. Estimation of dynamic labor demand schedules under rational expectations. *Journal of Political Economy* 86(6): 1009–44.

Sargent, T. 1987. *Dynamic Macroeconomic Theory*. Cambridge: Harvard University Press.

Scarf, H. 1959. The optimality of (S, s) policies in the dynamic inventory problem. In *Mathmematical Methods in Social Sciences*, ed. by S. K. K. Arrow and P. Suppes. Stanford: Stanford University Press, pp. 196–202.

Shapiro, M. 1986. The dynamic demand for labor and capital. *Quarterly Journal of Economics* 101: 513–42.

Smith, A. 1993. Estimating nonlinear time-series models using simulated vector autoregressions. *Journal of Applied Econometrics* 8: S63–84.

Stokey, N., and R. Lucas. 1989. *Recursive Methods in Economic Dynamics*. Cambridge: Harvard University Press.

Tauchen, G. 1986. Finite state Markov-chain approximation to univariate and vector autoregressions. *Economics Letters* 20: 177–81.

Tauchen, G. 1990. Solving the stochastic growth model by using quadrature methods and value-function iterations. *Journal of Business and Economic Statistics* 8(1): 49–51.

Tauchen, G., and R. Hussey. 1991. Quadrature-based methods for obtaining approximate solutions to nonlinear asset pricing models. *Econometrica* 59: 371–96.

Taylor, J. B., and H. Uhlig. 1990. Solving nonlinear stochastic growth models: A comparison of alternative solution methods. *Journal of Business and Economic Statistics* 8: 1–17.

Thomas, J. 2002. Is lumpy investment relevant for the business cycle? Manuscript. Carnegie-Mellon University, *Journal of Political Economy* 110(3): 508–34.

Topel, R. 1991. Specific capital, mobility, and wages: Wages rise with job seniority. *Journal of Political Economy* 99(1): 145–76.

Whited, T. 1998. Why do investment Euler equations fail? *Journal of Business and Economic Statistics* 16(4): 479–88.

Willis, J. 2000a. Estimation of adjustment costs in a model of state-dependent pricing. Working Paper 00-07. Federal Reserve Bank of Kansas City.

Willis, J. 2000b. General equilibrium of monetary model with state dependent pricing. Mimeo. Boston University.

Wolpin, K. 1987. Estimating a structural search model: The transition from school to work. *Econometrica* 55(4): 801–18.

Wright, B. D., and J. C. Williams. 1984. The welfare effects of the introduction of storage. *Quarterly Journal of Economics* 99(1): 169–92.

Yashiv, E. 2000. The determinants of equilibrium unemployment. *American Economic Review* 90(5): 1297–1322.

Zeldes, S. 1989a. Optimal consumption with stochastic income: Deviations from certainty equivalence. *Quarterly Journal of Economics* 104: 275–98.

Zeldes, S. P. 1989b. Consumption and liquidity constraints: An empirical investigation. *Journal of Political Economy* 97: 305–46.

Index

Printed in the United States
by Baker & Taylor Publisher Services